My Avatar, My Self

Identity in Video Role-Playing Games

ZACH WAGGONER

McFarland & Company, Inc., Publishers
Jefferson, North Carolina, and London

LIBRARY OF CONGRESS CATALOGUING-IN-PUBLICATION DATA

Waggoner, Zach, 1973–
   My avatar, my self : identity in video role-playing games /
Zach Waggoner.
      p.   cm.
   Includes bibliographical references and index.

   ISBN 978-0-7864-4109-9
   softcover : 50# alkaline paper ∞

   1. Avatars (Computer graphics)   2. Video games.
3. Virtual reality.   4. Online identities.   5. Shared virtual
environments.   6. Human-computer interaction.   I. Title.
QA76.76.I59.W34   2009
004.01'9 — dc22   2009009931

British Library cataloguing data are available

Cover image ©2009 Shutterstock

Manufactured in the United States of America

McFarland & Company, Inc., Publishers
   Box 611, Jefferson, North Carolina 28640
   www.mcfarlandpub.com

Table of Contents

Preface

This study investigates the relationships between virtual identity and non-virtual identity in video role-playing games. How do videogamers utilize liminal space to form connections between themselves and their avatars? To answer this question I use James Gee's identity theoretical constructs of real-world identity, virtual world identity, and projective identity as a frame for data collection and analysis. Phenomenological data (oral interviews and video gameplay transcription and analysis) was collected from four participants. Two "die-hard" videogaming veterans played *Morrowind*, one casual gamer played *Oblivion*, and one non-gamer played *Fallout 3*. These participants had varying levels of videogame literacy and interest in the role-playing genre of videogames; I wanted to see if these factors impacted user identification with their avatars. Findings indicate that the relationships between the virtual avatar and the "real-world" users were dynamic and complex: the real-world identities continually informed the virtual identities of the avatars, despite widely varying levels of user immersion and conscious diegetic identification. This study models one methodological approach for the collection, transcription, and analysis of videogame data. I also recommend the creation of two new terms to aid in the formation of reliable and consistent terminology in the field of videogame theory. First, the term "real-world" identity (used by Gee and other scholars to describe non-virtual identities) was found to be problematic. This study found that virtual identities, created and maintained by users' non-virtual identities, may be just as "real" to users as their non-virtual identities. Therefore, this study recommends replacing the term "real-world" with "non-virtual" for future studies on identity construction in virtual spaces, thus creating a more accurate terminological continuum. Second, the study also suggests creation of the term "verisimulacratude" to help describe how users identify with and become immersed in videogames set in fantastical simulacra-like gameworlds. Creation of the new terminological continua virtual/non-virtual and verisimulacratude/verisimilitude allows scholars to more accurately study the rhetoric of videogames and identity construction within virtual diegetic spaces.

1

1

Videogames, Avatars, and Identity

A Brief History

Our connection to the real world is very thin, and our connection with the artificial world is going to be more intimate and satisfying than anything that's come before.

— Marvin Minsky, MIT scientist, 1989

We may not want to acknowledge a connection between ourselves and the mechanical world, but to be alive in our time is to be faced with this reflection, like it or not.

— Janet Murray, technology theorist, 1997

It is September of 1999. A Thursday night. I should be asleep by now, but I'm not. Tomorrow is a teaching day, and I have to get up early. I roll over, pounding my pillow in frustration. I glance at the digital clock: the smug 11:53 P.M. mocks me. "*Only five hours until you need to get up,*" it seems to say. Dammit. I close my eyes, trying to drift down into sleep. But it's no use: my mind fills with images of giant geckos and plasma rifles, supermutants and radioactive ghouls. Frantically, I struggle to clear my head. Relax. Just relax. But I can't: I am Zach the Chosen One, and have much on my mind. Should I visit Redding or Reno next? Is my Small Guns skill high enough to help me survive if I'm ambushed in the Wastes? Will I come to regret not freeing the slaves in the Den? Should I have opted for a higher Perception skill when creating Zach, given my penchant for long-distance sniping? I can't stop these thoughts. I am powerless to control my mind. Sighing, I look at the clock once more: 12:17 A.M. What is wrong with me? How can I obsess this much over a videogame? Sure, *Fallout 2* is a great game: terrific story, open-ended gameplay, incredibly deep customization options. But it is still just a game, a fiction. Resigned to a poor night's sleep, I vow never to get this hooked on a virtual world during the middle of a semester ever again....

It is February of 2008. Groaning inwardly, I squint at the pale blue glow of my old nemesis: 1:02 A.M. Not again. Tomorrow is a long day, with committee meetings late in the afternoon after an early spate of classes. I needed to be asleep 75 minutes ago. When will I learn? I thought just an hour wouldn't hurt me, but here I am, unable to get that haunting music out of my head. It's triumphal and orchestric: great for inspiring me while grading papers, but lousy as a sleep aid. Plus, I'm reliving my last foray into the Oblivion gate near Kvatch. Those scamps really piss me off, and it is becoming increasingly clear that I'm going to need to improve both my Destruction magic skill and my Marksman skill before I go back in. I might need new armor too. Zach the Wood Elf just isn't as strong as he needs to be. *The Elder Scrolls IV: Oblivion* is consuming me, piece by mental piece. I can't stop playing, even though the demands of this semester's teaching load are calling for attention. Just one more hour, and I can finish the slaughterfish quest. Just one more hour, and I can buy Zach a new pair of boots. Just one more hour, and I can increase my Alchemy skill three times. Just. One. More. Hour.

Okay, I obviously didn't learn my lesson after spending more than 100 hours playing *Fallout 2*. It's almost a decade later, and I'm still investing copious amounts of time and energy in virtual videogame worlds. *Oblivion* is just my latest addiction. Somehow, video roleplaying-games (v–RPGs) speak to me, whisper to my soul. It is hard to explain why this happens, but this book is my attempt to do so. At least I can take comfort in knowing that I'm not alone: *Oblivion* has sold more than two million copies worldwide. Massively multiplayer online role-playing games (MMORPGs) like *World of Warcraft* have several million subscribers as well. Videogame revenue now reaches several billion dollars annually in the United States alone (with global figures expected to pass $50 billion in 2009). Clearly, other players enjoy videogames as much as I do. But do other v–RPGers care as much about their avatars as I do about mine? Am I alone in my virtual obsessions, having contracted some sort of virtu-virus or techno-schizophrenia? The words of videogame theorist Arthur Asa Berger, written in 2002, resonate with me, but offer cold comfort: "Playing video games may lead to alienation; this alienation can often lead to a sense of estrangement from oneself ... what is difficult to know is how being immersed will affect players. Will new video games become a kind of opiate for people who can find an outlet in simulations that seem better than those offered by their real-life experiences?" (107–108). Hmm. Estranged from my self. That doesn't seem to fit how I feel about Zach the Wood Elf. My relationship with my avatar seems more complicated than that. Exactly how I believe it is more complicated (for other videogamers as well as myself) and will take some explaining, as videogame technologies offer users interactive and immersive experiences that convey verisimilitude and beyond more with each passing year.

In the epigraphs that introduce this chapter Marvin Minsky and Janet Murray acknowledge humanity's connections to technologically-produced worlds. Indeed, they were among the first scholars to theorize and explore these connections. Berger was one of the scholars who first turned this critical gaze to the phenomenon of videogames; his statement above reflects the uncertainty felt by many about how exactly videogames affect the identities of those who interact with them. In this book, I continue this investigation into the relationships between virtual identities and non-virtual identities, primarily in video role-playing games. Using James P. Gee's identity theoretical constructs of real-world identity, virtual world identity, and projective identity, I analyze the connections (via projective identity in liminal space) between the real-world identities of videogame users and their diegetic avatars: virtual-world identities. To gather data for this project, I worked closely with four primary participants, conducting oral interviews, recording, transcribing, and analyzing their videogame play experiences in the v–RPGs *Morrowind*, *Oblivion*, and *Fallout 3*. I also collected data online from the devoted denizens of *Morrowind* and *Oblivion* to better understand videogamers' connections to the virtual personalities and bodies of their avatars. Who are we when we're also someone else in virtual play and space? The connections between videogamers and their virtual counterparts are complex indeed, as I hope you'll soon agree. In this first chapter I provide a brief history of the rise of videogames as a popular culture entertainment medium leading to the development of diegetic avatars in video role-playing games. I then discuss Gee's identity theoretical constructs and use them to analyze postings related to identity formation in the *Morrowind* and *Oblivion* online forums at Elderscrolls.com to demonstrate the need for my exploration into the connections between videogamers and their virtual identities.

A Brief History of Video Games

At the time of this writing in 2008, videogames have been in existence for over 40 years. In 1962, Massachusetts Institute of Technology scholars Steve Russell, Martin Graetz, Wayne Wiitanen, and Alan Kotok took advantage of access to MIT's powerful computers and in their spare time designed *Spacewar!*, widely considered to be the first computer game. *Spacewar!* displayed two spaceships (actually small "blips" of light displayed on the CRT monitor) trying to shoot each other while avoiding a star in the middle of the screen. Two people could play at the same time, each controlling one spaceship by manipulating several switches and knobs on the computer. *Spacewar!* was difficult to control and play, even for the designers, yet in the days and weeks that followed, MIT students waited in long lines to play *Spacewar!* or to simply watch fellow students play the game (Robinett ix).

Of course, few computers were as powerful as MIT's, and it took nearly ten years before videogame technology became feasible commercially and economically. In 1971, *Computer Space* officially became the first commercial videogame. *Computer Space* was modeled on *Spacewar!* with a simplified control lever (what we would recognize today as a "joystick"). Still, *Computer Space* was difficult to play, and the game was not a commercial success. The distinction of being the first commercially successful videogame belongs to *PONG* (a simplified version of table tennis), which debuted in 1972 in arcades across the United States. *PONG's* immense popularity encouraged the creation of other coin-operated video arcade games as well as the creation of the first home game console system[1] in 1972, the Magnavox Odyssey, which shipped with a version of *PONG*.

And so it all began. As Mark Wolf points out, videogames in arcades were the first computers many Americans ever used, and the home videogame systems were often the first home computers as well. In 1976, the Fairchild/Zircon Channel F was the first home videogame console system to offer cartridge-based technology: individual videogames were contained on "cartridges" that could be plugged into the game system. The Zircon Channel F was a colossal failure: users didn't find any of the games designed for it enjoyable to play. However, Nolan Bushnell was convinced that the idea of cartridge-based technology was sound, and in 1977 his company came out with a cartridge-based system of their own: the Atari 2600. It turns out Bushnell was right: the Atari 2600 became arguably the most important system in videogame history, selling millions of units and tens of millions of videogames on cartridges. Other manufacturers quickly moved to take advantage of the videogame demand created by the Atari 2600, and dozens of home videogame consoles flooded the market — too many, in point of fact.[2] In 1983 and 1984, the market for home videogames crashed (aided by the production of too many games in 1983 and too few in 1984), and many console videogame manufacturers in North America went out of business.

Yet videogames did not die out. Video arcades continued to do well, and in 1985, a new console system from Japan was introduced: the Nintendo Entertainment System (NES). By 1987, the NES's popularity rivaled that of the Atari 2600 at its peak (Wolf 5). Home computer technology also advanced to the point where "cartridges" became possible there as well: floppy disks (and later CD-ROMs) containing videogames created a healthy competitive market between videogame console games and videogames designed for home computers. This competition continues to this day, as "next generation" console systems such as the Xbox 360, Playstation 3, and Nintendo Wii compete against the ever-faster processing speeds, larger memory capacities, bleeding-edge soundcards, and DVD drives of home personal computers (PCs).

There are many other important "firsts" in the history of videogames in addition to the ones already mentioned. In 1980 the arcade game *Battlezone*, a tank simulator, offered a first-person point of view (POV), allowing users to play "through the eyes" of a tank commander. in 1982 *Zaxxon* unveiled an isometric perspective, showing three sides of an object (in this case the spaceship controlled by the user) instead of just one, which allowed for unprecedented visual depth and perspective. *Dragon's Lair* (1983) used laser-disc technology. *Wolfenstein 3D* (1992) filled in the first-person POV vector lines created for *Battlezone* and became the first truly "immersive" three-dimensional (3D) game, putting the user "into" the gaming world in a way that hadn't been done before. With the advent of CD-ROM technology in 1992, two 1993 PC games quickly became historically significant, breaking all past sales records: *Doom* and *Myst*. Interestingly enough, as games, these two offered immensely different gaming experiences. *Doom* perfected the visceral, high action "first-person shooter" formula created by *Wolfenstein 3D*, while *Myst* offered almost no action, focusing instead on spatial exploration and puzzle-solving. The 1980's saw the first online games, text-based multi-user dimensions (MUDs) played over modems. *Air Warrior* became in 1987 the first massively multiplayer online game (MMOG) to incorporate graphics, paving the way for *Ultima Online* (1997), *Everquest* (1999) and *World of Warcraft* (2004) to create elaborate graphical online worlds with hundreds of thousands of online users.

Avatars and Videogames

As this brief history suggests, there have been many landmark achievements in the history of videogames,[3] leading us to where we are now: in 2007, video and computer game software sales exceeded nine billion dollars in the United States. Over 267 million video and computer game units were sold in this country as well (Entertainment Software Association). The new medium of videogames is now poised to surpass cinema as the most lucrative entertainment medium the United States has ever known. Why? What is it about videogames that captivate so many users of all ages? Mark Wolf helps us understand this phenomenon by pointing out how truly unique videogames are from their main competitors, cinema and television: videogames are "the first [medium] to combine real-time game play with a navigable, onscreen diegetic space [and] the first to feature avatars and player-controlled surrogates that could influence onscreen events: real-time user interaction in one machine" (11, 5). Here, Wolf suggests that real-time user interactivity within the game space, via avatars, is crucial to videogame popularity and success.

Avatars. It's time I defined and complicated this essential term. What are they, and why are they so important to videogames? Videogame scholars apply the term in several different ways, but the origins of the word are clear. *Avatara*, meaning "descent," is a Sanskrit word that in Hinduism refers to an incarnation, a bodily manifestation, of an immortal being. Hindu gods and goddesses use avatars as necessary when they want to access the physical, mortal world of humanity. However, with the rise of computer technology and the virtual spaces made possible by this technology, the term "avatar" has been applied to videogames with several competing definitions.[4] In the broadest sense, an avatar is "the user's representative in the virtual universe" (Filiciak 89). Chris Crawford describes avatars in a similar way: "virtual constructs that are controlled by human players and function as a means of interacting with other characters" (Berger 33). These definitions combine Wolf's above notions of "avatar" and "player-controlled surrogates" and seem to cover any on-screen representation controlled by the user. Under these definitions, the small "blip" of light in *Spacewar!* representing the user's spaceship would be an avatar. Bob Rehak, using Miroslaw Filiciak's definition, provides a brief history of significant avatar moments in videogames beginning with *Spacewar!* He highlights *Pac-Man* as providing the first "alive" avatar: *Pac-Man* is portrayed as an organic creature, rather than a machine. All previous videogames had the user controlling either spaceships or other machines (like the ground-defense turrets of *Space Invaders*); being given control of an organic creature was a new idea. As previously mentioned, *Battlezone* allowed the user to operate from "inside" the avatar (a tank) from a first-person POV. *Myst* also provided a first-person POV, but was revolutionary for its emphasis on spatial exploration over narrative (an important distinction I'll return to later in chapter two). *Quake* was the first videogame that allowed the user to change the appearance of the avatar, offering several different "skins" the user could choose from. Using this simplified definition, avatars have been present since the inception of videogames.

At the beginning of this chapter, I provided the following statement from Marvin Minsky: "Our connection to the real world is very thin, and our connection with the artificial world is going to be more intimate and satisfying than anything that's come before" (161). Filiciak (perhaps influenced by the film *EXistenZ*) adds the following sentiments about the connections between real and artificial worlds: "In the foreseeable future [of videogames the] differentiation between artificial and real or between outside and inside will be blurred" (98). When considering these two statements it is difficult to imagine a user's connection to *Pac-Man* (or even *Tomb Raider's* Lara Croft) as being more "intimate and satisfying" than the interactions with friends at work or at school. So too is it difficult to imagine a user blurring the distinction between videogame play where she is "inside" her *Zaxxon* fighter jet or in control of Dirk the Daring in *Dragon's Lair* and "outside" activities like taking a calculus test or eating dinner at a pizza parlor. What is it about videogames and videogame avatars that lead to the notions espoused by Minsky and Filiciak that speculate on the blurring between real and virtual identities?

To begin to answer this question it is necessary to further refine the definition of "avatar" in relationship to videogames. Athomas Goldberg aids this process by distinguishing between "avatars" and "agents." He defines a virtual avatar as any "representations of 'real' people in computer-generated environment[s]" and agents as "any semiautonomous pieces of software that assume some visual embodiment" (161). Distinguishing between virtual avatars and agents is helpful, but Goldberg's definitions are still too vague: *Pac-Man* could be identified as either an avatar (since *Pac-Man* represents the user in the gameworld maze) or an agent (since it is the on-screen embodiment of semiautonomous software). Further refinement in the definition of avatar is needed to avoid this ambiguity, and Laetitia Wilson succeeds in providing it:

> [An avatar is] a virtual, surrogate self that acts as a stand in for our real-space selves, that represents the user. The cyberspace avatar functions as a locus that is multifarious and polymorphous, displaced from the facticity of our real-space selves.... Avatar spaces indisputably involve choice in the creation of one's avatar; there is substantial scope in which to exercise choice and create meaning [within the video game] [2–3].

This notion of creative choice is crucial to not only defining avatars in virtual spaces but also to understanding exactly how users connect with videogames and become immersed within them. Using Wilson's criterion of creative choice, it becomes much easier to distinguish between videogame avatars and agents. Pac-Man cannot be altered in any way by the user. He can only be controlled. His appearance and skills never change throughout the course of the game. This makes Pac-Man an agent. The same holds true for *Spacewar!*'s spaceship, Lara Croft of *Tomb Raider* fame, Mario of *Super Mario Bros.*, *Frogger*, *Sonic the Hedgehog*, *Duke Nukem*, *Grand Theft Auto: Vice City*'s Tommy Vercetti, and *Perfect Dark*'s Joanna Dark. All of these famous videogame characters are agents, as they can only be controlled by the user, never altered in appearance or skill level.

Users and Avatars: Relationships

In fact, when considering this much more restricted definition for avatars (the necessity for the user to have much creative control over the agent's appearance, skills, and attributes) it becomes clear that most of the controllable characters in video games are agents rather than avatars. What genre of videogame allows the user to have creative license to construct an avatar, then? To move forward in answering this question I must first go back: in 1997, Janet Murray's landmark *Hamlet on the Holodeck: The Future of Narrative in Cyberspace* was published. In that work, Murray focused on how computer technology would impact the evolution of narrative stories and established many terms and concepts that remain crucial to the theoretical landscape of computer and videogame technology. She acknowledged the importance of cyber-games and of game play in general:

> In games we have a chance to enact our most basic relationship to the world — our desire to prevail over adversity, to survive our inevitable defeats, to shape our environment, to master complexity, and to make our lives fit together like the pieces of a jigsaw puzzle. Like the religious ceremonies of passage by which we mark birth, coming of age, marriage, and death, games are ritual actions allowing us to symbolically enact the patterns that give meaning to our lives [143].

By placing game play as a rite of passage alongside such events as birth, marriage, and death, Murray reveals just how important she believes game play to be in human meaning-making. How exactly can videogames achieve this meaning-making? Earlier in her book, Murray describes her own experiences playing an arcade Western-themed shooter game named *Mad Dog McCree*, which used cinematic video and put a laser pistol in the user's hands to engage in gunfight after gunfight. Murray described the moment she became aware that she was both pacifist mother and cyber gunslinger: "I was conscious of being two very different people. I would not claim that *Mad Dog McCree* was a masterful piece of storytelling. But the moment of self-confrontation it provoked, the moment in which I was suddenly aware of an authentic but disquieting side of myself, seems to me to be the mark of a new kind of dramatic experience" (54). Clearly a rich and compelling narrative was not necessary for Murray's experience playing the game to be significant as it forced her to become aware of parts of herself she had been previously unaware of. And *Mad Dog McCree* is a game that provides neither agent nor avatar: the user simply points their laser gun at the video screen, aims, and attempts to hit the targets. If Murray could come to such self-awareness without any avatar present, and if, as Rehak and other scholars suggest, the most crucial relationship in video games is between user and avatar, then how much more powerful might Murray's experience have been if undertaken through an avatar? How can we characterize the relationships between a user and their avatar in a videogame world?

Several videogame scholars have theorized about the relationship between users and their virtual world avatars; this work reveals much uncertainty about the connections between the two. Katherine Hayles writes, "The avatar both is and is not present, just as the user both is and is not inside the screen" (38). Similarly, Rehak suggests:

> [The avatar's] behavior is tied to the player's through an interface: its literal motion, as well as its figurative triumphs and defeats, result from the player's actions. At the same time, avatars are unequivocally other. Both limited and freed by difference from the player, they can accomplish more than the player alone; they are supernatural ambassadors of agency [106].

Both authors here suggest a relationship between user and avatar that is filled with tension: the avatar is part of the user but at the same time remains separate, and the user makes decisions as to the nature of the avatar but the avatar also exists independent from the user (statically, frozen until the user returns to the game). Marie Ryan also recognizes this tension, but suggests that the user has control over how she relates to her avatar: "Will she be like an actor playing a role, innerly distanciated from her character and simulating emotions she does not really have, or will she experience her character in first-person mode, actually feeling [the emotions] that motivate the character's behavior or that may result from her actions?" (6). Wilson's definition of avatar privileges user choice, and Ryan's question here suggests that the user has complete conscious control over her relationship with her avatar. But when I read about Murray's experience playing *Mad Dog McCree*, or when I read Berger's comparison of videogames to an addictive drug, I am forced to wonder again about the nature of the user/avatar relationship and exactly how much choice the user has in this relationship. In an interview conducted by Celia Pearce, longtime LucasArts game designer Tim Schafer suggested that even as users may have complete control over their avatars in the early stages of a videogame, this relationship may change as the game play continues. In the beginning, he says, games "have to provide the character with motivation and you have to provide the player with motivation. Because the character will care about things that the player will not necessarily care about" (1). As game play progresses, Schafer hypothesizes that users begin to "ego-invest, they share the motivations of the character" (9). This notion of "ego-investing" is a complicated one and does indeed imply a reciprocal relationship between user and avatar.

Role-Playing Games

The concepts of ego-investing in an avatar and of seeing avatars as ambassadors of agency, provoking self-confrontation are interesting ones. It seems to me that these concepts, used by different theorists to try to explain the relationship between a user and her videogame avatar, are all related to one important concept: identity. How is human identity formed? Can videogame play impact identity formation? These are complex questions, as much research in identity theory and videogame theory can attest to. I will discuss this research in the next chapter. For now, I want to return my focus to avatars, since so many theorists agree that they are crucial to immersive videogame play. In distinguishing between agents and avatars earlier in this chapter, I eliminated most videogame genres from having true avatars, since most playable videogame agents are not customizable by the user. And so the question remains: which videogame genres have true avatars and provide the best opportunities for users to identify with them?

To begin to answer this question, I return to Murray's *Hamlet and the Holodeck* (1997) to highlight her prophetic talents. In this text, Murray made several speculative statements about how videogames in the future would best immerse users and impact them emotionally. Murray's predictions for immersive and emotionally evocative videogames dealt with several different aspects of videogame play. I share all of her prophetic statements here and then discuss their significance and relationship to the current status of avatars and videogame play. To sustain compelling storytelling in an interactive medium like videogames, Murray was convinced that the key was "to invent scripts that are formulaic enough to be easily grasped and responded to but flexible enough to capture a wide range of human behavior" (79). Regarding immersive game worlds, she envisioned the ideal spatial navigation:

> The potential of the labyrinth would seem to lie somewhere between the single-path maze adventure and the underdetermined form of the rhizome, in stories that are goal driven enough to guide navigation but open-ended enough to allow free exploration and that display a satisfying dramatic structure no matter how the interactor chooses to traverse the space [135].

For Murray, the key to immersive videogames lay in impacting the user emotionally: "We need to find ways of drawing a player so deeply into the situated point of view of a character that a change of position will raise important moral questions" (147). At the end of her text, Murray finally revealed the type of videogame genre she felt would best meet all these criteria as she discussed the virtual world of future videogames:

> Lushly realized places will turn from spectacle experiences to dramatic stages. We will move from the pleasures of immersion and navigational agency to increasingly active and transformational experiences.... Unlike a videogame, **a role-playing world** [emphasis mine] should allow each interactor to choose from several ways to go about the task,

including bartering as well as fighting.... The private pleasures of the digital environment are likely to continue to attract us. Solo play would allow the interactor to explore all the stories within the limits of the world and to play all the parts until they had exhausted all the possibilities of personal imaginative engagement within a nostalgically charged situation. As a domain in which we can actively participate in a responsive environment, **without consequence in the real world** [emphasis mine], the desktop story world may engage our most compelling transformational fantasies [264, 268, 270–71].

All of Murray's predictions have come true, and all of her suggestions have been realized in a particular genre of videogame. Not coincidentally, this is the same genre that allows users to construct true avatars: the video role-playing game (v–RPG).

The History of Role-Playing Games

Of course, v–RPGs owe their origins to table-top roleplaying games. *Dungeons & Dragons* (1974), created by Gary Gygax, was the first published table-top RPG. Eddie Dombrower provides a simple beginning definition for role-playing games, whether they be table-top or video: "The player assumes a persona that changes over time. The persona is assigned a range of physical and other attributes that change over time. These attributes also change as a result of the user's actions. The art of playing RPGs lies in mastering the complex relationships" (31) between the avatar and any given game situation. Gygax set *Dungeons & Dragons* (*D & D*) in a vast fantasy world inspired in part by J. R. R. Tolkien's Middle Earth, replete with magic and mythical creatures. Table-top RPGs need one person to perform the role of "dungeon master," who narrates the unfolding story for each individual gaming session, answers the players' questions about the gameworld, and takes on the role of any non-player characters[5] (NPCs) that were encountered during the session. *D & D* was enormously popular, and many additional table-top RPGs set in many additional fantastical worlds were quickly produced.[6] Table-top RPGs were epic open-ended affairs, with vast game worlds that could be expanded via the whims of dungeon masters' imaginations and endless adventuring and questing for the players' avatars. It didn't take long before techno-enthusiasts began to try to replicate the RPG experience virtually, and in 1975 several text-based v–RPGs came out for the PLATO[7] system. In 1980, Richard Garriott created *Akalabeth*, a graphical RPG that used vectoring lines much in the same way *Battlezone* did. Garriott's *Ultima* series, among the most successful v–RPGs of all time, was based on *Akalabeth*. The first v–RPG for a console system was created in 1982, when

Advanced Dungeons & Dragons: Treasure of Tarmin debuted for the Intellivision. In 2007, v–RPGs remain among the most popular video games, with MMORPGs such as *Everquest, Ultima Online,* and *World of Warcraft* each having hundreds of thousands of subscribers. However, single-player v–RPGs have been popular as well, with games such as *Final Fantasy X, Baldur's Gate, Knights of the Old Republic, Morrowind, Oblivion,* and *Mass Effect* all boasting strong sales and critical acclaim in recent years. With the continual development of computer technology, each new generation of v–RPG is now able to provide an arguably more immersive experience than table-top RPGs in all of the defining characteristics of the genre: a creative dungeon master (now "performed" by elaborate computer software), NPC interaction, a responsive, detailed environment, quantified assessment and evolution of the avatar's abilities, and a map of the game environment (Mackay 23–24). All of the v–RPGs mentioned here meet Murray's predictive criteria for immersive and emotionally meaningful videogames with open-ended game worlds and stories and most importantly for the purposes of this project, with customizable avatars. Indeed, it is the relationship between the user and their avatar that I explore to examine what identity connections exist. However, in order to study the relationships between the identity of the user and the identity of the avatar, a clear terminological framework is needed. For that framework, I turn to the writings of noted videogame scholar James Paul Gee.

Gee's Virtual, Real-World, and Projective Identities

In *What Video Games Have to Teach Us About Learning and Literacy* and *Why Video Games are Good for Your Soul*, Gee argues that in v–RPGs, three different distinct identities are involved. The first of these is a virtual identity: the avatar that exists in the fictionalized virtual gameworld. Gee provides the example of the half-elf named "Bead Bead" he created for the v–RPG *Arcanum.* The second type Gee calls real-world identity. For Gee, this is the "real-world character" (*What Video Games* 55) that sits down in front of a computer and plays the game. James Gee is a real-world identity: Gee has a physical body that exists (much of the time in Tempe, Arizona). However, Gee points out that each of us have many different "nonvirtual identities" at all times, identifying himself as a "professor, a linguist, an Anglo American, a middle-age male baby boomer, a parent, an avid reader, a former devout Catholic" (55) and so on. These multiple aspects of our identities are accessed by us as necessary as we encounter and react to life stimuli. Given Gee's notion of multiple identities, how does he characterize the interactions between his real-world identity (James Gee) and his virtual identity (Bead Bead)? Gee describes Bead Bead as a "delicious blend of my doing and not my doing" (54–55) and to explain this he creates his third type of identity, projective identity, which he describes as:

> The kind of person I want Bead Bead to be, the kind of history I want her to have, the kind of person and history I am trying to build in and through her is what I mean by a projective identity. Since these aspirations are my desires for Bead Bead, the projective identity is both mine and hers, and it is a space in which I can transcend both her limitations and my own.... In this identity, the stress is on the interface between — the interactions between — the real-world person and the virtual character [56].

Gee's projective identity then is the middle ground between the real-world identity and the virtual identity of the user: the avatar. Like Gee, I too am interested in the relationship between the real-world identity of the user, the virtual identity of the avatar, and the connections and tensions that exist between these two types of identity.

Even though he never uses the word itself, Gee's description of projective identity as the bridge between the real-world and virtual identities suggests that he sees the projective identity as liminal space. Liminality, from the Latin word meaning "threshold," was used by Van Gennep in 1908 as part of his three step sequence describing rites of passage: separation, liminality, and reincorporation. Liminality, the middle stage, was the phase where one belonged to both and neither of the other two phases: a phase of transition during which normal limits to self understanding are relaxed thus opening the way to something new. Seeing Gee's projective identity as a type of liminality clarifies the ways other videogame scholars also consider the relationship between user and avatar as intriguing yet problematic space. Rehak discusses avatars and liminality in the following manner:

> Movement back and forth across the border separating self from other might therefore be considered a kind of liminal play. We create avatars to leave our bodies behind, yet take the body with us in the form of codes and assumptions about what does and does not constitute a legitimate interface with reality — virtual or otherwise.... The worlds we create — and the avatarial bodies through which we experience them — seem destined to mirror not our wholeness, but our lack of it [123, 124].

Flynn defines a liminal experience in gaming as a "moment of heightened pleasure as the player is briefly suspended between one realm of experience and another" (2). Both of these theoretical descriptions seem consistent with Gee's explanation of projective identity. Even Murray spoke of liminal objects, "located on the threshold between external reality and our own minds" (99).

She described this balancing act: "In order to sustain such powerful immersive trances we have to do something inherently paradoxical: we have to keep the virtual world 'real' by keeping it 'not there.' We have to keep it balanced squarely on the enchanted threshold without letting it collapse onto either side" (100). All of these scholars, Gee included, seem convinced that the liminal, threshold space between the user and the videogame avatar is crucial to any identity formation that occurs as the result of v–RPG play. But is there reason to believe that such identity formation is actually occurring? Is there evidence to suggest that the real-world identities of v–RPG users are impacted in meaningful ways by their virtual identities? To find out, I turned my attention to two v–RPGs that I knew had large fan bases devoted to them, and in which I had personally felt strong connections to my own avatars: *The Elder Scrolls III: Morrowind* and *The Elder Scrolls IV: Oblivion*.[8]

Identity in Elderscrolls.com's Morrowind *and* Oblivion *Forums*

Both games are set in the Elder Scrolls fantasy universe[9] and are single-player v–RPGs. *Morrowind* was originally released in 2002 for PCs and the Xbox console system; *Oblivion* came out in 2006 for PCs and the Xbox 360. Both v–RPGs topped many video game critics' "Game of the Year" lists and remain popular today.[10] This popularity is evidenced by the large number of postings in the *Morrowind* and *Oblivion* forums[11] at Elderscrolls.com, a comprehensive website devoted to the Elder Scrolls universe depicted in Bethesda Software's games. It was to these avid *Morrowind* and *Oblivion* gamers in the Elderscrolls.com forums that I turned to begin my examination of just how closely connected users believed their real-world identities were to their virtual identities. Joining the *Morrowind* forum, I posted the following entry:

> Is your *Morrowind* identity any less "real" than your real-world identity? If many of us are logging hundreds of hours with our *Morrowind* avatars (a virtual identity), what impact does this have on our "real" identity? In other words, does the time spent in *Morrowind* carry over/impact when you leave that virtual setting? I'm interested in hearing how you see your identities (real, virtual, and the intersection between these two) being impacted/influenced by *Morrowind*. Do you find your virtual *Morrowind* identity to be as "real" in some ways as your non-virtual identity? How does one inform the other?

I also posted a similar question in the *Oblivion* forum. The replies I received to these questions were fascinating as they highlighted what appeared to be a significant, dynamic, yet poorly understood relationship between the users' real-life identities and their virtual identities. Dante Nerevar wrote:

In many ways I look at my character as me, except for the fact that my skin is not grey. I look at it like this: there are two of me, Nick [real-world identity] and Dante [virtual identity]. When not playing *Morrowind* I am Nick, but when I am I'm a completely different person. When I get lost in a virtual reality it is a good thing. Regardless, some of my characteristics influence Dante's and his influence mine [1].

Here, the user seems to contradict himself, at first stating that his two identities were "completely different" but later admitting to mutual influence between the two. Toastman shows a similar contradiction when he discusses the separation between his real-world identity and his *Morrowind* avatars:

For me, playing a character in a game is like playing a character in a play or movie. I love getting completely absorbed in a new identity, discovering how he reacts that is different from my reactions. I do things in character that I would never, ever think of doing in real life, [but] for some of my characters I make decisions based on my own values. While the [avatars] are fun to play, they're not me. Sure, maybe they represent subconscious aspects of my personality, but while I may act somewhat differently when I'm with family, or friends, or coworkers, I'm still essentially the same. Any differences are mostly superficial. Even though my own identity can change depending on who I'm with, my *Morrowind* identities are less real to me than my own identity. I know that when the lights go down on the stage, or when I power down my computer, that I will be myself again [1].

Toastman is willing to admit that his real-world identity is constantly shifting given different stimuli, but isn't willing to concede that his virtual identity (which also evolves thanks to Toastman's reactions to stimuli) is as significant as his real-world identity. His last phrase is provocative: if he wasn't himself during his *Morrowind* gameplay, then who was he? Did his avatar have a life of its own? Toastman seems unwilling to concede that the relationship between himself and his avatar might be substantial in any way. Another gamer, Anais, chooses to distance herself from her avatar. In writing about her favorite *Oblivion* avatar, she says, "I find that with my most played Bosmer [an elf] we often have disagreements. She has solutions to problems that wouldn't occur to me. I also have to respect her wishes" (1). Here, she seems to suggest that her Bosmer virtual identity comes up with solutions to problems without any input from Anais' real-world identity. Of course, this is impossible, since the *Morrowind* avatar takes no actions that are not explicitly triggered by the user. These users all seem to be in denial about the connections between themselves and their avatars.

Other *Morrowind* and *Oblivion* gamers seemed much more comfortable acknowledging the reciprocal relationship between their real-world identity and their virtual identity via their avatar. Syronj wrote, "Shaka [the avatar] is an idealized version of what I would look up to in a character: brave and unselfish, whenever possible. I found that I'm not good at playing evil characters in the game. At the same time, I sometimes think the game has made me more likely to take a chance in real life" (1). Syronj credits her virtual experience in *Morrowind* with making her real-world identity braver. Danile also readily admits that her avatars are:

> Mainly how I would like to be in real life. Tough, and not taking any put downs or anything from anyone. But, like me, they are caring and do not hurt anyone if they do not have to. One of my current characters likes to go pearl diving and all the pearls he gets he sells to get money for widows and orphans. It's beyond me to be evil [1].

I can't help but notice in Danile's posting how she seems to unconsciously move from the avatar ("he") to herself ("me"). This was a common phenomenon in many gamers' postings. James Gee himself demonstrated a similar connection to his *Morrowind* avatar Bead when recounting the shame he felt when Bead disrobed at the request of an NPC to obtain information. Gee confesses that he ended up killing that NPC out of rage and shame shortly thereafter. He also admits to having guilt over killing a guard while stealing a weapon out of a museum: "We felt guilty about this murder to the end. Many times we wished we had re-played that part of the game to clear our record" (*Why Video Games* 94). Note Gee's usage of "we" and "our" in this statement; this usage reflects the first person plurality of his videogame identity. Bobg seems to share Danile's identification with her avatar, saying that he does "feel what my [*Oblivion*] characters must be feeling given the person they are and their situation in the game. I try to play according to their world view" (1). Another user blames his virtual world struggles with addiction on his real-world identity's similar problems, as he admits to having logged over 1,000 hours playing *Morrowind* in a post that reminds me of Berger's statement at the start of this chapter. The vrrc writes, "I have spent entire days doing nothing but playing *Morrowind*. Quite literally 18 hours a day, sometimes for several days in a row. I have a very addictive personality ... which is also why I can't stay off the skooma"[12] (1).

The presence of a liminal projective identity between real-world and virtual identities was perhaps best articulated in these forums by the users named doctor44 and Bloom. Doctor44 acknowledges that his *Oblivion* avatars are really "expressions of myself. They express the darker sides of my personality that are inappropriate to express in the real world — it's a way to keep myself in balance in a safe and secure manner" (1). In describing his current *Morrowind* avatar Boris Karl, Bloom writes:

> It is amazing to me that Boris Karl is not even a level 5 character,[13] yet has walked around the entire circumference of Vvardenfell. He has

been killed several times, but never has he been all that interested in leveling up. It's not in his nature. When Boris encounters something that interests Bloom, the two have a tendency to overlap, although I try to resist that ... I think the middle ground between them (Boris and Bloom) is the arena of exploration and discovery. It is why I love the game as much as I do [1].

Other gamers expressed a similar and somewhat inexplicable fondness for their avatars. Cobb ruminated in the following manner about his *Oblivion* avatar: "I've stuck with the same character right through *Oblivion* — all 1000+ hours! She certainly isn't a 'perfect' character, in fact she's bloody useless — especially once mountain lions start appearing. I dunno, though, she's kind of grown on me even though I'm not sure what I was aiming for in the character creation stage. I've gotten so used to having her around" (1). Cobb's attachment to his female avatar is interesting indeed. Bloom and Cobb aren't alone in deriving pleasure from their Elder Scrolls videogame experiences as the following quote from Ice Troll illustrates: "Some consider *Morrowind* to be better than sex. I think they are exaggerating a bit, but it's pretty close" (1). Ice Troll's comment may well be tongue-in-cheek, but Bloom seems to believe that Boris and Bloom are both the same and different, joined and separate, that Boris has his own "nature" just as Bloom does. This tension between being/not being takes place in liminal space via Gee's projective identity as these replies from die-hard gamers strongly suggest.

Other postings in the *Morrowind* and *Oblivion* forums also suggest that the journey between real-world identity and virtual identity is not always instantaneous: it may take time for some gamers to complete the passage out of their virtual identity. One topical thread contained in both forums illustrated this clearly. It was entitled "You know you've played too much *Morrowind/Oblivion* when...." Each user was invited to share an example that completed this sentence. Brayf provided the following response: "When somebody walks into the room while you're playing, and you try to turn and look at them by moving the mouse" (1). Padalin made the following confession: "When you're mad with a friend and you say 'khajiit has no words for you'[14] and that actually happened to me whether you believe me or not" (1). Farterman suggested that "you know you have been playing too much when in REAL life you think of doing something bad that might affect you, and you ask yourself, 'Maybe I should save before I do this'" (1). Lonesniper admits to having real-world nightmares based on *Morrowind*: "When you have dreams about Corprus monsters[15] attacking you in the real world. Guilty" (1). Toastman posted the following response to this topic thread: "When this happens to you: I was doing the Sanctus Shrine Tempe Quest[16] and my housemate came into my room and asked me a question. It took me a few seconds to realize that I could actually talk to him without messing up the pilgrimage" (1). Toastman apparently needed a few seconds to move from his virtual identity to his real-world identity.

All of these postings seem to suggest that the virtual experiences the users had in *Morrowind* and *Oblivion* via their avatars were carrying over into their real-world experiences in certain ways, but exactly how was this happening? And to what extent does the level of immersive identification with the avatar and gaming world in question dictate the time needed to transition out of a virtual identity? This preliminary examination of *Morrowind* and *Oblivion* gamers using Gee's terminological identity construct led me to some very interesting questions indeed: How do the virtual identities of avatars in v–RPGs get constructed? Using *Morrowind*, *Oblivion*, and *Fallout 3* as representative examples, what is the relationship between real-world identity, virtual identity, and projective identity in video role-playing games? Before examining data collected specifically from players of these three v–RPGs I need to first provide an overview of the theoretical fields relevant to these questions. I turn now in chapter two to a closer examination of theoretical work related to identity, videogames, genre, and narrativity.

2

Locating Identity in
New Media Theory

Conscious agency is the essence of human identity. Sacrifice this, and we humans are hopelessly compromised, contaminated with mechanic alienness in the very heart of our humanity.

— Katherine Hayles, technology theorist, 1999

I no longer believe in a single reality, a single integrating view of the world, or even the reliability of a single angle of perception.

— Janet Murray, narrative theorist, 1997

Role-playing games can serve in [an] evocative capacity because they stand betwixt and between the unreal and the real; they are a game and something more.

— Sherry Turkle, technology theorist, 1995

To begin to understand the relationship between Gee's tripartite notions of identity (real-world, virtual, and projective) in video role-playing games several different themes need to be explored. In this chapter I first examine modern and postmodern theories of identity as identity formation is the main focus of this study. Next I trace important concepts and terms from videogame theory, as several technological aspects of this entertainment medium are essential to its immersive potential. Narrative theory is also discussed: narratives and stories are powerful instruments of meaning-making, both in the formation of personal identity and in v–RPGs. Finally, I discuss the importance of genre theory, as the fantasy role-playing videogame has at least three distinct generic levels (fantasy, role-playing game, and videogame). Each of these four major theoretical areas (identity theory, video game rhetoric, narrativity, and genre theory) make essential contributions to my examination of the identity formation that occurs between users and their avatars in video role-playing games.

Identity: Modernist Theories

It is essential to first explore the theoretical concept of "identity." What is identity? How is it formed? The answers to these questions continue to be much debated by scholars across disciplines. Most would agree that one's identity (or identities) is part of one's "self," but Jan Klein's scientific definition of "self" shows just how problematic this is: "[Self is] everything constituting an integral part of a given individual" (5). Rhetorically, it is easy to see this definition is open to much interpretation. For example, what constitutes an "integral" part for a given individual? Who gets to make that decision: the individual or the society around that individual? Much of the theoretical conversation revolving around identity is concerned with this very issue, with modernist and postmodernist perspectives central to the argument.

One of modernism's defining characteristics is the heavy emphasis it places on the individual. Alberto Melucci succinctly summarizes this view: "The most exalting and dramatic legacy of modernity [is] our need and duty to exist as individuals. Modern individuals think of themselves as subjects of action capable of purposive and meaningful behavior" (61). In similar fashion, Lester Faigley describes how modernism's notion of the individual is a "coherent consciousness capable of knowing oneself and the world" (16). With this concept at its core, Anthony Giddens' *Modernity and Self-Identity* is a pivotal modernist treatise on identity and identity construction. For Giddens, self-identity is connected to self-awareness:

> Existence is a mode of being-in-the-world. In doing everyday life, all human beings answer the question of being; they do it by the nature of the activities they carry out.... The identity of the self presumes reflexive awareness. It is what the individual is conscious of in the term self-consciousness. Self-identity has to be routinely created and sustained in the reflexive activities of the individual.... Self-identity is not a distinctive trait, or even a collection of traits, possessed by the individual. It is the self as reflexively understood by the person in terms of her or his biography [presuming] continuity across time and space.... A person's identity is not to be found in behavior nor in the reactions of others, but in the capacity to keep a particular narrative going. The individual's biography, if she is to maintain regular interaction with others in the day-to-day world, cannot be wholly fictive. It must continually integrate events which occur in the external world and sort them into the ongoing story about the self [52, 53, 54].

Giddens reveals some interesting assumptions about identity in this passage. It seems clear that he believes in a single self-identity rather than multiple self-identities for an individual. This identity is determined by a person's life narrative (again singular) that is created through the individual's self-awareness. In other words, each person becomes aware of their own identity by constructing a narrative about themselves: who they are and what they have done. Each new action the person takes must be able to be integrated with the identity they have already created in their life narrative (with change possible over time). He also suggests here that neither the person's actions nor the outside perceptions of those actions by other people greatly impact identity: the narrative within the individual's mind (and that individual's own awareness of the narrative) determines identity. Giddens' view here is very much in keeping with modernism's privileging of the individual and the sovereignty of the individual mind. He also makes many assumptions about the nature of stories and narrative theory which do not do justice to the complexity of narrativity.[1]

Giddens also stresses the importance of the body and embodiment to self identity:

> The self, of course, is embodied. To learn to become a competent agent is to be able to exert a continuous, and successful, monitoring of face and body.... Regularized control of the body is a fundamental means whereby a biography of self-identity is maintained.... The body and its practical immersion in the interactions of day-to-day life is an essential part of the sustaining of a coherent sense of self-identity [56, 57, 99].

For Giddens, embodiment is crucial to self-identity, even as his earlier quote suggested that the story of one's life that created identity exists in mental self-awareness. Giddens' modernist view on identity is complex in this regard. He suggests that the body's "immersion" in daily activities (external stimuli) is essential to sustaining self-identity, as the mind then processes and reflects on these external stimuli to create a coherent internal narrative. It is interesting to note here that Giddens also warns of the potential dangers of creating a disembodied false self "in which the body appears as an object or instrument manipulated by the self from behind the scenes.... The disembodied person may feel unimplicated in bodily desire, and experiences dangers as though they were threats to another person. When this dissociation happens as an unwanted feature of personality it expresses existential anxieties impinging directly upon self-identity" (59). Implicit here is the binary between true/false, another marker of modernity. I have found no evidence to suggest that Giddens ever studied videogames or considered them in constructing his theories of identity. Nevertheless, it is interesting to consider the relationship between users and their avatars in light of Giddens' ideas of disembodied notions of self. Later in this chapter I will examine whether or not videogame scholars consider the role-playing that takes place in v–RPGs as a dangerous, disembodiment of self-identity as Giddens likely would.

One of the biggest distinctions between modern and postmodern conceptions of identity is the debate over whether or not the self is unitary or multiple. Giddens articulates the modern view well as he critiques the postmodern notion of a fragmented concept of self-identity: "Some authors suppose that the self essentially becomes broken up — that individuals tend to develop multiple selves in which there is no inner core of self-identity. This is plainly not the case. The maintaining of constants of demeanor across varying settings of interaction is one of the prime means whereby coherence of self-identity is ordinarily preserved" (100). Yet later Giddens admits that this core is continually shifting: "A self-identity has to be created and more or less continually reordered against the backdrop of shifting experiences of day-to-day life and the fragmenting tendencies of modern institutions" (186). Even as Giddens is referring here to what he believes to be a stable self, this "reordered and shifting" identity suggests a multiplicity of identity in keeping with much postmodern theory.

Identity: Postmodernist Theories

Postmodern identity theorists privilege the "shifting experiences of day-to-day life" in postulating that individual identity is actually individual identities, fragmented and multiple. Whereas Giddens sees a core identity, many postmodern theorists question the very notion of a core at all. Feminist scholar Diana Fuss characterizes the postmodern view as she points out that identity is a disputed and unstable theoretical concept: "Identity is rarely identical to itself but instead has multiple and sometimes contradictory meanings ... [what is needed is] recognition of the precarious status of identity and a full awareness of the complicated processes of identity formation, both psychical and social" (98, 99). It seems clear that Fuss believes that both internal (psychical) and external (social) stimuli contribute to the multiplicity of identities within individuals. She goes on to say that her "own position endorse[s] identity as alienated and fictitious.... To the extent that identity always contains the specter of non-identity within it, the subject is always divided.... Fictions of identity are no less powerful for being fictions. It is not so much that we possess contingent identities but that identity itself is contingent" (102–104). The last sentence of this statement demonstrates that Fuss does not believe in any "core" identity but rather always shifting, contextual identities with none having any lasting primacy over the others. The notion of identity being closely associated with non-identity is also an important concept. To more fully explain this connection I return briefly to modernism and Kenneth Burke's concept of identification.

Identification

Burke was firmly situated in modernism, but his views on human identification remain relevant to modern and postmodern theorists alike and are crucial to understanding identity. For Burke, identification was a consubstantiation of merger and division: "In being identified with B, A is 'substantially one' with a person other than himself. Yet at the same time he remains unique, an individual locus of motives. Thus he is both joined and separate, at once a distinct substance and consubstantial with another" (20–21). Every day, people identify the stimuli they encounter as similar to themselves (merger) or dissimilar to themselves (division). Both are identifications, however, since as humans we are only ever able to define ourselves (what we are) in relation to what we are not anyway. Burke refers to this as the paradox of substance: a man is defined in relationship to not-man (woman); life is defined in relationship to not-life (death), and so on. Burke believed the transformation that occurred between life and death was one of the most important types of identification imaginable. Indeed, all identifications had the potential to be substantially transformative for Burke, whether the identification was merger or division. The influences of Burke's modern notions of transformation and identification can be found in the decidedly postmodern views of many videogame scholars, including Rehak, who explains just how crucial the transformation between life and death are to avatarial identification: "Avatars differ from us through their ability to live, die, and live again.... The simulated experience of death and resurrection is a key function of the avatar.... Systematic rupture of the agential and identificatory linkage between players and avatars is a defining characteristic.... Players derive pleasure from avatarial instability" (107, 114, 110, 123). Rehak clearly believes that users identify with their avatars through both merger (creating and controlling the appearance and skills of the avatar) and division (being forced to reload an earlier saved game point when the avatar dies, for example). Gee also echoes Burkean identification by stating that videogame "pleasure is a play between sameness and difference, a play between simplicity and complexity" (*Why Video Games* 13). For Gee, the tensions between being and not-being become pleasurable in videogames.

Fuss also explores the notion of identification in relation to identity but takes a different approach from Burke. She distinguishes between identity and identification in the following way:

> We tend to experience our identities as part of our public personas, the most exposed part of our self's surface collisions with a world of other selves—we experience our identifications as more private, guarded, evasive ... every identity is actually an identification come to light.... Identity is the Self that identifies itself. Identification is the psychical mechanism that produces self-recognition ... the detour through the other that defines a self [2].

Identification then for Fuss is the more personal, internal self-awareness that precedes and leads to the more public identities of individuals. This identification seems similar to Giddens' reflexive self-awareness in some respects, but Giddens would likely never agree that this self-awareness ever travels through an "other" to construct self-identity. Fuss' observation raises an interesting question when applied to a v–RPG avatar: can the user's avatar become this "other" through which the user produces self-recognition?

Fuss also resonates with Burke's paradox of substance when she discusses the concept of disidentification: an individual's willful choice to experience division rather than merger (to use Burke's terms). However, Fuss astutely points out that disidentification "may actually represent an identification that one fears to make only because one has already made it" (7). Murray's conflicted revelation about her dual role as pacifist mother and *Mad Dog McCree* gunslinger comes to mind as an example of the tenuous division between identification and disidentification. Fuss (drawing on Rey Chow's *Writing Diaspora*) also discusses identification as a "violent negation," pointing out that our identifications with cultural others are often "violent fantasies of displacement—fantasy idealizations that enact imaginary usurpations ... identification operates on one level as an endless process of violent negation, a process of killing off the other in fantasy in order to usurp the other's place, the place where the subject desires to be" (8–9). Here too we see echoes of Burkean transformation tied to life and death. Fuss also argues, contrary to Freud's psychoanalytical view, that identification (in Freudian language, the wish to be the other) and desire (the wish to have the other) are "fundamentally indissociable" (12): identification and desire for Fuss cannot be extricated from each other.

Other postmodern theorists see identity in still different ways. Filiciak acknowledges the influence of postmodernism in his definition of identity, calling it "cogitation on how to define our 'self' under postmodern living conditions" (88). Of course, as we know from Hayles' earlier observation, "self" is an equally problematic concept. Filiciak goes on to describe "conventionally understood human identity" as being a "constancy of physical and mental traits that allow us to differentiate our self from others" (93). He points out that in the past (before the industrial revolution), people had little opportunity to change social class and, therefore, social interactions, their residence, or type of work. Since the industrial revolution this has changed dramatically, Filiciak argues, thus increasing the number of social identities individuals now take on. Drawing on William James, Filiciak suggests that identity is determined only in reference to others. This idea resonates with Burke's paradox of substance and merger and division: self identities created in relationship to external stimuli that we identify as similar or different.

Feminist technology theorist Donna Haraway also critiques modernism's notions of self and identity. Despite her theoretical differences from Fuss, Butler, and other feminist postmodern theorists, Haraway sees the modernist, Western notion of self as inaccurate: "[The] concept of a coherent inner self, achieved or innate, is a regulatory fiction that is unnecessary.... Identities seem contradictory, partial, and strategic" (135, 155). Haraway uses the term "splitting" to describe the contradictory nature of self-identities:

> Splitting should be about heterogeneous multiplicities that are simultaneously necessary and incapable of being squashed into isomorphic slots or cumulative lists. The knowing self is partial in all its guises, never finished, whole, simply there and original; it is always constructed and stitched together imperfectly, and therefore able to join with another, to see together without claiming to be another [193].

Haraway describes self-identity as consisting of many distinct and unique parts (division) that nevertheless share enough (merger) to be able to join together. She stresses the importance of these different aspects of the self being able to "see" each other as crucial to the creation of self-identity, making the concept of vision central to this theory:

> Being is problematic and contingent. One cannot relocate in any possible vantage point without being accountable for that movement. Vision is always a question of the power to see. We are not immediately present to ourselves. Self-knowledge requires a semiotic-material technology linking meanings and bodies.... Vision requires instruments of vision. Instruments of vision mediate standpoints. Positioning is, therefore, the key practice grounding knowledge organized around the imagery of vision [192, 193].

Haraway's stance on vision here illuminates what seems to be a major problem: how to effectively switch vantage points to allow for alternative viewings to aid in self-identity? In other words, how can we position ourselves to see ourselves so that we might reflect on ourselves? I believe videogame theory related to avatars (which are typically offered in both first- and third-person points of view) can begin to provide answers to these questions and I will return to the issue later in this chapter.

Identity and Performance

Several postmodern theorists stress a performative aspect to identity. Among the most well-known of these is Judith Butler whose theory of performativity continues to influence many postmodern scholars. Butler focuses on gender, describing it as a repeated performance that produces the social belief in both a core gender and a distinction between interior and exterior. Butler stresses that both of these commonly held assumptions are fictions, that there is no core identity or any distinct demarcation between interior and exterior. In her own words:

> Persons only become intelligible through becoming gendered in conformity with recognizable standards of gender intelligibility. To what extent is "identity" a normative ideal rather than a descriptive feature of experience? The "coherence" and "continuity" of "the person" are not logical or analytic features of personhood, but, rather, socially instituted and maintained norms of intelligibility [16–17].

Performance (which can contain a mixture of language and bodily aspects) then could alter meaning in both internal and external ways. Butler seems comfortable theorizing language from both a Cartesian (language is understood through the mind processing ideas) and a Spinozan (language is a bodily transaction and transformation) perspective (Knapp 41).

For Butler, identity does have a type of durability that is created through culturally acceptable performances: not all roles are equally possible due to social limitations and influences. Jonathan Friedman seems to see identity as more easily altered, declaring that "identity is reduced to a mere mask or role to be taken on at will.... The ability to be able to shift from one identity to the next is a performative phenomenon" (76). Friedman identifies the mask as contributing to identity construction and indeed other scholars from Callois in 1961 to Filiciak in 2003 have investigated the importance of the mask in the history of societal identity play. Might not avatars represent a new incarnation of the mask? Mackay, in pointing out the obvious connections between performativity and table-top RPGs, suggests that role-playing experiences are as significant to identity construction as any other life experiences:

> Life, identity, and meaning are all understood as consisting of nothing more than language games, exercises in role-playing. Social reality is experienced through the performance of life, the performance of the everyday. In a world of manifest meaninglessness, devoid of any metanarrative by which to understand the events around us, it is only through relishing the role one plays that a person can find any sense of satisfaction [154].

For Mackay, all identity is performance, with the roles being played constantly in social motion (even as some identity performances are more culturally accepted than others). Butler would likely agree with him, just as she would likely agree with Melucci's connecting identity to body and language:

> Between the body and the various languages with which we give a name to our world we must be able to move with flexibility, open to change but respecting our limits. For individuals, this means accepting a finite existence and the possibility of change. Thus the theme of metamorphosis, of the ability to assume new forms, returns as a condition for coexistence [67–68].

Melucci also hypothesizes that identity is both a system and a process, pointing out that "the field is defined by a set of relations (making it a system), and is simultaneously able to intervene to act upon itself and to restructure itself (making it a process)" (64). Here, Melucci clearly states what many of the other postmodern theorists have implied about identity and the tensions and connections between the internal and external components that contribute to identity formation.

Identity and Computer Technologies

Identity theorists have also studied the prevalence of computer technology in the postmodern world. Sherry Turkle is among the most prominent in exploring how the Internet and other computer technologies have impacted the way we think about our self-identities. Identity, Turkle says, "refers to the sameness between two qualities, between a person and his or her persona" (12). She suggests that the notion of computer windows provides a "powerful metaphor for thinking about the self as a multiple, distributed system" (14). A computer user might have several different programs running at one time: a word processing program, an Internet browser, a calculator, and an Email account. Each program's window can be minimized at will, and the user can bring any of them to the forefront as desired. Turkle believes that this is similar to the different aspects of our self-identity: different facets can be given primacy depending on our needs and wants. Thus, the computer is "an object on the border between self and not-self" (30). To be sure, this belief echoes modernism, as it assumes an individual with the agency and power to shift between these "windows of the self." Nevertheless, Turkle seems to subscribe to the notion that an individual's identity is what Lifton has described as "protean": a self that is "capable of fluid transformations but is grounded in coherence and a moral outlook. It is multiple but integrated.... The essence of this flexible self is not unitary, nor are its parts stable entities. It is easy to cycle through its aspects and these are themselves changing through constant communication with each other" (258, 261). This "grounding in coherence" seems similar to Gidden's notion of a consistent demeanor that runs throughout the varying aspects of self-identity. Turkle's views on identity situate her between modern and postmodern theoretical positions as she embraces concepts from both.

Allucquere Roseanne Stone's work on cyber identities, transgendered peoples, and multiple personality disorders situate her as decidedly postmodern in her stance on identity. Like Haraway, she considers the Western notion of a single identity to be inaccurate:

> The self appears to be a constant, unchanging, stable product of a moment in Western history.... The societal imperative with which we have been raised is that there is one primary persona, or "true identity," and that in the offline world — the "real world" — this persona is firmly attached to a single physical body, by which our existence as a social being is authorized and in which it is grounded. [But this] Western idea that the body and the subject are inseparable is an exercise in wish fulfillment.... [Identity would] be better described as a process that is also palpably in continual flux [19, 73, 20].

For Stone, computer technologies make visible the essential fact that human identity is multiple: "The identities that emerge from [human-machine] interactions [are] fragmented and complex. I see these identities engaged in a wonderful and awesome struggle, straining to make meaning and sense out of their lives" (36). Stone describes this as a "struggle" because of the history of stigmatization of multiple identities and multiple personalities in Western culture. Stone sees the potential for computer technology to aid in reducing modern views of a single self by allowing viewpoints that increase the acceptance of identity-as-multiple.

Katherine Hayles' conception of identity is also heavily influenced by computer technology. Fearful about the direction humanity is headed due to its relationship to technology, she warns of a "posthuman" viewpoint of identity. A posthuman view, she says, privileges informational patterns over the material, "so that embodiment in a biological substrate is seen as an accident of history rather than an inevitability of life" (20). Through this lens, the human body is thought of as "the original prosthesis we all learn to manipulate, so that extending or replacing the body with other prostheses becomes a continuation of a process that began before we were born" (21). Finally, the posthuman view configures a "human being so that it can be seamlessly articulated with intelligent machines" (21). Hayles' views are extreme: humanity is certainly not in a posthuman stage yet. But the question of whether or not the body is necessarily essential to identities is an interesting one. Hayles uses anorexia as an example of how some people already view the body as an object to be controlled and not intrinsic to the self—she argues it is the mind not the body that seems to be crucial in these cases. Of course, few would argue that anorexia demonstrates a healthy sense of identity, and Giddens would no doubt share Hayles' concerns about any "posthuman" moves away from bodily connections to identity. Yet even Hayles admits to succumbing to posthuman thinking about her identity:

> I now find myself saying things like, "Well, my sleep agent wants to rest, but my food agent says I should go to the store." Each person who thinks this way begins to envision herself or himself as a posthuman collectivity, an "I" transformed into the "we" of autonomous agents operating together to make a self. The infectious power of this way of thinking gives "we" a performative dimension [24].

When considered in this way, Hayles' notion of posthuman identity seems in keeping with most other postmodern identity theories that privilege performativity and multiple, shifting identities These postmodern identity theories allow space for Gee's virtual, real-world and projective identities to form.

Debates between modern and postmodern identity theories continue. However, most theorists regardless of their camp seem to agree that communication media impact human identity construction. Even modern identity theorists such as Giddens recognize the importance of these external stimuli: "Mediated experience has long influenced both self-identity and the basic organization of social relations" (4). This statement is echoed by Jay David Bolter and Richard Grusin almost a decade later: "[People] employ media as vehicles for defining personal identity" (231). Bolter's and Grusin's *Remediation: Understanding New Media* is a pivotal text discussing the impact of media on human experiences and I use it here to mark a shift in this chapter into a review of theories related to technologies and their impact on humanity. To be sure, the identity theories discussed earlier in this chapter are present in much computer and videogame theory, as many theorists attempt to explore how and why users become immersed in computer technology. Predictably, most computer and videogame theorists subscribe to postmodern concepts of identity and identity construction.

Bolter and Grusin introduce two important terms that describe styles of visual representation that are applicable to videogame theory: immediacy and hypermediacy. Immediacy's goal is to "make the viewer forget the presence of the medium and believe that he is in the presence of the objects of representation" (272–273). When a filmmaker like Peter Jackson spends millions of dollars to create elaborate costumes, expensive sets, and hundreds of digitalized special effects for the *Lord of the Rings* film trilogy, this is done to make viewers feel as if they were "really there" (5) in Middle Earth as Bolter and Grusin put it. However, immediacy in videogames (and in most other media forms) is heavily dependent on hypermediacy: a style where the goal is to remind the viewer of the medium. How is it that these two styles with opposite goals actually work together? Bolter and Grusin illustrate this principle in the concept of the flight simulator, one of the earliest genres of computer game:

> The action unfolds in real time, as the player is required to monitor the instruments and fly the plane. The game promises to show the player what it is like to be a pilot, and yet in what does this immediacy of the experience consist? As in a real plane, the simulated cockpit is full of dials to read and switches to flip. As in a real plane, the experience of the game is that of working an interface, so that the immediacy of this experience is pure hypermediacy [11].

Bolter and Grusin here demonstrate the importance of the computer interface to computer/human interactions. Scholars have defined "interface" in a few interesting ways. Mackay calls interfaces "material objects that allow participants to perceive the imaginary realm" (78). This general definition would apply to the projection of film onto a movie screen and the pages of a fantasy novel as well as to computer hardware that allows the playing of a videogame. Wolf provides a definition more specifically tailored to videogames: "the boundary between the player and the video game itself. The interface is really a junction point between input and output, hardware and software, and the player and the material game itself, and the portal through which player activity occurs" (15). In this definition "interface" includes all peripheral devices like the keyboard, mouse, screen, and speakers and also onscreen graphical elements like buttons, scroll bars, and windows. Most interesting in Wolf's definition when considering identity is the last part where he suggests the interface is a "portal," a "junction," for activity. I am reminded here of how Gee describes projective identity: the middle ground identity between the real-world and virtual identity is also portal-like. Perhaps for experienced computer users, the windows-like computer interface becomes "transparent": it is easy for these users to see how to make the interface work, and how to negotiate between the different windows, so much so that they don't have to actively concentrate on the interface itself. It's like the tacit knowledge involved in driving a car: even as there is a complex interface, with multiple and continuous tasks to perform, soon enough we're able to work the interface almost unconsciously and get "beyond" it to focus on the external world through the windows. The internal workings of the car become transparent; so too do the external workings of the computer interface.

Most videogame scholars seem to agree that having the computer interface become transparent is one of the key criteria for a truly "immersive" video gaming experience. Immersion is a term that is used frequently by both popular and critical culture when discussing the appeal of videogames. Like so many key concepts, it has been defined in different ways. Murray's definition is the most often cited; she describes immersion as "the experience of being transported to an elaborately simulated place" (98). She believes that there is an "age-old desire to live out a fantasy aroused by a fictional world" (98) and that computer technology makes this possible in more tangible ways than ever before. Murray also believes that immersion does not so much suspend belief as it actively creates belief and that these elaborately simulated places can "become real through use" (11). Alison McMahan, acknowledging Murray's definition of immersion, offers a somewhat different, more videogame-specific, definition: "the player is caught up in the world of the game's story (the diegetic level), but [immersion] also refers to the player's love of the game and the strategy that goes into it (the nondiegetic level)" (68). She also identifies three conditions needed to create immersion in a video game: 1) user expectations for the game environment and the actual game environment must be aligned; 2) the user's actions in the game world must have a "non-trivial impact" (69) on the game world; 3) the conventions of the gameworld must be internally consistent. These criteria provide a useful guide to ascertaining what factors contribute to user immersion levels in v–RPGs.

Nicola Green's discussion of immersion connects well to Gee's tripartite notions of identity, suggesting that the immersion that takes place in virtual worlds is in fact not purely disembodied at all, but instead is heavily grounded in prior, non-virtual social experiences. He argues that the human-technical interface by necessity uses these pre-existing (prior to entry into the virtual world) experiences as referents (59–60). This seems to support the notion of a fluid ground between real-world and virtual world conceptions.

Few videogame scholars have contributed more terminology to help theorize the rhetorical approaches of videogames than Espen Aarseth. In *Cybertext: Perspectives on Ergodic Literature* he introduces the concept of "ergodic" literature, where "nontrivial effort is required to allow the reader to traverse the text ... it requires hard work in the form of concentration as well as conscious instead of automatic adjustment of eye focus and distance" (1, 180). These ergodic texts that require more active work to be understood (including hypertexts and adventure games) he refers to as "cybertexts": dynamic texts that require action (rather than passivity) on the part of the reader/player. Wolf provides a more simple definition of Aarseth's complex term ergodic: "the action has some physical aspect to it and is not strictly an activity occurring purely on the mental plane" (15). Aarseth uses this term to help differentiate videogames from not only movies and television shows (passive activities that require no physical work from the viewer) but also from traditional novels and stories: simply turning the pages of a book does not constitute "nontrivial" effort in Aarseth's eyes. Videogames, though, have a definite work aspect to them: "Gameplay requires all kinds of work including concentration, endurance, and coordination. Gaming requires strategy, skill, imagination — in essence hard work. A player's work interacts with the computer game's work to create the user experience" (Ruggill, et al. 299–302).

Of course, the title of Aarseth's book does refer to ergodic "literature," which seems to privilege story and sequentiality. Earlier in this chapter, I noted that Giddens suggested that self-identity was maintained by the individual's internal narrative; here too Aarseth's usage of the word literature (along with the examples his book provides) highlights his privileging of narrativity in identity meaning-making. But is a narrative essential to identity construction, particularly in new digital media like videogames? Before returning to discuss more of Aarseth's terminology, I pause here to turn my attention briefly to the relationship between narrative theory and videogame technologies.

Narrative Theory

As mentioned earlier, Murray focuses her theories in *Hamlet on the Holodeck* almost exclusively around narrativity (linear, sequential stories that help create meaning for individuals and society) and the impact of computer technology on narratives. Like Bolter and Grusin, Murray stresses "transparency" in communication technology, arguing that fictive works (regardless of medium) "help us understand the world and what it means to be human. Eventually all successful storytelling technologies become transparent: we lose consciousness of the medium and see only the power of the story itself" (26). Crucial to stories' powerful potential was something Murray calls an "objective correlative," a term she borrowed from T.S. Eliot. It describes the way "clusters of events in literary works can capture emotional experience" (93). The computer, Murray says, allows users to "create objective correlatives for thinking about the many systems we participate in, observe, and imagine" (93). She seems to feel that emotional experiences can be captured in computer spaces, just as they can in more traditional narrative spaces.

Rather than expressing apprehension over the changes that computer technologies might wreak on narratives, Murray seems optimistic that certain types of narrative experiences might be better "told" in digital spaces.[2] One of these she identifies as the multiform story: "A written or dramatic narrative that presents a single situation or plotline in multiple versions, versions that would be mutually exclusive in our ordinary experience" (30).

Video-RPGs seem well suited to this type of story: users can reload a saved game and replay sections using different tactics (stealth vs. brute strength vs. magic, for example) or can start an entirely new game and create a very different type of avatar with different attributes, gender, or race. The multiple possibilities allow the user/reader a "more active role, a more creative role, in the experience" (38).

Murray also believes narratives have transformational capabilities:

> Storytelling can be a powerful agent of personal transformation. The right stories can open our hearts and change who we are. Digital narratives offer us the opportunity to enact stories rather than to merely witness them. Enacted events have a transformative power that exceeds both narrated and conventionally dramatized events because we assimilate them as personal experiences [171].

This passage shows that Murray believes digital narratives have the potential to be more powerful than traditional narratives due to enactment. Sal Humphreys agrees, identifying the user as a co-producer of the narrative text:

> The line between production and consumption of the text has become blurred.... Computer games bring players into a productive relationship with the text. This is more than identity construction through consumption; this is an engagement which serves to create the text each time it is engaged. The engagement comes because the player is the performer, and the game evaluates the performance and adapts to it [37, 38].

Of course, whether or not this means one is transformed by the engagement is debatable. In some ways, though, videogame narratives are similar to traditional narratives in that they rely heavily on what Ryan calls "the most prominent reason for acting in life and therefore the most fundamental narrative pattern" (2–3): problem-solving. Murray too acknowledges that the "agon, or contest between opponents, is the most common form of game [and] also the earliest form of narrative. Opposition is one of the most pervasive organizing principles of human intelligence and language" (145). I am unable to locate a v–RPG that does not revolve around problem-solving and conflict, so in this sense digital narratives remain as predictable as traditional ones. However, the immersive potential of digital narratives as a result of the user contributing to the text is intriguing; whether or not this narrative production can help lead to identity formation is the open question.

Aarseth clearly believes that cybertexts (or digital narratives) are quite different from traditional narratives since he is adamant in his view that the cybertext reader is not a voyeur. Voyeurs, he says, operate out of safe positions—watching without involvement. But he sees the cybertext in an opposite light: "a cybertext puts its reader at risk: the risk of rejection" (4). There is uncertainty when "reading" a cybertext, as there is no clear linear, sequential narrative path to follow. He uses the term "aporia" to describe the way that a cybertext prevents the user/reader from making sense of the whole text by withholding access to a particular part of the text. Aarseth points out that the dialectic between aporias and epiphanies (the connection between searching and finding) is typical of games in general and "is not a narrative structure but a more fundamental layer of human experience" (92). Cybertexts (and v–RPGs) also provide an immersion-inducing balance between anamorphosis and metamorphosis. Anamorphosis occurs when there is a clear, final state of resolution, where all is revealed. A user can achieve anamorphosis in a single-player v–RPG if they choose to play the game long enough. Yet many single-player v–RPGs (and all MMO-RPGs) are also metamorphic texts, having the potential for near endless transformation with no final state reached. Murray calls this "refused closure," suggesting that "because of its ability to both offer and withhold, the computer is a seductive medium in which much of the pleasure lies in the sustained engagement, the refusal of climax" (174–75). *Fallout 2* demonstrates videogames' abilities to both offer and withhold quite clearly. Completion of the v–RPG's main narrative arc is continually delayed. First, the Chosen One's task is to save his village, Arroyo, by finding a Garden of Eden Creation Kit (GECK). The GECK is reputed to be able to allow life to flourish in the post-apocalyptic world the game is set in. However, once the Chosen One finds the GECK and returns to Arroyo, the gamer learns that the people of Arroyo (the Chosen One's family and friends) have been taken prisoner by the Enclave, an organized gang made up of the last remaining members of the former U.S. government. The Chosen One must now track the Enclave, learn where their hideout is located, and free the villagers of Arroyo. The Chosen One must search the Wastes, moving from town to town, seeking clues as to the location of the Enclave. In this way *Fallout 2* is clearly metamorphic, requiring several dozen hours of gameplay before the narrative's final anamorphosis (destroying the Enclave's headquarters and escaping with the Arroyo villagers) can be achieved. But *Fallout 2* offers continual opportunities for many smaller anamorphic moments along the way as well. In each town, the Chosen One encounters NPCs who need help with problems of their own, each of whom are willing to trade information about the Enclave for the Chosen One's help. These mini-missions can often be completed relatively quickly, thus providing the gamer with the satisfaction of closure and a job well done while still promising many more opportunities to explore and develop the avatar and the game's larger narrative. The v–RPG genre seems to be able to transcend either/or dichotomies (aporia vs. epiphany, anamorphosis vs. metamorphosis) and blurs the boundary between these binaric terms. The genre also takes full advantage of epistemophilia in general: the human desire to know things and to be able to exact some measure of control over the obtainment of knowledge (Mulvey).

Aarseth points out another way cybernarratives are different from traditional narratives through his usage of the terms "intrigue" and "intriguee." Intrigue, he says, describes the plot of which the user is the target "with an outcome that is not yet decided — or rather with several possible outcomes that depend on various factors, such as the cleverness and experience of the player" (112). The target of the intrigue he names the "intriguee."[3] Aarseth explains how the intriguee is different from the main character of a linear novel in the following way: "The user assumes the role of the main character and, therefore, will not come to see this person as an other, or as a person at all, but rather as a remote-controlled extension of herself" (113). The player becomes the main character of a cybertext in a way that a reader of novel never does: the user-as-producer notion described by Humphreys earlier here. Again, *Fallout 2* typifies the way v–RPGs situate the user's avatar as intriguee. In the cinematic cutscene that begins the game, the village Elder of Arroyo recites the following speech to the user/avatar:

> Truly, you are the Chosen One. It is to you that we turn as our Arroyo — our village, our home — faces its hour of greatest need. In all the years since our ancestor, the vault dweller, founded Arroyo, our people have known hardship many times. But never before has our village suffered so long a period of trial. The wells are almost dry, crops wither in the fields, the old and the young alike sicken, and our Brahmin are dying. We have hope, Chosen One — an object spoken of in the sacred text of our ancestor. It is the birthright of our people, the Garden of Eden Creation Kit, the wondrous GECK. Only that can save us now.... You must travel the Wastes to find the GECK. This is the only way our people may yet be saved.... Fear not, Chosen One — the strength of the Vault Dweller runs strong in your veins. I know that you shall not fail us... [*Fallout 2* strategy guide, x].

The Elder's speech clearly identifies *Fallout 2*'s setting (the village of Arroyo, in the middle of the radioactive Wastes), the main character (the avatar as the Chosen One), and the initial plot (find a GECK somewhere in the Wastes, and return it to Arroyo). The speech also references the avatar of *Fallout,* the Vault Dweller (thus linking the narratives of the two games together). The Elder's usage of the word "you" in this speech comes to represent both the Chosen One avatar and the "real-world" user, creating identificatory fusion.

It seems clear that for Aarseth and other narrative theorists that the interactive qualities of cybertexts and videogames, the creative, productive powers given to the reader/user, are crucial to the immersive potentials of these texts and to their potential to aid in identity construction. Jill Walker provides yet another definition of interaction that highlights the connected, reciprocal nature of the relationship between user and computer: "Users must perform physical actions beyond perceptual actions (such as looking and listening) in order to access digital works ... there is a feedback loop between user and machine where the user has some influence on the machine and the machine has some influence on the user" (1). Walker refers to this merger of the actual and fictional worlds as "ontological fusion": the user is able to "imagine both her perceptual actions and her manipulation of the work as being fictional as well as actual" (8). The reciprocity of this ontological fusion is crucial to Gee's notions of identities as well.

Earlier, I discussed Bolter's and Grusin's demonstration of immediacy and hyperimmediacy as applied to flight "simulators" leading to immersion. Simulation is an important concept invoked by many videogame theorists to explain the transparent, immersive nature of a videogame experience. Gonzalo Frasca defines a simulation as an artificial system that models a more complex system while retaining some of original system's behavior (Walker 2). Sid Meier's famous *Gettysburg!* is a good example of a simulation: it recreates the Civil War battle of Gettysburg for the user in virtual space. This includes not only the regiments of the Union and Confederate armies, but also the geographical terrain the battle was fought on: the game's theme and content are based on events that have real, non-virtual world equivalents. Simulations attempt to provide verisimilitude: they attempt to be life-like and realistic even as they are copies rather than originals. As Turkle points out, in the postmodern technological world, it becomes continually easier for users to immerse themselves in computer simulations: "We have learned to take things at interface value. We are moving toward a culture of simulation in which people are increasingly comfortable with substituting representations of reality for the real" (23). However, not all videogames are simulations. What about a videogame such as *Final Fantasy X*, which invites the user to explore a mythical world that has no real-world equivalent, and offers the user's avatar the opportunity to use magical powers that don't exist outside of that virtual space? If this type of videogame space is not simulation, what is it?

Simulacra and Virtual Space

Jean Baudrillard provides another possibility by introducing the term "simulacra": copies without originals. The most famous example of this Baudrillard cites is Disneyland, which aims to recreate an innocent version of America that never really existed in the first place: "This world wants to be childish in order to make us believe that the adults are elsewhere, in the 'real' world, and to conceal the fact that true childishness is everywhere — that it is that of the adults themselves who come here to act the child in order to foster illusions as to their real childishness" (13). Disneyland's Main Street USA is therefore a copy of an American street that exists nowhere else. Many v–RPGs are simulacra rather than simulations, as they offer virtual copies of worlds that have no real-world equivalents. In Turkle's words: "The objects on the screen have no simple physical referent. In this sense, life on the screen is without origins and foundation. It is a place where signs taken for reality may substitute for the real. Its aesthetic has to do with manipulation and recombination" (47).

Baudrillard refers to "worlds" and Turkle to "places." Both terms imply a spatial aspect to virtual reality, and the notion of "space" is significant to videogame interaction. Turkle's own definition of virtual reality displays this connection: "the metaphorical spaces that arise only through interaction with the computer" (181). Later in her book, Turkle quotes William Gibson in discussing virtual space: "Everyone who works with computers seems to develop an intuitive faith that there's some kind of actual space behind the screen" (265). Of course, different genres of videogames present space in different ways. Wolf describes eleven different types of videogame spaces; video role-playing games fit into his tenth and eleventh categories as they are both "interactive three-dimensional environments" and also typically "mapped space."[4] In interactive 3D, "spaces and objects can be viewed from multiple angles and viewpoints which are all linked together in such a way as to make the diegetic world appear to have at least enough spatial consistency so as to be navigable by the player" (66).[5] As videogame worlds grew (thanks to expanded computing power) and became more complex, conceptual maps became important to aid the user in virtual navigation. In essence, they are onscreen representations of off-screen spaces.[6]

Bernadette Flynn, drawing on Lefebvre's *The Production of Space*, identifies three levels through which spatial practices can be analyzed. First are material spatial practices: experiences that have taken place in the non-virtual world. Second are representations of space: perceptions. Third are spaces of representation: imagination. I find the distinction between these last two tenuous. Perception seems to require external stimuli, some space that can be seen. Imagination need not draw on sight; one need only hear about a space to be able to imagine it (or a form of it). Yet all three seem connected when Flynn says, "Navigation is a pilgrimage where the imagination is shaped by the spaces it passes through and which may in turn shape the spaces it passes through" (2). So, the mind also has a spatial aspect to it. Later, drawing on de Certeau, Flynn points out that the act of walking "opens up a place to human creativity and articulation, transforming it into a space of enunciation ... repeated exploration of a game environment and its cultural contents creates a mnemonic of the landscape where associations within the game world trigger other cultural and imaginative associations" (2). It is interesting to note that avatars in v–RPGs traverse their gameworlds mainly on foot (as opposed to in spaceships, race cars, or in airplanes as is more typical in many action-oriented videogame genres); additional research is needed to explore whether or not this on-foot navigation contributes to identity transformation.

Aarseth would characterize the traversable spaces of v–RPGs as multicursal labyrinths where there are a series of critical choices in which path is taken through the gameworld. He distinguishes this type of labyrinth from the unicursal labyrinth where there is only path. Aarseth's notion of labyrinths differs from Umberto Eco's. In *Semiotics and the Philosophy of Language* Eco describes three distinct labyrinth types: the linear, the maze, and the rhizome. The linear (only one path is possible) and the maze (many choices for travel exist) correspond to Aarseth's unicursal and multicursal, respectively, but the rhizome has no parallel in Aarseth's terminology. In *A Thousand Plateaus* DeLeuze and Guattari describe a rhizome as a theoretical net where every point can be connected with every other point; Murray refers to it as "a tuber root system in which any point may be connected to any other point" (132). Murray suggests that videogame agency, "the satisfying power to take meaningful action and see the results of our decisions and choices" (126), can be obtained through navigation and identifies two navigable configurations in videogames: the solvable maze (similar to Aarseth's unicursal maze and Eco's linear labyrinth and maze) and the tangled rhizome. A rhizomatic text would be one that does not privilege any one order of reading. Murray suggests this "frustrates our desire for narrational agency" but then goes on to admit that the unsolvable rhizomatic maze "does hold promise as an expressive structure. Walking through a rhizome one enacts a story of wandering, of being enticed in conflicting directions, of feeling helpless to orient oneself, but [the experience] is oddly reassuring. In the rhizome, one is constantly threatened but also continuously enclosed. The fact that the plot will not resolve means that no irreparable loss will be suffered" (133). Filiciak believes the rhizome to be "the perfect metaphor to describe the user of electronic media; we cannot talk anymore about a single identity that produces temporary identities subordinate to itself. Thus, we should rather talk about hyper-identity. It is more a process than a finished formation" (96–97). Here we see Melucci's concept of identity formation as a system and a process echoed.

Point of View

Whether video game space is labyrinthine or rhizomatic, it seems clear that users must feel as if they have a presence in this space in order to be immersed and identify with the gaming experience. But, of course, the user remains present in the non-virtual space they occupy as well. Taylor uses the term "telepresence" to describe this ability of an individual to be present in multiple spatial domains. For Taylor, point of view within the gameworld is crucial to any theorizing of how the user perceives the game space and identifies with their avatar. She explains the connections between avatarial identification and point of view (POV) in the following way: "The player identifies sufficiently with objects or characters of the game space to function in response to that game space through a self-image that is inserted into the constructs of the game space and then internalized by the player" (5). This self-image Taylor refers to is the avatar. In videogames, two types of POV are possible: first-person POV and third-person POV.

In chapter one, I described *Battlezone* as the first first-person POV video game: the user played "through the eyes" of a tank commander. First-person POV places the user inside the body of the avatar or agent: the gameworld is seen as if looking through these virtual eyes. Typically, the only parts of the avatar that can be seen in this view are the hands, extended in front of the virtual, invisible body. Third-person POV allows the user to see the avatar or agent's whole "body," usually from a camera position above and behind the avatar. *PONG* allowed the user to control the table-tennis racket (depicted as a small rectangle on the screen), but did not place the user inside the racket; rather the user looked down upon the virtual table from an overhead perspective.

Exactly which POV, first- or third-person, allows for greater identification between avatar and user is debated among scholars. Taylor's argument in favor of the identificatory power of first-person POV shows this uncertainty:

> Players have more direct agency in first-person shooters, due in large part because FPS games are identified by their predication on action and control, and that this sense of agency creates a sense of primary identification with the player as being within the game. Yet, FPS games also disrupt the gaze by removing the player from the field of the gaze.... Playing first-person I play as me so I never pass through the medium of screen; acting on the screen rather than within the screen because I have identified with and taken in only my own actions instead of a character's. Essentially, from a position alone the player cannot enter into the game space as part of that game space because of the lack of context which embodiment, in third-person point of view games, provides [6, 8].

It seems reasonable that more agency might lead to greater identification (and Taylor claims the first-person perspective provides the greatest agency): control over one's own actions and relative freedom to act as one chooses allow actions that will be embraced more readily by one's identity. However, it also seems that for a gamer to identify as completely with their avatar as possible, they ought to be "passing through the medium of the screen" and "within the screen" to experience immediacy. But this quality Taylor gives to the third-person perspective. Stephen Clarke-Willson suggests that third-person POV is more complex (and therefore has greater identificatory potential) because it allows the user to see the avatar in the gameworld; the first-person POV he sees as more visceral. Gee sees both perspectives as contributing to identity construction: "First-person mode feels closer to the character and allows you to identify tightly with [the avatar's] situatedness in the world. Third-person mode allows you to see [the avatar's] body, actions, and reactions and identify with him from a thematic point of view, since you now have images to help with the identity play you are engaged in being [the avatar]" (*Why Video Games* 71). Bolter and Grusin choose not to take a side in this debate, but instead simply stress the significance of POV in videogaming experiences: "Empathy is highly regarded as a means of knowing [and] the path to empathy is the occupation of another's point of view" (245–46). So, taking on another's viewpoint leads to empathy which is a way to obtain knowledge. This leads to an interesting question: what knowledge can v–RPG users hope to gain by taking on the viewpoint of their avatars? Perhaps the answer lies in part in the following observation from Bolter and Grusin: "Fascination with media works as the sublimation of the desire, central to the Western tradition, to be immediately present to oneself" (236). Perhaps avatars in v–RPGs make elements of the user's self present to themselves, tangible in ways that might not be possible in non-virtual spaces. Perhaps gamers hope to come to know parts of their self better through the empathy they experience with their avatar.

These are existential speculations, and I am reminded here of a statement made by Giddens as he contemplates the formation of self-identity: "All humans live in circumstances of existential contradiction: we are of the inanimate world, yet set off against it, as self-conscious beings aware of our finite character.... [A key] existential question concerns the existence of other persons. Although the individual can perceive the body of another person he or she cannot perceive that individual as subject" (49, 50). Giddens' words here are interesting when applied to v–RPG avatars, which are effectively immortal. Users can continually reload from earlier saved points if the avatar dies in the game world. Also, avatars are individuals that can be perceived as subjects and objects, both other and not other at the same time. To be both self and not-self is likely existentially enticing for some users.

This virtual identity experimentation is made even more enticing when the bricolage aspect of videogame play is considered. Turkle explains how this works in virtual environments:

> Bricoleurs approach problem-solving by entering into a relationship with their work materials that has more the flavor of a conversation than a monologue.... The revaluation of bricolage in the culture of simulation includes a new emphasis on visualization and the development of intuition through the manipulation of virtual objects. Instead of having to follow a set of rules laid down in advance, computer users are encouraged to tinker in simulated microworlds. There, they learn about how things work by interacting with them [51, 52].

Any experienced videogamer is aware that trial and error plays a substantial role in how the user learns to be successful in the videogame space. Turkle certainly acknowledges the element of play (pleasurable repetitive learning processes, Grodal 153) in videogames: "To learn to play you have to play to learn" (70). Nikos Papastergiadis directly connects bricolage to identity construction:

> Identity is never fixed once and for all, never coheres into an absolute form.... Identity always presupposes a sense of location and a relationship with others.... Any theory of agency must also include the process of bricolage. Identity is always conceived in the 'twixt of displacement and re-invention; representations of identity are at best a rear view of a part of the past that is pushing us forward into the future [277–78].

In this passage, the author points out identities are defined in relationship to external stimuli, similar to Burkean merger and division. This quote is also reminiscent of Friedman's notion of a fluid and ever-changing identity.

Papastergiadis mentions another factor that makes it easier for some videogame users to experience identification within virtual spaces when he notes that identity "presupposes a relationship with" another. Several examples illuminate an interesting truth: humans have a tendency to ascribe to computer technologies too much intelligence: in a sense, we anthropomorphize them. Turkle, citing famous examples like the Turing test-inspired bot "Julia" and the ELIZA tests, concludes that often humans "treat responsive computer programs as more intelligent than they really are. Very small amounts of interactivity cause us to project our own complexity onto the undeserving object ... the fake seem[s] more compelling than the real" (101, 237). It is not difficult to imagine this happening when a user "projects" an identity into/onto a virtual avatar, but Wolf hypothesizes that the computer can actually have an identity as a player in a videogame, an active opponent that competes with the human user: "By assigning an identity (consciously or not) to the computer player, competition becomes possible and emotional stakes are raised" (15). McMahan echoes this sentiment, arguing that the non-player characters (NPCs) within a gameworld can contribute to immersion: "The use of a synthetic social actor (NPC) can lead to a heightened sense of presence, [since] users respond to the computer itself as an intelligent, social agent.... Conversing with artificial characters is social interaction" (78–79, 80). Of course, the more "synthetic" the NPCs are (the more interactive and "realistic" they appear) the higher the gamer presence is likely to be.

So, where does this labyrinth of identity and videogame theories and terms lead? I believe that the content of video role-playing games may indeed allow for some users to experience identification with their avatars in those virtual spaces, thus lending credence to Gee's theories on real-world, virtual, and projective identities. Of course, the v–RPG is but one genre of video game, and I would be remiss if I did not explore the connections between genre theory and identity in this chapter.

Genre Theory

Like so many of the terms essential to this study, "genre" has been defined differently by scholars. For Halliday, genres are "configurations of semantic resources that members of the culture associate with a situation type" (Coe et al. 111). For Green genres are "structuring devices for realizing meaning in specific contexts" (Coe et al. 86). Miller defines them as "typified rhetorical actions based in recurrent situations" (Coe et al. 103). These definitions share much common ground: essentially, genres are discursive forms that are socially acceptable for responding to recurring situations (2). Since these forms are socially created they are not neutral nor are they value-free. Pierre Bordieu's famous notion of the "habitus" is consistent with much genre theory:

> The conditionings associated with a particular class of conditions of existence produce habitus, systems of durable, transposable dispositions, structured structures predisposed to function as structuring structures, that is, principles which generate and organize practices and representations that can be objectively adapted to their outcomes without presupposing a conscious aiming at ends or an express mastery of the operations necessary in order to attain them [53].

Essentially, the habitus guides individuals in the course of their daily lives on how to act, influencing their actions and inclinations by providing a sense of what is appropriate.

Genre impacts video role-playing games on three distinct levels. First is the genre "videogame." Videogames are forms of electronic entertainment that use computer communication technologies. Earlier discussion in this chapter has differentiated them from other media like film and television due to the interactive, productive, participatory, and "work" aspects of videogames (all leading to the potential for high levels of immersion and identification). At this point I find it important to define "game" as doing so will show the connection to genre theory. Videogame designer Crawford defines games as "closed formal systems that subjectively represent a subset of reality" (Thorhauge 2). Callois suggests that games are accompanied by a "certain conscience of a second reality or of utter unreality in relation to ordinary life" (Thorhauge 2). Video-RPGs fit both of these definitions well. These theorists also believe that games require players to take on a "lusory" attitude: a willingness to accept the rules of the game so that the game can be played. This notion seems closely tied to genre: the conventions of a genre must be accepted and understood in order to have an identificatory experience. Second is the genre of videogame: "role-playing games." In chapter one I described how the v–RPG is unique in its usage of true avatars (as opposed to agents), and the freedom of choice given to the user in navigating the gameworld. The third type of genre relevant to v–RPGs is the "gameworld" and its setting: the vast majority of v–RPGs (and table-top RPGs for that matter) have fantasy settings reminiscent of Gygax's *Dungeons & Dragons* (who was, if you'll remember, influenced heavily by Tolkien's Middle Earth). Technologically limited worlds replete with magic and mythical creatures have become canonical in the fantasy genre and most v–RPG worlds are riffs off of this formula.

Other theorists provide more tangible connections between genre theory, videogames, and identity. Charles Bazerman speaks of genre as if it was physical space: "If you hang around a certain place long enough you will become the kind of person who hangs around that kind of place ... the places you habituate will develop those parts of you that are most related to and oriented towards the activities of that space" (14). Does Bazerman believe that it is the actual physical space where the person is hanging around that will cause this change? No: it is the discourse(s) happening in and at that place and the individual's internal reflection on that discourse that will alter identity. Given this chapter's earlier discussion on videogame space, Bazerman's connection of space to identity and genre is interesting. He takes his explanations of these connections even further:

> Going to the place is only the first step, for once you are there you need access and encouragement to engage in particular roles, use particular resources, and take part in particular experiences and activities. When [you occupy the space of a genre] you begin thinking in actively productive ways that belong in that form of life and you take on all the feelings, hopes, uncertainties, and anxieties about becoming a visible

presence in that world and participating in the available activities. You develop and become committed to the identity you are carving out within that domain. The particular ranges of feelings, impulses, and stances that you adopt in orienting to that world develop in interaction with the people and activities within that world [14].

Bazerman's view resonates provocatively when applied to the virtual spaces user avatars "live" in. I am reminded of Coe's words as he speculates on the inevitability of identification with and within genres: "To what extent and for how long can people [experience] a particular subject position without identifying themselves with that position and all it entails?" (4). I would instead ask a similar question: to what extent can one play a video–RPG from a particular subject position without identifying themselves with the position (avatar) they've taken up, particularly when the user has chosen from the start, willfully and purposefully, to identify with the avatar?

Of course, Bazerman points out that it is the "discourse" within the genre that influences identity. This leads to another important question: do the interactions with videogames constitute discourse? Coe defines discourse as "strategic response to situation" (6); the choices made in v–RPGs certainly seem to fit this definition. In *Genre and the New Rhetoric* Freedman and Medway even suggest a game metaphor for the social nature of generic discourse, suggesting that such discourse requires at least two genres and two "players" who react to each others' "moves." These reactions may be tacit. As I've already shown in Turkle, Wolf, and McMahan, users treat the videogame world and the NPCs encountered there as a second "player" who responds to the user's choices based on the system guidelines created by the game designers. Given these definitions, discourse and therefore identity construction is possible via videogame interaction.

In this chapter I have examined postmodern and modern theories of identity. I have also explored a range of videogame theories introducing crucial terminology such as immersion, simulacra, diegetic space, interface, and point of view. To fully analyze identity theory and videogame theory it has been necessary to discuss narrative theory and genre theory as well. Exactly what the relationship is between Gee's real-world, virtual, and projective identities remains unclear, as does the means by which the avatars of video role-playing games might influence these identities; knowing which variables in a user's gameplay experience are essential to identity formation has yet to be pinpointed in existing research. It is these gaps in identity and videogame theory that this study attempts to fill. I close this chapter with one final statement from James Newman, who argues that the visual appearance of the avatar is overrated and is relatively insignificant to an immersive videogame experience (10). Instead, he views the pleasures of videogame play as "kinaesthetic:" every aspect of the gameworld is simultaneously important. This is a belief similar to Friedman's, who Newman cites here. Newman points out that gamers talk about "being" rather than "playing" or "controlling." Therefore, he argues, "The level of engagement, immersion or presence experienced by the player is not contingent upon representation ... the notion of an identifiable and singular entity embodied by the player may be an oversimplification indicative of an implicit reliance on existent models of audience" (8, 11). Newman suggests that identification within videogame space is overdetermined: there are likely many factors that contribute, including avatarial construction freedom, interaction with NPCs, the narrative (or lack of one), the space of the gameworld, point of view, and the ability for the interface to become transparent enabling immediacy. I agree with Newman; all of these variables play crucial roles in avatarial immersion. Therefore, in this study, I have selected video role-playing games that allow users much freedom not only in constructing their virtual identities but also in navigating the gameworld. These v–RPGs are *Morrowind*, *Oblivion*, and *Fallout 3*. I thought it important to collect data from different types of videogame players for this study to ascertain how varying perceptions of the connections between virtual identities and real-world identities impacted avatar construction. In the next chapter, I analyze data from two "hardcore" fans of single-player v–RPGs using *Morrowind* as the representative gaming experience. How did their pre-existing proclivities for videogame identification aid or hinder their connections to their diegetic avatars? In chapter four I analyze data from a more casual videogame player (one with no particular interest or experience with v–RPGs) using *Oblivion*. Would his initial lack of interest in open-ended avataristic gameworld exploration lead to more division than merger? In chapter five I examine the gaming experiences of a non-gamer, someone who thinks videogames are "a waste of time." What happens when this person plays *Fallout 3*? Does she identify at all with her avatar? Stay tuned. I turn now in chapter three to a more detailed discussion of the first of these v–RPGs: *Morrowind*. In this chapter I describe the challenges of collecting videogame data and provide background information on the two "hardcore" gamers who participated in this portion of the study. I also share their *Morrowind* gaming experiences and provide analysis of their diegetic decisions related to identity construction.

3

Morrowind

Identity and the Hardcore Gamer

Computer games are perhaps the richest cultural genre we have yet seen, and this challenges our search for a suitable methodological approach.
— Espen Aarseth, videogame theorist, 2001

All in all, these were happy times, exploring, fighting, and pearl-diving, in a vast landscape filled with countless others. I even learned to fly.
— Aarseth describing his experience playing *Morrowind*, 2003

How do the virtual identities of avatars in v–RPGs get constructed? Is there a relationship between real-world identity, virtual identity, and projective identity? If there is, how can we study it? As Aarseth's first epigraph to this chapter suggests, selecting an appropriate methodology to effectively study videogames is not easy. This is partly because of the relative newness of the videogame theory field; too few detailed studies have yet taken place in a discipline still deciding on terminologies and theoretical approaches. Another reason designing methodology for the study of videogames is challenging is the multimedia aspect of videogaming experiences. Wolf explains:

> The main reason for the [theoretical] neglect of the video game is that it is more difficult to study than traditional media. The video game as a text is much harder to master.... Instead of fixed, linear sequences of text, image, or sound which remain unchanged when examined multiple times, a video game experience can vary widely from one playing to another. More time is needed to experience a video game. Sometimes it is not even clear how many choices a player has, and discovery of alternate narrative paths is also a part of game play [7].

Wolf's observation is directly applicable to v–RPGs which are arguably the most problematic genre of videogame to study due to exactly the challenges Wolf describes: open-ended gameplay makes every user's experience unique, with many gameplay variables contributing to the immersive and potentially identificatory experience. What methodological approach best enables a researcher to answer the questions about identities I ask at the beginning of this chapter?

Videogame theorist Kurt Squire suggests that "the study of games and learning might begin with qualitative study of game players" (4). I heartily agree, and after studying the research design suggestions of Norman Denzin, Yvonna Lincoln, and John Creswell, I decided on a qualitative, phenomenological research approach.[1] Creswell identifies several key theoretical terms important to a phenomenological approach. Among these is the notion of intentionality of consciousness "where experiences contain both the outward appearance and inward consciousness based on memory, image, and meaning." Intentionality of consciousness assumes a refusal of subject/object dichotomies: "The reality of an object is only perceived within the meaning of the experience of an individual" (53). Following Husserl's work, Creswell also suggests that a phenomenological approach "suspends all judgments about what is real until they are founded on a more certain basis" (52). If phenomenological approaches suspend judgment on "reality" and refuse traditional dichotomies, then my study (exploring the tensions and connections between virtual and real identities via videogame play) is certainly phenomenological in nature.

Creswell points out when selecting participants for a phenomenological study purposeful sampling is crucial: "It is essential that all participants experience the phenomenon being studied" (118). Therefore, for this first portion of my study, I selected two participants who had a high probability of being able to identify strongly with their avatars. This meant selecting participants who already identified themselves as "hardcore gamers": people who enjoyed playing videogames and did so often for enjoyment and immersion. I also selected gamers who enjoyed the role-playing genre of videogames, and who were used to manipulating the complex mouse-and-keyboard interface of personal computing v–RPGs because I did not want differing levels of videogame and computer literacy to be an impediment to these two participants being able to immerse themselves in the gameplay experience or keep them from identifying with their avatar. Therefore, I only selected participants for this portion of my study with very high levels of videogame literacy for whom the interface could "disappear" fairly quickly (even as each new videogame requires a learning curve to master the control scheme). After preliminarily considering several different candidates, I selected the following two participants for this portion of the study:[2] Vishnu, a 26-year-old Caucasian male and a recent college graduate with a B.A. in English Literature, and Shiva, a 23-year-old Caucasian female university library assistant, also a recent college graduate with a B.S. in Biology.[3] Vishnu and Shiva described themselves as being avid videogamers for most of their lives. In preliminary interviews both participants demonstrated they met the necessary criteria to participate in this study as "hardcore" gamers.

Participant Gaming Histories

Vishnu described himself as a life-long videogame player: "I've been gaming actually almost as long as I can remember. My dad got his first degree in computing and he always had gadgets and computers and stuff [at home] before I was even born." Vishnu explained that his brother also influenced him as a videogamer: "[My] older brother [was] a big part of it. He's two and a half years older so as he was starting to get into gaming, you know, I was also. I'm going to do whatever my brother is doing! Simultaneously we had a computer, Coleco, Atari, and the TRS 80." Vishnu speculated that his first experiences playing videogames at home began when he was four or five. Soon the Nintendo Entertainment System (NES) was added to his family's collection of videogame console systems, and Vishnu was gaming not only with his brother and father, but also with other children in the neighborhood:

> Vishnu: We all went over to each other's houses to play *Contra*, and *RBI Baseball*, all that good stuff. So I've been a gamer, pretty much, my entire life.
> Zach: For all of your conscious memories.
> Vishnu: Yeah, have been gaming memories.

Vishnu's history as a videogame player extends as far back as his earliest memories. The social influences on his interest as a videogame player are clear, with his brother and father playing pivotal roles in his initiation into videogames. Vishnu expressed a desire to play videogames several times a week, but since becoming employed as an office manager for a major airline and recently getting married, he admitted to having less free time to devote to playing videogames. These variables had reduced his videogame play to just once or twice a week. Vishnu did admit to videogame play binges, however: "Sometimes I go on kicks where I play for three straight days, I'll play ten hours a day." During this study Vishnu gamed sporadically and in spurts when windows of opportunity presented themselves.

Like Vishnu, Shiva has been playing videogames for most of her life. Shiva described her introduction and instant attraction to videogames:

> I started gaming so young! I think my earliest memory was when I was playing at my friend's house when I was eight; I think we were playing *Super Mario Bros. 2*. I remember, I played with them once, and it was just so much fun and so new. I was like, "I want to play more!" I drove my friends nuts; I would go over to their house and play videogames quite often.

Shiva was hooked, but had to wait until she was ten to be able to play videogames in her own home, when her parents bought an NES for Shiva and her brother to share. With the NES in the home, Shiva admitted that she gamed every day, but had to compete with her younger brother for playing time on the system, leading to some of the biggest fights she can ever remember having with her sibling. Like Vishnu, much of Shiva's early gaming experiences involved her brother and her father, who also liked to spend time gaming. Shiva recalled early frustrations when her father monopolized the NES: "A lot of times my dad would game, and he'd be like, 'I'm playing,' and I'm like, 'No, it's not your turn!' and he'd say, 'Go do your chores.'" Despite this continual household competition for gaming time, Shiva continued to game throughout her years in school and now that she is employed as a university library assistant she speculated she has increased her videogame play: "I think I do it (gaming) more now since I have more free time. In school I got busier. I would [have] liked to do it daily but sometimes there wasn't time. I still stuck it in as much as I could." During this study, Shiva gamed several times a week.

Both Vishnu and Shiva have a life-long passion for playing videogames that I felt was crucial to this portion of my study. But it was just as important that both participants' love of videogames did not keep them from seeing that all videogames are not created equally wonderfully; they have high expectations for their videogame experiences and weren't shy in finding fault with games that didn't hold their interest. Vishnu complained that he is continually less impressed with new video games: "Perhaps the fact that I'm getting older and I see through some of the tricks they pull. Also, most games are just so redundant. I've done it [all] a hundred times before." As an example, Vishnu cited videogames set in the *Star Wars* universe. Although he admits to being a big fan of all things *Star Wars*, Vishnu explained he was tired of "playing the level of Hoth. I can't tie up those AT-AT walkers any more. I've done it."[4] He also complained about the predictability of first-person shooter (FPS) games, saying the lack of innovation in the genre kept the gameplay from being very rewarding. Shiva also expressed frustration with the redundancy of many videogame experiences, complaining that too many role-playing games "feel like they get old, like very similar, like [the] *Final Fantasy* [series]. I've played them all, but I've never [finished] them because I get to the point where I just, eh (shrugs shoulders)." Both Vishnu and Shiva enjoy becoming immersed in video games but this doesn't happen automatically; enjoyable game play and innovation seem necessary.

Of course, what constitutes "enjoyable" game play is variable from user to user. What specific gaming preferences made Vishnu and Shiva good matches for the initial portion of this study? First, both participants stressed the importance of narrative as integral to videogaming immersion. When asked what the qualification was for an enjoyable and immersive videogame experience, Vishnu replied, "I don't know! Something that's not easily described. It's gotta be engaging. You know, I look for a good story." Later, when explaining what separated good role-playing games from "lousy" ones, Vishnu said, "I think narratives. There is much more empathizing in role-playing games and I think it takes on even more importance in that [type of] game. The good narratives, there is something interesting happening, I'll forgive a lot of other flaws— graphically or gameplay — if the narrative is there." Shiva expressed a similar attitude about the importance of narrative in videogames admitting that many of the fights she had with her brother growing up that revolved around videogames had to do with the plots of the game they were playing. He would play further ahead in the game and then reveal crucial plot elements to Shiva, which she hated. Shiva, like Vishnu, also indicated a willingness to overlook certain gameplay weaknesses if she is interested in a videogame's narrative: "If the gameplay is kind of bad, like maybe I don't like the system as well, but the story's really good, I'll get past it; I'll work past it." An interesting narrative had been a key component of videogame engagement for both Vishnu and Shiva prior to their *Morrowind* experiences for this project.

As mentioned earlier, it was important that these two participants have a high level of videogame literacy so that the *Morrowind* gaming system would not be an impediment to the user accessing the gaming world. Like many v–RPGs, *Morrowind* has a complex interface, requiring the user to manipulate the computer mouse with one hand and the keyboard with the other (with as many as 30 different keys potentially needed to control the avatar). PC gaming interfaces are typically more complex than console gaming interfaces; playing *Morrowind* on an Xbox with an Xbox controller requires the manipulation of less than half as many buttons as the PC version. Both Vishnu and Shiva had experience gaming on both platforms (PCs and consoles), but Shiva in particular expressed an enthusiasm for PC role-playing games: "I like to play more complicated [RPGs] on the computer, because you can have more complicated goals with the key commands, when it is a little more difficult." Shiva clearly enjoys the challenge of mastering complicated gaming interfaces. Vishnu, on the other hand, admitted to a predisposition toward the gaming controllers of console systems:

> Part of my bias is growing up with controllers and paddles; I've always had a control pad. Whenever I go and game with a mouse, to me it's awkward. I don't like the wrist positioning. I think the [console] controller for me is just very comfortable though I've been trying more [recently] with PC games to get more comfortable with using the buttons.

Motivated by the purchase of a new PC with more computing power, Vishnu had recently been doing more PC gaming than console gaming, thus increasing his PC gaming literacy. To maintain a consistency of interface for this portion of the study both participants played *Morrowind* on PCs.

The gaming interface represents the extra-diegetic part of a videogame system; diegetic parts of gaming systems can be just as complicated. Understanding the rules is essential for any game if the user wants to play the game effectively. In videogames "playing effectively" usually means winning. This might include winning a football game in *Madden '08*, killing all your opponents on a *Halo 3* map, or completing the narrative of an adventure game (freeing Atrus in *Myst*, discovering who the serial killer is in *Still Life,* or helping Kate Walker find her way to *Syberia*). Most genres of videogames have simple linear parameters for winning and effective gameplay. However, *Morrowind* is much more open-ended and the strategies for effective gameplay vary enormously depending on each situation and the type of avatar the user chooses to play. Due to the many ways *Morrowind* can be "effectively" played this genre of videogame requires a much deeper understanding of the complexities of the game system and this understanding can only come through trial and error over time spent in the gameworld. Not every videogamer has the patience for this type of videogame.[5] Therefore, it was crucial that Vishnu and Shiva enjoy not only playing *Morrowind* but also figuring out how to play *Morrowind* effectively. In chapter two, I provided the following statement made by McMahon: "The player is caught up in the world of the game's story (the diegetic level), but [immersion] also refers to the player's love of the game and the strategy that goes into it (the non-diegetic level)." Vishnu in particular professed a love for the non-diegetic aspects of immersion when asked why he likes playing v–RPGs: "I guess the obvious answer is entertainment, [but] I like learning the rules of the game and learning how the game operates. I guess it's something about figuring out the rules, and exploiting them. Or at least, doing well with them.... There's something about that, learning and even mastering the system. I like figuring out the system of the game." Vishnu admitted that he likes puzzles and puzzle-solving within videogames and it is clear that he considers learning the game system of videogames to be an extra-diegetic puzzle. This only aids his videogaming immersion. Although she did not directly mention the non-diegetic gaming system in explaining why she enjoys videogames, Shiva's above quote about enjoying mastering complex key commands suggests an interest similar to Vishnu's. Shiva readily admitted that videogames containing puzzles and problem-solving were among her most memorable gaming experiences, and she often found the sub-quests and mini-games as enjoy-

able as the main quests. Her fascination with a mini-game involving cook-
ing in *Star Ocean 2* illustrated this:

> SHIVA: I usually like sub-games, like cooking, or something. I get
> involved with that.
>
> ZACH: What game has a cooking contest? You've referenced that a cou-
> ple of times, there must be something you played that sticks with
> you.
>
> SHIVA: *Star Ocean 2*. I played that a long time ago and I played it sev-
> eral times and every single time you get to a certain part where
> you can do cooking and I never get past that part, because I love
> cooking too much to go past [it].

In this example, Shiva was willing to forego the game's main narrative and
spend her time instead on *Star Ocean 2*'s sub-quests. Like Vishnu, Shiva listed
puzzles, numerous quests, and a good story as her three favorite components
of videogames.

In keeping with their interests in puzzle-solving and character development, both participants also emphasized that one of the aspects of v–RPGs
they liked the best was not feeling as if they were "on the clock" to make decisions. Shiva explained why she preferred v–RPGs to FPS games: "It just seems
like, with *Halo*, you're always shooting, always running, always dying. I play
games that are a little slower [paced]." Vishnu agreed, admitting that he
wouldn't enjoy playing fast-paced shooters and sports games if he wasn't able
to hit the "Pause" button on his computer whenever he needed to. One of the
aspects of v–RPGs he likes best, Vishnu said, is that they allow you to "think
about the repercussions of your actions." This internal reflection is also crucial to identity formation, as I discussed in chapter two.

I argued in chapter one that v–RPGs are distinguished from other genres of videogames through the continual development of avatars. Therefore,
it was also essential that Vishnu and Shiva enjoy the character development
inherent to playing *Morrowind*. Shiva stressed that customizing and devel-
oping her avatar was in fact the component of role-playing games she enjoyed
the most: "I like leveling up, I like changing my character. It's unique!" Vishnu
also explained that character development was one of the main reasons he
plays v–RPGs: "I like character development. The customization of characters is something that I get more and more into.... With [the] customization,
I like that because it lends itself to, like, personality." Vishnu's reply here is
interesting as in it he directly connects avatar construction to "personality."
Personality is a term that is closely tied to real-world self-identity.

Finally, it was important to select participants for the *Morrowind* portion of this study who could become immersed in their avatars and who had
a history of and proclivity for videogaming identification. Both Vishnu and

Shiva expressed these characteristics in a few ways. I asked both participants to talk about some of their most memorable gaming experiences. In the games Shiva mentioned (such as *Thunder and Lightning* and *Galerians: Ash*) she had beaten them (completed the games' levels and story) before her brother or her father. Shiva admires both male members of her family and seeks positive attention from them constantly. Shiva's gaming identification in these instances was clearly tied to her real-world identity and relationships: the games she remembered playing were ones where she had displayed more gaming skill than her brother and father and thus earned their real-world respect. Vishnu revealed similar connections, listing *Final Fantasy VII* as among his most memorable experiences:

> *Final Fantasy VII* was a huge one! It might have to do with the age that I played it, I was seventeen maybe, and there was a pretty strong love story going on, and there was you know this whole, [as] if he was that kind of teenager too. There was a lot of identification, with the character, with the story going on. It just really clicked for me.

Here, Vishnu's real-world identity (a teenaged boy) identified strongly with the virtual teenaged boy of the gameworld. Vishnu also cited *Super Mario Bros.* as being "seminal" in his gaming experiences and tried to explain why: "I think it's sort of who I was at the time I was playing the game. I was like eight and my brothers were always playing it and I was trying to get in so I really wanted to play the game. I was like, 'Let me play, let me play!'" Like Shiva, Vishnu had to compete for videogame playing time at home. In both of these instances Vishnu's real-world identities contributed to making his videogame experiences memorable.

Both participants also made statements that hinted at a blurring of the line between their real-world and virtual world identifications. One of Vishnu's favorite videogames is *Madden*, the popular professional football series (a new edition comes out each year with up-to-date rosters and players for each National Football League team). Vishnu attempted to describe the sense of accomplishment he felt when compiling gaudy statistics for his customized virtual quarterback:

> ZACH: Is feedback one of the key reasons you play videogames?
> VISHNU: I think so. Like *Madden* for example, something that is customized to me like where it gives stats; my quarterback does this; that's me; I did that. I threw 50 touchdowns, whatever, and it's almost in a strange way like I accomplished something, you know, even though I didn't. I know that it's not me and yet still, games allow you to sort of lose that.

Vishnu's statement here seems to indicate confusion, or at least a tension, between his real-world identity and his virtual identity (Vishnu's *Madden* quarterback). Here, Vishnu admits that it was not him accomplishing these virtual feats. This raises an interesting question: who was it then, if it was not Vishnu? Vishnu seems willing to discount the validity of the experiences of his virtual identity after the fact. Why does he do this, when the experience was so real to him while experiencing it? This question is an important one, and one I will return to in chapter six.

Vishnu also provided evidence of a time when his virtual gaming experiences continued to affect him in the "real" world. *Grand Theft Auto III* was the top selling videogame of 2001 and has spawned five equally successful sequels at the time of this writing. In the game's virtual Liberty City, the user's avatar can carjack, murder, steal, solicit prostitutes and drive recklessly in freeform fashion; the open-ended gameplay and kairotic temporality leave these choices up to the user. Vishnu remembered vividly the first time he played *Grand Theft Auto III* and described the impact it had on him:

> VISHNU: The first time I played it I was just sitting in my brother's house and just hangin' out. I'd watched for about a half hour and played for about a half hour. And I got in my car, I'm waiting at a stoplight, and I just, I felt really compelled to just peel out and you know, with just no regard for the traffic, cross the light. That [game] really had a response, a response within me.
> ZACH: Did you have to consciously say to yourself, I can't do that, I shouldn't do that?
> VISHNU: Yeah! It was very surprising to me, a little bit disturbing. I really felt compelled, almost, to do that.

After having spent very little time (30 minutes watching, 30 minutes playing) in Liberty City, Vishnu's passage from his virtual identity in a virtual world to his real-world identity when driving his car took a little time. This lag time he experienced is fascinating and reveals the presence of liminal space between the virtual and real-world identities: Gee's projective identity. In this particular instance for Vishnu, the passage out of virtual space was not instantaneous.

Shiva seemed less convinced that her videogaming experiences had ever directly impacted her real-world identity. When I asked her if she thought videogaming experiences had ever changed her life, she replied, "I don't know. The games I play are so fantastical that I don't really relate them to real life.... I mean, I play [some] games that it's like real where you're trapped in a castle and there are these maniacs coming after you, that could be real." This statement demonstrates what appears to be an unconscious connection between fantasy and reality. Being hunted by maniacs in a castle, although possible, seems pretty far down the fantastical end of the "reality" continuum. The chances of having this experience in a virtual setting are far greater than encountering it in the real world. Shiva's statement here may provide evidence that the many virtual videogame experiences she's had over the course of her life (where monsters and madmen appear with much greater frequency than they do in the real world) may have influenced her more than she is willing to admit or is consciously aware of. The following statement from Vishnu typified both participants' gaming experience: "I've been gaming actually almost as long as I can remember." Both participants enjoyed playing v–RPGs yet neither of them had yet played *Morrowind*, making them ideal for participation in this portion of my study.

Videogame Selection: Why Morrowind?

Selecting the videogames for this study was enormously important: what videogames would best provide opportunities for the real-world identities of users and the virtual Identities of their avatars to inform each other? As my discussion in chapter one suggested, I believe that only the role-playing genre of videogame offers the opportunity to construct true avatars (in the purest sense of the word) as opposed to mere agents that can only be controlled, but never altered or shaped. I selected Bethesda Softworks' *The Elder Scrolls III: Morrowind* as the representative v–RPG for this portion of the study.[6] *Morrowind* was one of the most popular video games of 2002, winning several critical and popular awards. Perhaps most crucial to this study, *Morrowind*'s avatarial construction opportunities are continual and many. At the outset, *Morrowind* allows the user to select the name of the avatar, the gender (male or female), and race. Ten different races exist in Vvardenfell (the island setting of the game, within the larger world known as Morrowind). Four of these races are humanoid (Nord, Redguard, Breton, and Imperial), three are elven (Dark Elf, High Elf, and Wood Elf), and the other three are more animalistic in appearance (the reptilian Argonian, the feline Khajiit, and the porcine Orc). Each race has predetermined values in the eight character attributes: strength, intelligence, willpower, agility, speed, endurance, personality, and luck. Attributes like these (and often these very eight) are canonical in v–RPGs and the variability in choosing which of these attributes will be strongest and which weakest for the avatar is an essential characteristic of strategic gameplay in role-playing games. Each race offers a limited number of facial and hairstyle options the user can pick from when deciding on their avatar's appearance. Races also receives a bonus to particular skills based on that race's inherent abilities and attributes. For example, Khajiit characters receive a 15 point bonus to the Acrobatics skill (since Khajiit have a very high natural agility). Like the attributes, customizable skills that can be improved over the course of the gaming experience are central to video role-playing

games. *Morrowind* offers 27 different skills, designed to help the avatar interact with the gameworld via physical combat (Axe, Block, Blunt Weapon,
Hand-to-hand, Heavy Armor, Light Armor, Long Blade, Marksman, Medium
Armor, Short Blade, Spear, and Unarmored), magic (Alchemy, Alteration,
Conjuration, Destruction, Enchant, Illusion, Mysticism, and Restoration),
or non-combative means (Acrobatics, Armorer, Athletics, Mercantile, Security, Speechcraft, and Sneak). All skills have a rating between 5 (very
unskilled) and 100 (mastery of the skill). Skills can be improved simply by
repeatedly using them in the gameworld (e.g., using a spear in combat will
gradually improve your "Spear" skill rating). Each time the avatar increases
ten total skill points from among their Major Skills,[7] "leveling up" occurs
and the user can improve three attributes by one point each. Within the
v–RPG genre, *Morrowind* allows each user a great range of freedom to select
the skills and attributes they are most interested in when constructing their
avatar both at the beginning of the game and throughout the duration of the
gameplay experience.

It was also important to me to select a single-player only v–RPG for this
(and each) stage of the project; *Morrowind* is such a game. The user interacts in the game world only with pre-established NPCs; *Morrowind* is not
played online with other "real-world" users like in popular MMORPGs like
World of Warcraft and *Everquest.* I have not selected MMORPGs for my study
because identity construction in this type of v–RPG is more problematic and
unpredictable. Janet Murray also explains why she prefers single-player
v–RPGs to MMORPGs: "Collective fantasy can be fraught with problems.
[Online gamers] tend to fight with one another both in and out of character. Wizards and gods can eavesdrop, reassign treasure, and kill or revive
players. Because of the improvised nature of [online gaming], a lot of time
is spent in negotiating appropriate [social] behavior rather than in story making" (150–51). In a MMORPG, there is great potential for the user's immersive identification with their avatar and the gameworld to be complexified
and potentially disrupted by factors outside their control: the behaviors of
other users. In a single-player v–RPG like *Morrowind*, the potential for these
external variables disappear, as the gameworld system is "closed" in a sense.
The user's level of identification with their avatar is reliant only on the immersive properties of *Morrowind*'s programming and the user's own decisions
within the game's spaces. This reduction in unpredictable non-diegetic variables enacts a measure of control over the experiences of the participants, and
allows these experiences to be compared and contrasted as I attempt to discover the relationships between their real-world identities and their virtual
identities. Certainly, MMORPGs offer many opportunities for socialization
and community-building; much scholarship exists on these aspects of

MMORPGs.[8] However, I believe single-player v–RPGs offer better opportunities to specifically study the connections between virtual identity and real-world identity via projective identity.

Morrowind is also a good choice for this study because it follows RPG generic standards by having an archetypal plot and a fantasy setting. Ryan identifies the archetypal plot of the role-playing genre in describing the "quest of the hero across a land filled with many dangers to defeat evil forces and conquer a desirable object" (13). Certainly the main quest (or central narrative) in *Morrowind* fits this description well. *The Morrowind Prophecies*, the official guide to *Morrowind*, offers the following summary of the game's main plot:

> In an earlier era, Lord Nerevar, the great hero of the Dunmer people (as Morrowind's native Dark Elves call themselves), defeated the Dwarves and their ally, the Dunmer traitor Dagoth Ur, in a great battle at Red Mountain. But Dagoth Ur somehow survived, and, dwelling in darkness under the volcano, he lusts for revenge. Technically, he is imprisoned. The Tribunal Temple (essentially, the church of Morrowind) ringed the volcano's crater with magical wards (the Ghost-fence). [But] the Ghostfence has begun to fail. Dagoth Ur's minions roam the ashy wastes around the volcano. Nerevar lost his own life defeating Dagoth Ur. The earthly gods of the Tribunal Temple have retreated from the field, and the Temple suppresses as heresy the hopeful belief in a prophesied resurrection of Nerevar. The Great Houses and the Guilds are busy fighting one another, or simply indifferent to the threat. This is where you come in. You are the prophesied hero behind whom the land might unite [1].

Of course, at the start of the game, the avatar is unaware of any of this, having been unceremoniously released from prison by the Emperor and sent by ship to the small fishing town of Seyda Neen, where the avatar is instructed to deliver a package of documents to Caius Cosades in Balmora and receive further orders there. However, the user can deliver the package to Cosades in Balmora or not: the avatar is free to go anywhere in the gameworld at any time and need never follow the steps needed to complete the main quest if they so desire. Unlike so many other genres of videogame, *Morrowind* users do not have time constraints or pressures placed upon them.

Without time constraints, *Morrowind* users have the luxury of reflecting on and learning from their decisions, which many faster-paced genres of videogames do not allow for. Gunther Kress defines learning as "the process of inward meaning-making and the resultant change to the state of an inner semiotic resource" (40) stressing the need for "reflection, for assessment, for the quiet moment of consideration and review" (174). Even as Kress concedes that "the process of outward meaning-making also has a transformative effect" (174) he clearly believes that being able to reflect internally is essential to learning. The identity theorists discussed in chapter two would doubtless agree, as the "self" needs time to consider how to not only identify with a given stimuli, but also how to make sense of the interaction in terms of the ongoing internal narratives necessary for self-identity. Without time for reflection, no learning can take place, and identity cannot be (re)formed. *Morrowind*'s meaning-making and learning potential is integral to the identificatory possibilities of the gaming experience.

To understand how time functions in *Morrowind*, it is helpful to think about time in terms of chronos and kairos. Chronos refers to measurable, quantitative time: "the specific time or duration of some event or action as conceived in terms of a socially agreed-upon temporal measure" (Yates 108). In contrast, kairos is a qualitative term referring to the "opportune or appropriate moment to perform an action" (108). But is kairos objectively given or humanly constructed? Theorists have been divided on the issue, but Miller (1992) suggests a third option encompassing both views: kairos as a dynamic interplay between objective and subjective. Kairotic moments may present themselves to vigilant rhetors, but in turn rhetors can craft a kairotic moment as well. Both avenues are possible.

Temporality in *Morrowind* demonstrates the cooperative relationship of kairos and chronos quite well; this is an important reason I selected the game for this study. As mentioned, there is a linear story (the main quest) that can be followed. Accomplishing each of the 24 essential tasks (many of these requiring substantial time and sub-tasks to complete) will progress the storyline presenting a kairotic moment (an appropriate time to act). However, how far apart these staged kairotic moments are from each other in terms of chronos is variable. In *Morrowind*, gamers are free to wander Vvardenfell as they please, potentially never taking on the main narrative spine (and thus missing out on these pre-established kairotic moments). The chronos of the game time runs continually regardless: days and nights pass within the game world regardless of the player's actions. Does this mean a user who chooses not to undertake main quests (those crucial to advancing the Dagoth Ur/Nerevar storyline) cannot find kairotic moments within the game? No: spontaneous kairotic moments still abound because of the many dozens of side quests and random encounters with NPCs that can be found in *Morrowind* (there are literally hundreds of NPCs and mini-quests to discover).[9] Each time, the user faces a kairotic moment: should they have their avatar attack the NPC in the distance with a sword? With a bow and arrow? With a magic spell? Should the avatar run away (or sneak by) and avoid an encounter? In a videogame, of course, users are freer to take chances. If the user attacks the NPC and the avatar is killed, perhaps the kairotic moment for fighting that NPC hasn't yet arrived; maybe the avatar isn't yet powerful enough. Or maybe the user just tried the wrong strategy. This can be explored by simply reloading the last saved game point and trying again. Through this trial and error method, kairotic moments in the game can be continually discovered. The game's design gives the user control over time, in a sense: chronos continually runs,[10] but no kairotic moments will be missed — each waits statically somewhere in Vvardenfell for the user to find and trigger, and then retry if the outcome doesn't meet their satisfaction (if the user is willing to reload their game from an earlier point). Just as importantly, *Morrowind* gameplay can be paused at any time, thus allowing the user as much time as needed to think about the gameplay experience: the reflection Kress identifies as essential to learning. Even when the game is not paused, *Morrowind* is still relatively slow-paced, with more time devoted to exploring Vvardenfell and talking to NPCs than to combat.

As a result of the narrative freedom *Morrowind* allows, the user becomes a producer in the way that Murray and Humphreys have hypothesized, and is able to interact internally and ontologically with the game. Ryan explains that *Morrowind* is internally interactive in the sense that the avatar is a member of Vvardenfell, not outside of it (as is the case in many sandbox-type games or other "God" games[11]). *Morrowind* is also interactive in an ontological sense because the user makes decisions that determine what story will emerge; no one linear narrative must be followed. With this dual type of interaction, "the user and the fictional world produces a new life, and consequently a new life-story, with every run of the system" (Ryan 12). I should also note here that Murray, citing Tobias' guidebook for writers, provides a list of what she considers to be the twenty master plots that exist, corresponding to the basic patterns of human life (variations of desire, fulfillment, and loss, essentially): quest, adventure, pursuit, rescue, escape, revenge, the riddle, rivalry, underdog, temptation, metamorphosis, transformation, maturation, love, forbidden love, sacrifice, discovery, wretched excess, ascension, and descension (186–87). Most narratives offer at least one of these, or perhaps a few. However, an examination of the quests and encounters listed as possible in *The Morrowind Prophecies* reveals that *Morrowind* offers users the opportunity to experience potentially all of these over the course of the gameplay experience (depending, of course, on the exploratory path taken through Vvardenfell). These transformative opportunities, along with *Morrowind*'s open-ended approach to narrativity, make it ideal for this study.

Another reason I selected *Morrowind* as the v–RPG for this study was the game's space. In *Hamlet on the Holodeck* Murray identified four properties of digital environments essential for allowing immersion. First, they must be procedural: the defining ability of computers is to execute a series of rules

(71). In chapter two, I discussed computer users' propensities to ascribe to computers more human characteristics and intelligence than they deserve. *Morrowind* has a complex interface, and all interactions within the game-world (combat, conversation, bartering, lockpicking) are decided by statistical rules. For example, if the user's avatar tries to pick the lock on a treasure chest, whether or not the attempt succeeds is determined by the Lockpick skill level of the avatar, the lock level of the chest (how complicated a lock it is), and the quality of the lockpick the avatar is using. All of these numbers are weighed against each other and the chance-to-open-the-lock-percentage is calculated by the game's programming. Of course, these calculations are opaque and happen instantaneously for the user. In this way, the user feels like the game is continually responding to their input. This is Murray's second essential property: the digital environment must be participatory. My discussion of *Morrowind*'s open-ended gameplay and freedom in avatarial construction earlier in this chapter demonstrate the highly participatory nature of *Morrowind*. The procedural and participatory properties of *Morrowind* are what make it interactive for users in Murray's terms.

Murray's third essential property for digital environments is that they be spatial: they must represent navigable space (79). In chapter two, Aarseth, Flynn, Murray, and Taylor stressed the importance of space in videogames, particularly in relation to point of view, labyrinthine structures, and walkable navigation. The island of Vvardenfell in *Morrowind* is vast: *The Morrowind Prophecies Official Guide* breaks the island down into eighteen distinct regions, providing a detailed map for each region. The smallest of these regions highlights the town of Seyda Neen (located on the southwest coast of Vvardenfell) and the region around the town. Despite this map's small size, twenty-three different spots of interest are listed, many of these tombs, caves, grottos, and buildings that each have their own internal labyrinthine maps. To explore even this small region of Vvardenfell thoroughly would take a user several hours of chronos time. The guide lists 812 total spots of interest in the eighteen different regions of Vvardenfell. *Morrowind* places the avatar on foot; therefore, walking is the primary means of navigation through Vvardenfell. This supports Flynn's theories of immersion and navigation in digital spaces. Much of Vvardenfell's terrain is rhizomatic as well, with the avatar free to wander from any point to any other point (albeit not instantaneously as the world is "flat"). However, all caves, grottos, tombs, and buildings are single-path mazes (with many of these requiring extensive exploration as well). *Morrowind*, therefore, offers several different types of navigable space. Just as importantly, *Morrowind* allows the user to choose either first-person or third-person point of view when navigating the game space, thus increasing the opportunities for immersive identification within the gaming experience, since each user is able to choose the point of view they prefer the most and find most immersive.

Murray's fourth essential property for a digital environment is that it must be encyclopedic, with the capacity to represent and contain vast quantities of information. Few v–RPGs are as encyclopedic as *Morrowind*. I've already mentioned the hundreds of NPCs in Vvardenfell who can be interacted with. Many will share information on a variety of topics: the history of Vvardenfell, rumors, locations of interest, creatures to be avoided, and more. Vvardenfell also contains many dozens of books that can be discovered (whether it be from the shelves of the towns' libraries, from wizard towers, or in the holds of shipwrecks) and read. Most of these books describe the histories and lands of Morrowind, over time providing extensive encyclopedic knowledge about the gameworld. The spatial and encyclopedic natures of *Morrowind* work together to make the game immersive in Murray's sense of the term.

For all of these reasons, *Morrowind* seemed like an excellent v–RPG to choose for this portion of the study. The game's high customizability, narrative and temporal freedoms, vast navigable game space, and generic fantasy role-playing conventions allow great potential for immersion and avatarial identification. I collected data for this study in the following ways. First, each participant played ten hours of *Morrowind*; this gameplay was recorded directly onto an external hard drive. After compressing this raw audio/visual data down into smaller file sizes, the gameplay data was moved onto DVDs. I then transcribed the diegetic decisions of each participant (see the appendix for a complete transcription example) and analyzed this transcription to pinpoint crucial decisions made by the avatar. *Morrowind* users make diegetic decisions continually; for my analysis I concentrated on diegetic decisions that were substantially and purposefully tied to the development of the avatar's identity construction (in terms of ethics, narrativity, and attribute and skill development). I then used this transcription analysis to generate specific questions about each participant's *Morrowind* experience, and interviewed Shiva and Vishnu using these questions to guide the interviews. These follow-up interviews were then transcribed and analyzed to ascertain what connections existed between each user's real-world identity and their virtual identity in *Morrowind*. I turn now to a description of both participants' identificatory decisions and my analysis of those decisions.

Choosing the Avatar's Name

In chapter one I provided the following question asked by Marie Ryan on the relationship between user and avatar in v–RPGs: "Will [the user] be

like an actor playing a role, innerly distanciated from her character and simulating emotions she does not really have, or will she experience her character in first-person mode, actually feeling [the emotions] that motivate the
character's behavior or that may result from her actions?" (6) This question,
representing two ends of an identity continuum, is an important one: how
"real" was each user's identification with their avatar? In *Morrowind* there are
many opportunities for users to identify with their avatars. Each new game
begins with a cinematic that provides minimal backstory for the avatar: the
avatar has been mysteriously released from prison on the Emperor's orders
and sent on a slave ship to the small village of Seyda Neen for release. This
explanatory cinematic takes less than two minutes, and then the avatar is
woken by a fellow prisoner, Jiub, in the hold of the slave ship. Jiub asks the
avatar what her/his name is. This is the first opportunity for *Morrowind* users
to begin constructing their avatar. How did Vishnu and Shiva decide on their
avatars' names?

"Steve!" was the name of Vishnu's avatar. This choice was surprising.
Vishnu was an experienced v–RPG gamer: he knew *Morrowind* was set in a
fantasy world with monsters and non-humanoid races. I was expecting a less
ordinary name inspired by Gandolf or Saruman (*Lord of the Rings*) or Bib
Fortuna or Boba Fett (the *Star Wars* trilogy). Certainly not Steve! (Vishnu
was adamant that the exclamation point was an important part of the name).
Vishnu described his reasons for choosing this name: "It's sort of a long-running personal joke, really just with myself. For some reason I have this alter
ego that I love, Steve Grabowski. It's this great name." Vishnu went on to
explain the significance of the name:

> VISHNU: It actually comes from two places. Um, the [*Simpsons*] episode
> where Homer goes to New York to get his car back, after Barney
> takes it? It's in between the World Trade Center. And he calls in
> to get the boot taken off his car, and the automated phone serv-
> ice is like, "Your request has been denied by Officer Steve
> Grabowski." And then I just thought that was really funny. And
> then in the movie *Grosse Pointe Blank,* she's [Joan Cusack's char-
> acter] talking about the hitmen that have been hired to assassi-
> nate John Cusack's character and she, she, one of them is named
> like, "Steven La Poo Belle," and she goes, "AKA, Steve!" and the
> way she said that, with an exclamation point, for some reason I
> just thought that was the world's funniest thing, and ever since
> I use Steve Grabowski for all kinds of secret stuff.
> ZACH: So it's the kind of thing you do quickly for your own amusement.
> VISHNU: Yeah, pretty much. No one really would get it other than me.

Even though Vishnu did not select a name for his avatar that seemed in keeping with the fantasy RPG genre, the name did have personal, "secret" mean-

ing to him. Vishnu admitted that he had named his head coach in *Madden 06* Steve! Grabowski. Vishnu's choice for his virtual identity's name in *Morrowind* was directly influenced by his real-world identity's sense of humor and predisposition for a long-running personal joke. That he refers to Steve! Grabowski as an "alter-ego" shows his level of investment and identification with the name and the persona it represents.

Shiva named her avatar "Shi." I asked her to explain why: "I'm not creative with naming and I feel this pressure to name it (the avatar) cool, but then I don't know what's cool. I feel like I want to name it something I like. And I like my own name a lot. Shi is my default name; I don't know why. [Actually] I guess I do: it's me." This reveals that Shiva's real-world identity has primacy at this stage of the avatar's creation: her virtual world identity shares her name. *Morrowind*'s decision to have users select the avatar name before selecting the race and gender is an interesting one: if the user hasn't read the game manual to learn about what these choices entail, the name selection at the beginning of the game comes with almost no contextual diegetic data to aid the user. Users must rely on their extra-diegetic real-world identities when naming the avatar as Vishnu and Shiva have illustrated here.

Learning the Gaming Interface

After the avatar is named, *Morrowind* users are then allowed to begin moving around in the gameworld: a guard on the slave ship asks the avatar to follow him up from the storage hold to the main deck. As I discussed earlier in this chapter, it is important that the game's interface become intuitive as quickly as possible so that the user can become immersed in diegetic aspects of the game. Here at the beginning of the game, the avatar is controlled in first-person POV.[12] Vishnu admitted that at first it was "kind of tough" to learn *Morrowind*'s complex interface particularly when trying to control the Y-axis. To control the direction the avatar (and therefore the user) is looking within the gameworld the user must move the mouse up and down (the Y axis) and left and right (the X axis) corresponding to the movements of the avatar's head. However, most videogames have a default Y axis setting similar to airplane controls: pushing forward actually looks down and pulling the mouse backward looks up. This feature in particular bothered Vishnu, and in the first ten minutes of his *Morrowind* gameplay, he entered the game's Settings feature to examine the control scheme and experiment with the vertical axis seven different times. Thereafter, however, Vishnu was comfortable with the gaming interface:

> After the first ten minutes it was pretty good. Having gamed a lot, usually one of the first things I'll do, I'll go look at the controls and find

out at least the major ones. In this instance I went and scrolled through
the control list and as I started gaming I tweaked a little bit. After about
an hour of playing I was [comfortable], using the hot keys, refining
them, stuff like that.

That it took Vishnu ten minutes to become comfortable with the gaming
interface is a tribute to his gaming acumen: ten minutes is a very short
amount of time, especially for a v–RPG offering potentially hundreds of hours
of gameplay. Shiva was more comfortable with the interface immediately
likely due to her more extensive experience with PC gaming interfaces.
Describing herself as "really flexible" when it comes to gaming interfaces,
Shiva, in contrast to Vishnu, never entered the game's Settings at any time
during her *Morrowind* gameplay. She relied on the default game settings and
the control settings reminder on the back of the game manual instead. The
interface never interfered with Shiva's *Morrowind* immersion.

Selecting Race and Gender

The next step in *Morrowind*'s avatar creation is selecting race and gender. The avatar is escorted off of the slave ship, where a waiting guard asks
where she/he is from. This triggers the racial and gender selection screen from
which the user can select a male or female from any of the ten playable *Morrowind* races (with ten different facial and twenty different hair options for
each). This selection screen defaults to a Dark Elf male. After examining all
the racial options (spending more than five minutes to make his selection)
Vishnu ultimately selected Dark Elf as the race for his avatar. Had he been
influenced by this being the default race in the selection screen? When asked,
he said that this had no bearing on his selection. He explained that his decision was more tactical: "I know from other RPGs and stuff, usually Elves are
quick, and they're decent magic users, decent fighters, so you know they have
a good balance. I think that's why I ended up taking it." Vishnu used his
knowledge of genres (both v–RPG genre and fantasy genre) to help him hone
in on the three Elven races. He then relied on his love of "number crunch-
ing" to examine the starting attributes of each race. A statistical examination
reveals that the Dark Elves do indeed have the highest Speed value of any race
(50, the highest initial value possible for any attribute) and also have strong
starting values in Strength (40, important for fighters) and Intelligence (40,
important for magic users). Vishnu relied on a combination of diegetic
knowledge (the specific attribute values for Dark Elves in *Morrowind*) and
extra-diegetic knowledge (past experiences with Elven characters in v–RPGs
and knowledge of Elven fantasy mythology) to select Steve!'s race.

Like Vishnu, Shiva also selected Dark Elf for Shi's race. She was influenced by each race's starting attribute values to a certain degree. She also expressed a desire for a "balanced" character saying since she wasn't sure whether combat or magic skills were going to be more beneficial in the game, she "wanted to be able to do both." However Shiva was influenced even more by her wish to identify with the avatar:

SHIVA: I wanted to choose a race that would match my stats,[13] so I was trying to think, and I usually have a hard time choosing the other-worldly races in role-playing games.

ZACH: So there was an Orc (porcine), there was a Khajiit, which was catlike, and there was the Argonian which was a lizard. Were those eliminated right off the bat?

SHIVA: Basically.

ZACH: But of course the Dark Elf doesn't look particularly human...

SHIVA: It's more human to me, I don't know why. A lot of times I do a magic user that looks a lot like me and I wanted to get away from that a little bit

ZACH: You wanted to get away from which one?

SHIVA: Me always choosing something that looks like me. I was like, "I can just be different!" and that's why I chose the Dark Elf. It was a bit about her appearance. I think I decided it was maybe a little bit different, but not too different. So I was going to be an Elf.

Shiva made a conscious effort to select a race for her avatar that was different physically from her real-world identity. At the same time, she was careful to make sure that the avatar's racial identity would not be so different (animalistic in appearance) that she wouldn't be able to identify with it. She seemed to find a careful balance here between merger and division in connecting Shi to her real-world identity.

To aid in the merger aspects of her avatarial identification Shiva selected female for Shi's gender. This selection, she said, was the easiest part of the selection process:

SHIVA: I'm female and I want to go with a female. I sometimes go male, but usually I'm like, there are enough male [avatars]. I'm female. I want it

ZACH: So you want your avatar to be female and named Shi?

SHIVA: Yes, basically me, I guess.

Shiva's desire to create an avatar that resembles her real-world identity's appearance was shown as she scrolled through the different races before deciding on Dark Elf. Shiva showed clear gender identification: she was eager to play as a female. Historically most videogame avatars and agents have been male. Shiva exhibited a strong feminist identity throughout this project, decrying the impossible physique of *Tomb Raider*'s Lara Croft and boycotting

Shiva's avatar Shi, initial creation.

Grand Theft Auto III because of the degrading depiction of women in the game. Shiva was eager to create a female avatar that she could roleplay as strong and independent, characteristics she felt were too infrequently available in female videogame characters. Ultimately, she chose between a red-headed Dark Elf female and a brunette Nord female (one of the human races). Shiva admitted that the Nord avatar she was considering was "me being egotistical, just being myself." Ultimately she rejected this option partly due to her above-mentioned desire to try something "different" but also due to her inability to find any Nord facial options that really looked like Shiva:

> SHIVA: I didn't like any of the [Nord] faces. All the faces were not that great. And so, if you're a Dark Elf, or some other race...
> ZACH: It's okay for it not to look real?
> SHIVA: Right, because you don't know what's [real]. But here (the Nord), it's obviously not a good enough likeness. It's not pretty enough.

For Shiva there was safety in selecting the Dark Elf since there is no physical reality against which to weigh its appearance. If the *Morrowind* avatar cre-

Vishnu's avatar Steve!, initial creation.

ation system had been sophisticated enough to allow Shiva to create a Caucasian female that more closely resembled her real-world appearance, she likely would have done so given her stated desire to create avatars as similar to her extra-diegetic self as possible. Shiva's selection of gender and race reveal an interesting paradox. She selected the avatar's gender because it matched her real-world identity. However she selected the avatar's race because it decidedly did not match her real-world identity. Yet both selections only strengthened her identification with Shi In an interview conducted after her *Morrowind* gameplay Shiva said she found her avatar Shi memorable and stressed how much she liked the avatar. This example echoes Gee's description of his creation of his avatar Bead Bead: "a delicious blend" (54) of both merger and division leading to strong identification with the virtual identity. This phenomenon is central to v–RPGs and I describe it further in chapter six.

Shiva's desire to try something "different" with her avatar was mirrored by Vishnu, who also selected female for his Dark Elf. A female named Steve! was certainly unexpected but it was in keeping with Vishnu's sense of humor and desire for self-amusement. He admitted that he didn't usually choose female avatars but that this time he decided to "do something a little different." When asked why he normally selected male avatars, he replied that male avatars made identification easier for him: "I guess part of it is that it is transferring identity into the game. You want [the avatar] to kind of reflect yourself a little bit." Vishnu attempted to create an avatar that physically looked like him before ultimately deciding that the closest possibility (in this case, a Caucasian Breton) wasn't close enough. Vishnu did admit that he was able to create a Khajiit character that closely resembled his pet cat but decided that was an identification he wasn't willing to embrace for the duration of his *Morrowind* gameplay. Vishnu's desire for a balanced character and willingness to try something different led him to select the Dark Elf female. Vishnu and Shiva, both heavily influenced by their real-world desires, selected Dark Elf female avatars.

Selecting Class and Skills

After the user selects race and gender, the avatar is escorted into Seyda Neen's Census and Excise Office, where the next phase of avatar creation, class, takes place. *Morrowind*'s game manual describes "class" in the following way: "Class defines your way of life and which skills are most important to you" (Hines and Cheng 21). In the Census and Excise Office non-player character (NPC) Socucius Ergalla offers the user three ways to generate avatar class. First, she can select from the 21 pre-existing classes that exist in the game. Seven of these classes emphasize combat as the primary means of interacting with the game world, seven emphasize magic, and seven emphasize stealth. Users are free to select any one of these 21 from the list provided. Each of these 21 classes has five Major Skills and five Minor Skills associated with them. The second option allows the user to create their own custom class by choosing the Major and Minor skills they want to emphasize and naming this class.[14] For the third class-generation option, Ergalla offers to ask the avatar a series of ten questions; he will then assign a class (from the 21 pre-existing classes) to the avatar based on the answers. Each question has three possible answers with each answer demonstrating a propensity for combat, magic, or stealth; combined, the ten answers will match one class given pre-established systemic parameters.[15] However, each question is vague and it isn't readily apparent what the answers might mean. The eighth question Ergalla asks represents this ambiguity: "Your mother asks you to help fix the stove. While you are working, a very hot pipe slips its moorings and falls towards her. What do you do?" The user has three choices: "Position yourself between the pipe and your mother," "Grab the hot pipe and try to push it away," and "Push your mother out of the way" (*The Morrowind Prophecies* 7). It's impossible to know which of these choices the game designers have decided is related to combat, magic, and stealth. This adds an element of surprise to the avatar class selection.

Both Vishnu and Shiva chose this third option. Shiva in particular enjoyed selecting Shi's class in this way even as she found the questions "silly" and "strange": "I really like the way you could choose. I liked the idea of using it to see what you are in the gameworld. I wanted to see what Shi would be in this world according to these questions." Shiva here admitted that she answered the ten questions "completely honestly" in keeping with her real-world identity's ethics and morals.[16] After answering the questions Shiva was assigned her avatar's class: Witchhunter (six magic answers, two combat answers, and two stealth answers). This pleased her: "I liked Witchhunter, I liked it a lot. I was excited!" When asked why this appealed to her so much, she explained that part of the reason was the balance in the class's skills between the three gameplay approaches (magic, combat, and stealth). Witchhunter satisfied her earlier desires for an avatar flexible enough to problem solve in different ways. Vishnu's Steve! was also assigned one of the magic-based classes: Spellsword (five magic answers, five combat answers, and no stealth answers). Vishnu was more ambivalent about this classification and examined the Major and Minor skills of this class closely but ultimately kept all of them except the Minor Skill Axe, replacing it with Short Sword. The rest of the Spellsword's skills satisfied his initial desire, like Shiva's, to play a balanced avatar.

Selecting Birthsign

The final step in the initial avatar creation process is selecting a Birthsign. The *Morrowind* game manual explains the Birthsign's significance: "Persons born under certain constellations are said to be 'fortunate in their aspects.' Such persons are often blessed — or cursed — with remarkable abilities or weaknesses as a result of the magical conjunctions of celestial influences" (Hines and Cheng 25). As is fitting for a videogame set in a fantasy world, *Morrowind* has its own unique constellations (which are in fact visible in the night sky during gameplay). Shiva chose Shi's Birthsign carefully. She admitted that she tried hard to match the Birthsign's abilities with her Witchhunter class, ultimately deciding "The Lady" (with Fortify Personality and Fortify Endurance abilities) fit the best:

> I was a little sad, I looked, I was trying to match [the Birthsign] with my character's strengths and my class, and The Lady didn't quite do it, so I didn't know if I wanted to choose her. But I looked at the other ones and they didn't work for me either. And I think Personality was

one of the options I wanted for my character so it was like, one match and one extra benefit and I was like, "I can do that!" Because she (The Lady) had all positives, no negatives. I liked the idea of if I had two main attributes I would be so pumped up. I loved it!

Vishnu, however, expressed ambivalence for most of the Birthsign options, saying they "seemed pretty worthless." Initially, he wasn't even sure he remembered which Birthsign he had selected. After looking at the list of possibilities he remembered selecting "The Ritual" which gave the avatar the ability to heal herself and "turn" undead creatures.[17] Vishnu explained that his previous experiences playing v–RPGs influenced his decision to select a Birthsign that would allow Steve! to heal herself:

> ZACH: Why did you think [healing yourself] was going to be impor-
> tant?
> VISHNU: Just knowing that early in the game you generally get your ass
> kicked.
> ZACH: Are you saying the avatar is incompetent, early on?
> VISHNU: I think it's the player that is incompetent, probably. I know
> the style of the game or even some of the particulars of that game
> you just get killed really quickly. [With] the ability to heal I was
> trying to cover all the bases. I just thought, "Well, if nothing else
> you can heal yourself." It's always a good thing to be able to heal.
> ZACH: We know that from role-playing experiences for sure.
> VISHNU: Having played far too many role-playing games, yes.

As with his other decisions so far, Vishnu relies on the extra-diegetic knowledge he has accumulated and internalized from his previous experiences. This accumulation is interesting: it represents a combination of virtual experiences (past v–RPG gameplay) that have been collated and stored in Vishnu's mind. These experiences influence Vishnu's decisions in creating Steve! Vishnu is able to articulate these virtual world decisions in real-world, extra-diegetic ways.

It is evident that both Vishnu and Shiva chose their Birthsigns with the intent of giving their avatars as much of a chance to be successful in the game-world as possible. Without any hands-on experiences yet in *Morrowind* to aid in determining which Birthsign attributes would be most beneficial to their avatars both participants drew on other sources of information to make decisions. Shiva couldn't imagine wanting any negative attributes associated with her avatar. The influence of her real-world identities is clear here. It was unimaginable to Shiva to consciously choose characteristics that would impact her avatar negatively (even as the idea of playing a heroic yet flawed Achilles-like avatar might appeal to some users). Shiva was either unwilling or unable to set aside her goals for her real-world attributes when constructing Shi.

Vishnu drew on his memories of past virtual experiences to guide his Birth-sign selection. Perhaps it goes without saying, but clearly virtual experiences are stored as real memories by the user and are accessed as needed. How should Vishnu's memories of past videogame experiences be characterized? Are they virtual memories? Real memories? Real memories of virtual experiences? These are interesting questions that demonstrate the problematic nature of Gee's terminology. I address this problem in greater detail in chapter six.

Morrowind's avatar creation process is a lengthy one: it took Vishnu just over twenty-two minutes to complete all of these steps and Shiva just over twenty minutes. This is a long time to spend in a videogame essentially setting up the game to play. In many videogame genres entire levels and multiple objectives can be completed in twenty minutes. It is easy to imagine many gamers getting frustrated by having to wait so long to actively play the game. But in v–RPGs, this experience (which is both diegetic and extra-diegetic) actually aids in identity construction. Vishnu explained how this worked for him: "I think it sort of engages you a little bit more, as you become 'your' character a little bit more than if you were just watching cut scenes or being pushed forward. I think here you're actually creating some sort of identity in the game that you're going to relate to in the game. You created it (the avatar)." The many steps in the avatar creation process in *Morrowind* as demonstrated by Vishnu and Shiva allow the user's real-world identity to make decisions about her/his new virtual identity. This insures that the avatar and user are connected, since all of the decisions the user made for the avatar have real-world justifications and reasons behind them. In this way the avatar is both virtual and non-virtual. In chapter one Gee described the creation and playing of his avatar Bead Bead as a "delicious blend of my doing and not my doing" (54–55) to help explain the concept of projective identity. The initial creations of Vishnu's Steve! and Shiva's Shi seem to share this blend.

Point of View

As I note in chapter two vision for Haraway is crucial to the construction of self-identities. For Haraway, being able to see a potential subject position is essential to being able to inhabit that position and, thus, relocate identity. This argument is predicated on some bodily aspect as there must be something tangible to be seen by the viewer. Haraway describes the need for a "semiotic-material technology linking meanings and bodies" (192). Other scholars agree on the importance of the connections between vision and the body as well. Spinoza believed that language was a bodily transformation.

DeLeuze described images as "the traces of an external body on our body" (73). Walker suggested that in visual depictions "the phenomenal character of the perception is inseparable from the imagining that takes it as an object. The seeing and imagining are inseparably bound together, integrated into a single complex phenomenological whole" (4–5). *Morrowind* too seems to consider vision and seeing the body as important to identity construction as the game design allows users to select either first-person point of view (POV) or third-person POV. Was being able to have this choice important to Vishnu and Shiva? Was being able to see their avatars crucial to the identification process?

Morrowind defaults to first-person POV for the duration of the initial avatar creation process: it is not until Socucius Ergalla instructs the avatar to take their release papers from his desk that the user can switch to third-person POV if they wish. This process took over twenty minutes for both Vishnu and Shiva and both participants admitted that initially they forgot about the option to switch to third-person POV. The *Morrowind* avatar cannot be seen in first-person POV.[18]

Representative first-person point of view.

Representative third-person point of view.

As I discussed in chapter two, the connections between identity, the body, and vision are important ones. How then were the participants going to be able to see their avatars enough to identify with them? This problem was solved by *Morrowind*'s inventory windows. As I explained in chapter three *Morrowind*'s chronos time runs continually during gameplay but is paused when the user enters the inventory.[19] In the inventory screen, the user can examine the map of the gameworld, the avatar's attributes and skills levels, items the avatar is currently carrying and perhaps most importantly in this case, a full body image of what the avatar looks like. Each of these inventory windows can be enlarged or reduced at the user's discretion. By changing the clothing and armor the avatar is wearing, the user can continually change the appearance of the avatar which is reflected in the inventory screen. In other words, each time the user enters the inventory she is presented with a bodily image of her avatar, thus increasing the chances of identification (particularly since the user has control over this appearance, from the choices during the initial avatar creation to the clothing and armor choices throughout the gameplay). Vishnu described his satisfaction with this component of the inventory screen:

VISHNU: I think it gave you a good, as far as visualizing your avatar,
     you can see the changes you make, um, in apparel and weapons.
ZACH: Is that important to you? Is it something that matters to you as
     a gamer in this genre?
VISHNU: Yeah! I mean again it's sort of that customization, making it
     your own, and obviously you're limited here in [in the begin-
     ning to] what they give you, but as you get further into the game
     you can sort of choose what kind of armor you want. I know I
     stuck with some armor that probably wasn't the best because I
     liked the way it kind of looked. I'm trying to remember, [maybe
     it] was the Bonemold [armor]. I liked the way it looked, espe-
     cially in the third person, when you're out, sort of looking at
     yourself.

In ten hours of *Morrowind* gameplay Vishnu entered the inventory screen 219
times, sometimes for several minutes at a time. Even if he had played exclusively in first-person POV Vishnu still had multiple opportunities see his virtual body and thus identify more completely with it.

   However, Vishnu did not play exclusively in first-person POV; in fact,
after one hour and nineteen minutes of gameplay he switched to third-person POV and never returned to the first-person perspective. Vishnu cited
two main reasons why the third-person POV in *Morrowind* was much more
immersive for him. First, he found it much easier to engage in close-quar-
ters combat in third-person POV. He explained his frustrations with first-
person combat:

   I felt like I had no depth perception in terms of swinging. So I think I
   went in and changed it because you have a little bit more of a peripheral vision. You can see things a little bit more fully in that third person view and I kind of like that a little bit more. In combat you can
   see what's going on a little bit more around you, especially if you're
   surrounded.

The second reason Vishnu cited for his third-person preference was also
related to depth perception and visual bodily identification. For Vishnu seeing the full body of his avatar greatly aided his identification with the avatar
and his immersion into the gaming world:

   VISHNU: You get a better feel of your environment in a 3D sort of way.
        I think personally depth perception is better in third person. You
        get a feel and sense of your size in comparison to the world
        around you that you sometimes don't get in first person. You can
        see what you yourself are doing, not just your actions, but [what]
        your character [is] doing.
   ZACH: How do you distinguish between those two, not just your actions
        but your character's actions?

VISHNU: Like not only swinging, or blocking, or walking, but to actually watch the avatar, viewing, swinging the sword, and walking.

ZACH: So not just the sword, but seeing the whole body in action, the world, is important?

VISHNU: To me, yeah, I think so. It gives it a little bit more of a sense of realism in sort of a strange way because in a first person mode, there is no sense of the body around you as opposed to in life you can see your arms.

ZACH: You can look at your body at any time.

VISHNU: Yeah, you can see it in sort of, you know, even if you're focusing forward you can still sort of see your extremities or something like that that you don't get in a first person. I think it gives you a better sense of again your character in the world, um, that is just cool to look at.

ZACH: Cool to look at because it's a different body frame, there is interesting armor...

VISHNU: Right, cool armor and stuff like that.

ZACH: And all those things contribute to Vishnu's identification with Steve! the female Dark Elf?

VISHNU: Yeah, I think so in sort of a weird way. I've always felt it's a little easier to get into the game in third person than it is in first person. First person obviously gives you a through-the-eyes viewpoint, but in a way I think it disconnects you a little bit more because you don't have that peripheral which is a big part of our vision and our perception.

ZACH: So third person feels more real to you than first person does in the gaming world.

VISHNU: Yeah, in a lot of ways, yeah!

Notice that throughout his explanation here Vishnu refers to the avatar not in the more distant third person "he" or "she" but rather with the more intimate "you": "You get a feel and sense of your size in comparison to the world around you that you sometimes don't get in first person. You can see what you yourself are doing, not just your actions." This pronoun choice indicates that Vishnu closely identifies with his avatar. Vishnu also stressed how important it was to him to be able to see Steve! in the gameworld. Vishnu's perception of the avatar was greatly aided by his ability to see the avatar's virtual body. For Vishnu, identification was greatly aided by vision. Seeing the avatar made the virtual identity more real to him: "It gives it more of a sense of realism." This is interesting: it suggests that for Vishnu his perceptions of the importance of the avatar's virtual body and his "real" physical body are intersecting. The kinesthetic argument Vishnu makes here indicates the liminal space between Vishnu and Steve! is shrinking in these instances.

Shiva's *Morrowind* gameplay took place almost exclusively in first-person POV. She took pride in describing herself as a flexible gamer capable of playing effectively from either perspective: "Whatever you've got, just give me and I'll go with it." She said she felt like both POVs were "equal" when it came to her ability to become immersed but she did state a fondness for third-person POV similar to Vishnu's: "Sometimes I try to put myself in first person and I don't like it. I can't see around the person. I like being there. [But] in *Morrowind* I did it in first person, I guess, so I could be more in character." Shiva also said that she found the combat in the game easier in first-person POV: "In third person you couldn't always see where the monster was." Shiva's statements here show her flexibility when it comes to POV immersion. Both first-person (helping Shiva feel "in character") and third-person (helping Shiva feel "there") POV can lead to immersion for her. Point of view wasn't as crucial to avatar identification for Shiva. Her identity as a veteran gamer skilled enough to enjoy both POVs was very important to her; she was proud that she was able to identify with her avatar via either perspective. Instead, Shiva stressed that her v–RPG immersion and identification was dependent on whether or not she liked the avatar she was playing. What might lead to her not liking an avatar she has created? Shiva clarified with the following example, explaining why she preferred the v–RPG *Bard's Tale* (which gives the user limited control over the avatar's creation and development) to *Fable* (a v–RPG with more open-ended gameplay and choices for avatar construction):

> [With] *Fable* I was really excited because you can change your character and I liked some of the options you could do with your character, I guess more freedom, but sometimes I just felt that world was harsher, was meaner, or something. I didn't connect with my character as much. In *Bard's Tale* it wasn't me as much, but he [the avatar] was funny! And I think of myself as funny, so it was nice to see a funny character, and because I liked the character I felt more [connection to him].

In this instance Shiva identified more strongly with the gameworld of *Bard's Tale*: the mood (for lack of a better word) of *Fable*'s setting didn't appeal to Shiva's real-world sensibilities. In the non-virtual world, Shiva is optimistic, cheerful, quick to laugh, and is eager to please those around her. I mentioned earlier Shiva's indignance at aspects of *Tomb Raider* and *Grand Theft Auto III*: Shiva carries her real-world sensibilities into her videogaming experiences. She wants to spend time in a virtual world that resonates with her own pleasant worldview. *Fable*'s gameworld did not do this, but the light-hearted approach of the *Bard's Tale* was a better fit. Fortunately, Shiva was sufficiently interested in *Morrowind*'s gameworld to become invested in her avatar (more on the participants' *Morrowind* gameworld immersion later in this chapter). Shiva also entered the inventory screens even more than Vishnu did: she accessed those windows 318 times. This gave Shiva ample opportunities to

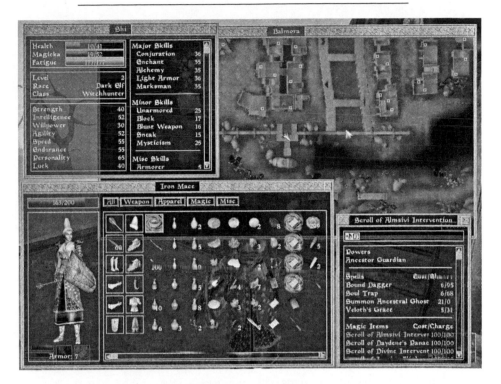

Shi's inventory screen.

view Shi's appearance. The avatar's appearance was certainly important to Shiva as she had rejected several racial and facial options for Shi because they were "not pretty enough." In a fashion similar to Vishnu's identification with Steve!, Shiva's identification was aided by her perception of Shi's virtual body.

Killing, Stealing, and Dying: Avatar Ethics and Diegetic Experimentation

After users makes their final decisions about the avatar's race, gender, class, and birthsign, Socucius Ergalla instructs the avatar to pick up her release-from-prison papers from his desk and show them to the guard at the door. This action is necessary so that the avatar can leave the Census and Excise Office. From this point forward, the user is now free to explore *Morrowind* in whatever manner they wish. Interestingly enough, at this point, both Vishnu and Shiva made gameplay decisions that were influenced by non-diegetic knowledge. For example, Steve! immediately attempted to Intimidate Socucius Ergalla in conversation, resulting in Ergalla having a much lower disposition toward Steve![20] Vishnu also attempted to steal items off of the table in front of Ergalla, causing the NPC to admonish Steve! Why would Vishnu attempt to bully the man who had just set Steve! free? I asked Vishnu to explain his actions:

> VISHNU: I think two reasons. Mainly, just to see what the commands actually did, you know, just getting used to the interface, and knowing how the gameplay actually worked.
> ZACH: Did you fear repercussions from your bullying and intimidating?
> VISHNU: That was the second thing. I figured in this room in this section you probably aren't going to get punished for it, you know, trying to steal things, trying to punch people, you know.
> ZACH: Why did you think that?
> VISHNU: Again, familiarity with gaming. Generally you know something that initiates you into the world isn't going to punish you or have the repercussions that normal gameplay would.
> ZACH: And you got the sense you were in kind of safe, "newbie" space? In other words, you could try out things that there might be greater repercussions for [later]?
> VISHNU: Yeah. In terms of initiating you, that generally, they'll give you a little bit of leeway and I think I was taking advantage of that as well just to get the gameplay down.

Here, Vishnu uses his knowledge about v–RPG conventions to test the *Morrowind* game system, learning what repercussions certain actions will have. Steve!'s attempts to bully Ergalla is clearly Vishnu making the decision for Steve! based on Vishnu's past v–RPG experiences. This influence can also be seen in Vishnu's decision to join the Fighters Guild in Balmora. I asked Vishnu why he only joined this guild instead of the Guild of Thieves or the Mages Guild. Vishnu again cited his past videogaming experiences as the reason why he made this selection:

> I think because again familiarity with the (RPG) genre, a Fighters Guild will probably give you better armor, better weapons, so from a practical standpoint I thought the Fighters Guild would probably give you some items that you would need in order to survive a little longer. As opposed to joining a Mages Guild, probably, you might get some power-ups, some magical items, I don't know, something, but it may not be as beneficial up front in the game as better armor or better weapons was probably my thinking on that.

Is the knowledge Vishnu is drawing on diegetic or extra-diegetic? It seems to be a little of both: his real-world identity is remembering past virtual experiences that appear relevant to his current *Morrowind* videogame play. Virtual experiences stored as real memories help Vishnu make decisions for

Steve! This is significant in that it again shows how virtual memories function similarly to real-world memories for Vishnu: both types of memories are stored and are then accessed as needed to aid in predicting appropriate behavior to guide the individual's actions.

Shiva made choices for Shi in a similar manner. Like Vishnu, Shi immediately tried to steal a tankard off of Ergalla's desk only to be chastised by the NPC. She explained this decision by saying that she "wanted to see what the gameplay was like, if they allowed for stealing or whether there were consequences." Interestingly enough though Shiva finds a book in the Census and Excise Office's "newbie room"[21] and chooses not to take it opting instead to read the book and then replace it on the shelf. When asked why she didn't take the book and sell it later, Shiva replied that "in a lot of games you can take books but they're worth like one gold and they take up tons of space so I guess maybe I've been trained to think that." Prior v–RPG experiences influenced this decision. Shiva also had Shi join several different organizations as soon as possible: the Temple, the Mages Guild, the Guild of Thieves, House Hlaalu, the Imperial Cult and the Fighters Guild. This struck me as odd: why would Shi the ethical Witchhunter want to take orders from so many different people? When asked, Shiva was quick to explain how this strategy actually dovetailed perfectly with Shi's projective identity: "I didn't think I was playing by their rules. I just wanted their free stuff! I wanted access. If you join the guilds, you get good advice, and they like you better, and you get more stuff. So I was like, 'Cool!' And I just wanted to see what it was like to join. If they gave me orders I didn't want, I'd just ignore them." Shiva's plan was to use the guilds to gain experience and items; she didn't really consider herself loyal to any of them. Shiva was influenced by her memories of earlier v–RPG experiences in joining so many different factions but at the same time she was able to justify this decision through the projective identity she was creating for Shi. The explanations given by both Vishnu and Shiva here rely heavily on memories that are paradoxical in terms of identity and show a clear passage between real-world and virtual-world identity. Diegetic experiences (past v–RPG gaming sessions) become extra-diegetic memories that are stored within the real-world identities of the user. These memories are then accessed to aid the user in decision-making in future diegetic experiences (even if the future diegetic experiences are with a different video game). This movement from virtual to real-world and back to virtual demonstrates the convergent and fluid nature of identity construction.

As a result of their ability to access earlier diegetic experiences, both Vishnu and Shiva had no hesitations about stealing items in *Morrowind*. This conduct was a definite departure from both participants' real-world identities: Vishnu and Shiva were adamant that they would never steal anything outside of virtual space. Shiva admitted that her ethics "are a bit looser" in the virtual worlds of video role-playing games. She believed that many items exist specifically to be stolen: "It seems in gameplay, all the stuff is just for you. They put barrels and stuff in to give you life experience and money. People aren't going to use it!" Vishnu seconded this notion, justifying Steve!'s continual thievery in *Morrowind*: "Usually in other RPGs I know some of the best stuff you get you have to steal, or have to get in means other than buying [or] purchasing: sometimes you actually have to go and take [it]. You know you're in a world, a virtual world, you can do things you can't do in the real world." Vishnu very clearly distinguishes between *Morrowind*'s world and the "real" world to justify his avatar's behavior. Shiva does as well, explaining why she had no qualms about having Shi loot the body of a slaver she had just killed in Addamasartus:[22]

> ZACH: Shiva, how ethical is it to loot the body that you just killed?
> SHIVA: It's a slaver!
> ZACH: Why did you do it?
> SHIVA: Cause it's not real world. And I guess I always loot the corpse, in any game I play, even role-playing. I'm the first person to loot! They're dead, they're not going to need it, and I probably will.
> ZACH: No ethical dilemma?
> SHIVA: No. I guess if I'm willing to kill them, that is not an issue. So why can't I steal their stuff? Who else is going to use it?

Here Shiva demonstrates just how fluidly she can move between diegetic and non-diegetic thinking. She defends her willingness to kill and loot diegetically by pointing out Vvardenfell is not "real world." Yet she is still compelled to provide rationale for her actions: the NPC is a vile slaver and therefore can be ethically killed. And if one is willing to kill (arguably the least ethical action possible), looting must therefore be acceptable as well. Shiva takes the diegetic actions of Shi seriously enough to justify them rationally.

Vishnu also routinely looted corpses in *Morrowind* and like Shiva rationalized and defended the ethics of these decisions, going so far as to suggest that he believed the *Morrowind* gameworld expected this behavior. Vishnu describes why he looted the body of the Addamasartus slaver he had killed (interestingly enough the same slaver killed and looted by Shiva):

> VISHNU: You have to. [Laughing.]
> ZACH: Ethical behavior? Why was it okay to loot that body?
> VISHNU: Uh, primarily, he was the aggressor so I probably won't get punished; um, secondly I think you have to loot people in this game, well because he probably has better armor than you or something or at least would have money.

ZACH: So there is no ethical doubt, there's no hesitation in the killing of the character and in taking anything you want off of the dead body?

VISHNU: I think if he is a villain, or an enemy, I think it's alright. Again if it's an unprovoked thing and you just mug someone and kill them, I probably would still do it, but it's less ethical. This I would have no problems.

ZACH: There's no hesitation.

VISHNU: No, because that's fair game. He attacked me, that is my reward. It's the character's reward.

ZACH: And that's typical in your RPG experience prior to *Morrowind*?

VISHNU: Yeah. I think so. I think it extends beyond this world.

In their explanations here, both Vishnu and Shiva clearly make a distinction between their real-world ethics and their virtual ethics: stealing and killing become acceptable virtually. Here the distinctions between the two types of identity are clear and the participants have no difficulty articulating these differences. Yet earlier during the creation of the avatar's name, gender, race, and class both participants demonstrated that this demarcation isn't always as clear cut. The passage between real-world and virtual-world identities is a complicated one. Immersion within *Morrowind* for the participants resonates with Gee's "delicious blend" of virtual and non-virtual memories and identities.

Both participants stressed in their initial interviews that they enjoyed learning the individual systems of videogames. Several examples seem to confirm this same interest in learning *Morrowind*'s diegetic rules for both Vishnu and Shiva. Just as Vishnu had experimented by attempting to "Persuade" Socucius Ergalla through Intimidation, Shiva had attempted to "Persuade" Ergalla through Admiration. Shiva explained that she was merely testing her abilities, seeing how the Persuasion component of the game worked. Both Shiva and Vishnu also readily admitted that they had read most of the fifty-page manual that accompanied the videogame before playing *Morrowind*. Vishnu chose to "Persuade" through Intimidation, a choice that resonated with his real-world masculine identity and sense of humor: he considered Intimidating Ergalla to be both a "manly" and funny action. Shiva chose Admire, a less aggressive persuasive attempt. This too reflects her real-world temperament and easy-going personality. Through their interactions with Ergalla here the participants identify via merger with their avatar's actions; earlier when looting and killing they identified via division. Both types of identification contribute to the overall avatar identity construction within *Morrowind*. Vishnu even considered the death of his avatar as nothing more than a learning experience. After one hour and eighteen minutes of gameplay, Steve! is killed in Addamasartus by a magic-wielding slaver.

When asked about how this affected him, Vishnu explained that it upset him only because it meant he would have to replay from his last saved game (which had been eleven minutes earlier representing a substantial amount of gameplay). But Vishnu saw even this inconvenience as an opportunity to learn how to succeed in *Morrowind*:

> VISHNU: I was more than anything mad because I don't think I'd saved for awhile. And I had to go back and do all that stuff again! But you know I think because you have that option, you treat it more as a learning experience. You learn that you save more frequently, which is something that you should do in any game but also what sort of tactics work with different characters; with melee characters you can just walk up and stab them; with a mage who will attack you from a distance you have to approach it a little different.
>
> ZACH: So you hadn't gone into your *Morrowind* gameplay experience thinking, I'm going to try to play this whole game through and never die?
>
> VISHNU: No! I don't think it's a realistic expectation.
>
> ZACH: So you knew death would come for your avatar at some point?
>
> VISHNU: You know, it comes for us all. And probably, a lot more for this guy than for me personally. With the save option I knew you could just reload, and you're back.

Steve! died 26 times in Vishnu's recorded gameplay; Vishnu clearly accepted this as a normal part of the gaming experience. In the above statement Vishnu alternately refers to Steve! as "this guy" and "you." This demonstrates how easily and unconsciously Vishnu moves between considering his avatar as an external other (the female avatar he refers to as "this guy") and as an extension of himself (his usage of the first- and second-person "I" and "you").

Vishnu made it clear that he didn't consider it a "realistic expectation" for the avatar to avoid dying in *Morrowind*. Certainly, his attitude toward virtual death as an inevitable and common occurrence to be learned from contributed to the frequency with which Steve! was killed. Vishnu's expectation that Steve! would occasionally be killed and his propensity to put Steve! in danger led Vishnu to save his game progress sixty-six times. Up until the point where Steve! died for the first time, Vishnu had only saved the game one time (in one hour and eighteen minutes of gameplay). Therefore, over his final eight hours and forty-two minutes of gameplay, Vishnu saved his progress more than seven times an hour. This shows evidence of his penchant for learning how to succeed within the diegetic space. Vishnu also rested[23] frequently as well to replenish Steve!'s health, magicka, and fatigue. All of these gameplay decisions reflect Vishnu's experimental approach to

Morrowind. Steve! served as the guinea pig through which Vishnu tested the gaming system and explored the gameworld.

However, Shiva cared much more deeply about her avatar's virtual life: Shi never died one time during Shiva's recorded gameplay. Shiva had a dramatically different view of avatar death than Vishnu did. It became clear that there was considerable overlap between her virtual identity and her real-world identity:

> ZACH: How important was that to you, to try to play Shi where she is never killed? There are times when it was close, there are battles, but you cast the Intervention spell that teleports you away.
>
> SHIVA: It was really important to me. I guess I just want to survive! I could run; I could just leave. And that's why I also stayed away from the water. I don't know if you noticed, but I rarely ever entered the water. It's like a phobia. I got into a fight with my boyfriend, he told me to go in, and I was like, "No!" I don't like dying.
>
> ZACH: So dying in *Morrowind*, you took it pretty seriously.
>
> SHIVA: Yes. I get into the games, and, I don't know. I don't want to die.
>
> ZACH: I was impressed.
>
> SHIVA: I think it just depends on how you play. I think I almost get too into it, which is why I get scared of the water.
>
> ZACH: Shi's life was important to you in the gameworld.
>
> SHIVA: Yes!

Shiva's real-world unease around water carried over to Shi in *Morrowind* as did the care with which she handled the avatar's mortality. Shiva did admit that Shi was killed later during her *Morrowind* gameplay (outside of the ten hours recorded for this study) but speculated that it didn't happen more than half a dozen times or so. That's a very small number given the many threats to the avatar's mortality within the diegetic space and the dozens of hours of gameplay Shi spent in Vvardenfell. As a result of her more careful exploration, Shiva saved her game progress with much less frequency than Vishnu did. She saved the game for the first time after fifty-two minutes and thirty-two seconds; overall she saved her progress forty-four times. Shiva also faced many fewer combat situations than did Vishnu. As a result, she rested to heal Shi only seven times.

Shiva and Vishnu demonstrated markedly different approaches to playing *Morrowind*. Yet each participant's approach was a reflection of their real-world identity. Vishnu's matter-of-fact handling of Steve!'s death as an opportunity to learn more about *Morrowind* gameplay definitely shows a more clear distinction between his real-world identity and his avatar's virtual identity. Yet at the same time learning the rules of the gaming system aided Vishnu's immersion. Vishnu explained how this worked as he slowly learned the nuances of the complex *Morrowind* interface:

VISHNU: [Because] you're spending hours and hours and hours, you do learn some shortcuts and stuff, clicking and dropping on your character, clicking and dropping in the world, to drop things. Up front, I remember it took me a long time and I could get a little frustrated sometimes.

ZACH: Does that frustration pull you out of this gaming experience or does it pull you in? Is part of the challenge of figuring it out something that keeps you invested in a way?

VISHNU: Yeah, a little bit. Sometimes the better you get at a game, the less interesting it is, the less you want to play it because you've learned the system and learned the rules.

ZACH: Once you figured out the limitations of the system, figured out the inventory, how to manipulate it, what new challenges did you set?

VISHNU: I think that became a challenge to accumulate things. I don't know how far I got into the gaming that you recorded but by the end of the character I had a huge inventory: items and potions and weapons and gold, currency, whatever it was, I had like 68 million dollars, you know, after, it became kind of a "how much can I get" kind of thing. You set new little mini games; you create your own challenges I think in a lot of ways.

An open-ended v–RPG like *Morrowind* offers numerous opportunities for users to create mini-games even after they have mastered the game's systemic rules. Vishnu treated death as a type of puzzle to solve: what actions could he have taken that would have kept Steve! from dying? Approaching diegetic encounters as puzzles to be solved aided in Vishnu's immersion even as his cavalier attitude toward death showed a clear distinction between his real and virtual identities. Shiva however took her avatar's death much more seriously and demonstrated less distance between Shiva and Shi in this aspect of identification.

Avatar Ethics and Diegetic Experimentation Continued: Fargoth & Hrisskar

Both participants' initial decisions in *Morrowind* (generating their avatars and moving around in the newbie space of the Census and Excise Office) relied heavily on their real-world identities' proclivities. Did the virtual identities of Steve! and Shi begin to separate themselves from Vishnu and Shiva as gameplay continued? Immediately after leaving the Census and Excise Office, *Morrowind* users face one final mandatory encounter. Fargoth, a Wood Elf, approaches the avatar and tells a sad story: his engraved Ring of Healing has been stolen. Not coincidentally, the avatar has found this ring in a barrel in the courtyard of the Census and Excise Office (a message from the game system having prompted the user to look in the barrel earlier). The avatar is now faced with a choice: either tell Fargoth she found the ring and give it back to him or pretend not to know what he is talking about and keep the ring for herself. This scenario forces the user to make an ethical decision, one of many such decisions that must be made over the course of *Morrowind*'s gameplay, each helping to construct the avatar's diegetic history (and thus projective identity). What factors influenced Vishnu's and Shiva's decisions?

When prompted about her decision regarding Fargoth's ring, Shiva immediately remembered that Shi had chosen to give the ring back to him. When asked why (she could have either sold the ring for extra gold or kept it to heal herself after combat), Shiva admitted that the decision reflected the desire of her people-pleasing real-world identity:

> I was playing a really ethical character. I'm such a nerd. I never even thought about selling it. That was never in my mind. I think when I get into the world, it is real, and the characters are real to me. I vote for the underdog, so I was like, "Here, have your ring, it's your ring!" and I knew it would make him feel happy. I guess it was good for me to create a happy world for the NPCs.

In this instance there is very little difference between Shiva's morals and Shi's morals; real-world identity and virtual identity are indistinguishable. Shiva's interactions with Fargoth seem to have been internally, extra-diegetically motivated. Vishnu also remembered Fargoth immediately when prompted and, like Shi, Steve! also opted to return the ring to him. But Vishnu's rationale for doing so was much different than Shiva's and indicated motivation in keeping with his real-world identity's passion for figuring out the rules of videogames:

> VISHNU: A lot of times knowing the genre you, you'll get rewarded for making choices that the developers deem as "good" or morally right.
>
> ZACH: "Good" in this case means ethical? It isn't like your character stole the ring from Fargoth.
>
> VISHNU: Yeah, ethical. Right, but it was stolen from him. You want to right the wrong, you know. I think in a lot of ways I wanted to see if they rewarded you for doing the "right" thing.
>
> ZACH: Because your experience in RPGs before had been "Do the ethical thing, there is probably going to be a reward."
>
> VISHNU: Especially in like the *Final Fantasy* world. Any time you do the right thing you generally get rewarded: they'll give you an item. Sometimes they'll even give you it back; you generally are rewarded, and if you do the wrong thing you are usually punished, in the *Final Fantasy* universe. So I wanted to see what happened I think in this universe.

Vishnu's decision reflects his ongoing desire to test the limits of the gaming system; this interest in systematic testing is a characteristic of Vishnu's real-world identity. Vishnu wanted to see if his decision would be rewarded with money or a special item. However, the only reward for returning the ring to Fargoth is a dramatic increase in Fargoth's Disposition towards the avatar. As Fargoth is not a major NPC in *Morrowind* (he has no items to sell nor plays a role in any more quests) this doesn't represent much of a reward. This was Vishnu's first opportunity to learn that *Morrowind*'s designers haven't created a diegetic space that precisely reflects real-world ethics. The user is freer to experiment with ethical decisions and test the ramifications of actions. Vishnu's desire to do this can also be seen in the next significant ethical decision Steve! is faced with. Upstairs inside Arrille's Tradehouse (Seyda Neen's only emporium and hostel), the avatar can encounter Hrisskar Flat-Foot who promptly attempts to strike a deal with the avatar. He asks the avatar to spy on Fargoth and discover the secret stash where Fargoth keeps his valuables. In return for this service he offers to pay the avatar 100 gold (a substantial amount of money for the newbie avatar). Steve! refused to help Hrisskar. Vishnu's attempt to explain why he chose not to aid Hrisskar demonstrates his continued interest in learning the gaming system but it also reveals the influence of his real-world identity's ethical code:

> VISHNU: I'm not sure. Maybe it was a way to stick it to The Man: he represented the police, the factions, the ones with power I think.
>
> ZACH: This is amongst the group that has been bullying Fargoth?
>
> VISHNU: Right, right. I think I was still trying to see again what the rewards were for doing certain ethical actions. I think I was still trying to find out specifically what happened. If there was no reward or punishments, either route, I probably would have done the right thing.
>
> ZACH: The right thing being?
>
> VISHNU: Tell the guy, Hrisskar, tell him to go to hell, that I wasn't going to do what he was asking me to do.
>
> ZACH: Now why would you do that? Here's a chance for you to come into some loot.
>
> VISHNU: Uh, I don't know. I'm not sure I have an answer. That's what I would do, I think.
>
> ZACH: Is that what Vishnu would do, is that what Steve! would do, or was there no difference?
>
> VISHNU: I think, in this instance, there was no difference. I think it was Vishnu doing that, the gamer doing that, as opposed to the character in the game doing that.

In this case Vishnu's desire to learn how the gaming system would reward ethical behavior and his real-world code of ethics dovetailed nicely. Vishnu's desire to have Steve! "stick it to The Man" directly reflects his real-world identity as a liberal anti-authoritarian. Vishnu admitted to having had his own run-ins with law enforcement officials in the past, mostly revolving around actions that were illegal that he considered to be perfectly ethical. Vishnu's disdain for what he considered to be ridiculous laws and the occasional bullying tactics of law enforcement officials influenced his decision to reject Hrisskar's overtures. Like the encounter with Fargoth, *Morrowind*'s designers offer no particular reward to users who take this more ethical course of action: Hrisskar accepts the refusal of service calmly and informs the avatar that he'll just find someone else to do the deed. If anything, *Morrowind* rewards the more unethical action. If the avatar spies on Fargoth and reveals the location of his hiding spot to Hrisskar, Hrisskar rewards the avatar with gold. The two encounters with Fargoth and Hrisskar establish for users that there is no particular pattern for ethical actions in the gameworld: some ethical actions will be rewarded and others will not be, just as some unethical actions will have tangible rewards. This allows users to make diegetic decisions based on how they want to roleplay their avatar without worrying about whether or not these decisions match the ethics of the game designers.

Shiva continued to demonstrate a strong identification with Shi in her own encounter with Hrisskar. She also refused to aid Hrisskar in his scheme to rob Fargoth, saying that Hrisskar came across as a "jerk" who she despised: "I didn't like him. I didn't like him at all, and I was like, 'I'm not going to help you. I am not going to help you.'" As previously mentioned Shiva's real-world identities are friendly, relaxed, and gentle. Hrisskar's arrogance and strong-arming tactics offended Shiva; Hrisskar displayed characteristics that Shiva associated with real-world men she considered to be "jerks." Just as Shiva attempted to avoid men with this personality, she wanted Shi to avoid them in Vvardefell as well. Witchhunter Shi's ethics and Shiva's ethics are the same in this instance.

It is clear that ethics were important for both participants: Vishnu and Shiva adamantly defended their avatars' rights to steal and loot dead bodies, claiming these actions were ethically acceptable in *Morrowind*'s virtual world. Vishnu even defended one NPC in Seyda Neen's lighthouse who attacked Steve! for attempting to steal one of her books. Steve! was still a newbie character at this time (he had not yet even leveled up once) and took a severe beating from the woman before fleeing the lighthouse. After a few hours of gameplay, a much stronger Steve! returned to Seyda Neen but never reentered the lighthouse to seek revenge for the savage beating he had taken. Vishnu explained the ethics behind his decision:

> VISHNU: I think I was trying at that point not to kill anyone, to murder anyone. I mean you can kill people, you know, but you don't want to murder anyone. I think the game makes that distinction as well.[24]

ZACH: They do talk about it, they make it clear if you're attacked, that's
    not a murder.
VISHNU: Right. Exactly.
ZACH: If you initiate, kind of unprovoked. But didn't that woman attack
    you?
VISHNU: Yeah. But I stole from her.
ZACH: You thought she was justified in her attack?
VISHNU: Yeah, exactly.

Vishnu's statement here reveals just how immersed he is in *Morrowind*'s game-world; he has begun to internalize the habitus of *Morrowind*, justifying the actions of the NPCs within this virtual space. McMahan (drawing on Turkle) reminds us that interaction with NPCs can often aid a user's immersion into and identification with a video game: "The use of a synthetic social actor can lead to a heightened sense of presence [since] users respond to the computer itself as an intelligent social agent" (78–79). Vishnu's interactions with the woman in the Seyda Neen lighthouse and Shiva's interactions with Fargoth and Hrisskar demonstrate this phenomenon. Both participants have rational and ethical explanations justifying their interactions with the NPCs mentioned here. These explanations seem to be a combination of the participants non-diegetic personalities and experiences (experiences tied to their real-world identities), the users' awareness of *Morrowind*'s systemic rules, immersion in *Morrowind*'s gameworld, and identification with their avatars (tied to their virtual and projective identities).

Real-World Interests, Virtual Tendencies: Morrowind *Books*

Vishnu's and Shiva's avatars' decisions were clearly influenced by their real-world identities in other ways as well. Shi spent time reading each of the books she discovered in *Morrowind*. Slowly turning the pages of a virtual book doesn't appeal to every videogame player; when asked why she took the time to do this reading, Shiva replied that she simply loved books, saying they "fascinated" her.[25] In her initial interview she had revealed that before she discovered videogames she spent most of her spare time reading books, particularly science fiction and fantasy novels. Interest in these genres obviously carried over to videogames. Shiva also revealed that she is still a voracious reader and her love of books dictated Shi's interest in the many dozen books in *Morrowind*. Vishnu's reaction to *Morrowind*'s books was a little different: whereas Shi read each book she came across and usually left them where she found them, Steve! took each book he found (which often meant stealing them) yet never spent any time reading them during these ten hours of gameplay. I asked Vishnu why he did this:

ZACH: Some of the books you kept but never read could have been sold for more money than some of the other loot that you found that you did sell.

VISHNU: Yeah, I don't know.

ZACH: You didn't read any of them. But you kept them all.

VISHNU: I don't know, it's true, it's a lot like my house; I have stacks and stacks of books that I have not read but I keep them.

ZACH: Why keep them around?

VISHNU: Because I may eventually go read them, I think.

An English Literature major, Vishnu loved books and collected them in his non-virtual house. This component of his real-world identity dictated Steve's compulsion to hoard books as he found them: Vishnu could not bear to have his virtual identity sell any of the books. Several of the books in *Morrowind* are valuable and sell for hundreds of gold pieces. As Steve! never read any of the books, there is clearly no value in having the avatar hold onto them: the desires of Vishnu's real-world identity actually hurt his virtual-world identity here, as the books merely take up the limited carrying space in Steve!'s inventory without providing any benefit in money or knowledge.[26]

Choosing One's Own Path: Gameworld Exploration and Narrative

In their initial interviews, both Vishnu and Shiva stressed the importance of a compelling narrative story for memorable videogame play. Both participants recalled times when they had stopped playing videogames because they were unable to immerse themselves in the game's narrative. Both Vishnu and Shiva remarked that they enjoyed their experiences playing *Morrowind* very much; each went on to log many more hours beyond the ten required for this project. Yet interestingly enough, neither participant expressed much interest in the game's main quest narrative: having the avatar fulfill the Nerevarine Prophecies and defeat Dagoth Ur under Red Mountain. The avatar receives specific orders in the Census and Excise Office that will propel this main narrative forward: take a package to Caius Cosades in Balmora. It is true that both Vishnu and Shiva visited Balmora within their first ten hours of gameplay, and delivered the package to Cosades. These actions seemed to indicate that they were interested in pursuing this narrative path. But when asked about the importance of this narrative, both participants revealed they had more pressing interests within *Morrowind*. Shiva eschewed the main narrative because she felt doing so was in keeping with the virtual identity she was establishing for Shi: "My Witchhunter was an ethical rebel [and] I didn't want to do what they said." In this case the "they" were the administrators in the Census and Excise Office, working in conjunction with Caius Cosades. Shiva pictured Shi as rebellious and blindly following orders didn't fit with that projective identity. Shiva stressed that instead she wanted to "see what the world was like, get a grasp of the world a little bit."[27]

Exploration of *Morrowind*'s gameworld was also Vishnu's main interest. When asked if he was interested in progressing in the main narrative he replied, "No, I wanted to explore the world. I wanted to see what was around, and stuff, knowing that it was pretty open ended. I was much more interested in seeing what the world looked like and finding out what types of interactions you could have with characters, with items." If he was not interested in progressing the main narrative, why had Vishnu chosen to head to Balmora (where Caius Cosades is located) rather than any of *Morrowind*'s other locations? I pressed Vishnu on this point and he revealed that his decision reflected his desire to both improve Steve! and explore Vvardenfell:

> VISHNU: I think you know obviously you want to move [the narrative] along a little bit. I wanted to, I guess I should go back and say it was mildly important to progress [the story] because obviously you need to get some tasks in in order to build up the character, to level up, to do sorts of stuff like that.
>
> ZACH: So only toward the ends of making your character level up, improve, get stronger, did you care about missions at all?
>
> VISHNU: And just progressing the game a little bit because you do want to perform some sort of narrative, you know, and I knew that was where they were trying to push you; the programmers and the developers want you to go. In order to open up the game more and progress the story, you have to go that way. I think I headed that way but got lost along the way.
>
> ZACH: And were okay getting lost along the way.
>
> VISHNU: Yeah, and I knew that was the ultimate destination, and so I think it was a bit of going towards moving the story along and also seeing what was around.
>
> ZACH: But it doesn't sound like story was your driving thing, even though from our earlier interview, a good story was the thing you kept coming back to over and over as what made for memorable gaming.
>
> VISHNU: Right. Uh, I think I was really impressed by the design of the world and everything. I think I wanted to see a lot more of it before I got into some story development.

It was interesting to discover that *Morrowind*'s vast game world (illustration six) contributed significantly to both participants' level of immersion in the game space. When asked if she found exploring Vvardenfell with Shi immersive Shiva replied, "Oh yeah, definitely. I liked [how] it changed, you had swampy land, you had different types of monsters, and then it got greener with lakes." Vishnu also stressed that the look of *Morrowind*'s world really impressed him: "Visually it was pretty stimulating.... I just remember thinking that visually it was very striking, with purples, reds, just really good, um, and really different. I mean, I think they did a pretty good job making it a dynamic world; there was a lot of variety in terrain, and characters around, and just items, and things to look at."

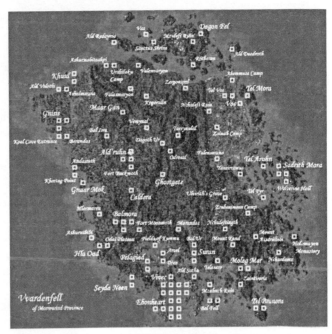

Vvardenfell, *Morrowind*'s island setting.

When asked what stood out the most about his experience playing *Morrowind*, Vishnu adamantly said the gameworld rather than his avatar. Vishnu stated that he was also impressed by the game's sound and the world's vast size: "It's a huge map! [That] really struck me, as I started to wander, and I think I didn't realize how big [the world] was, heading towards Balmora the first time. I read online it's somewhere like 23 square miles, or something like that." Vishnu also stressed that having Steve! navigate this space on foot really helped to impress this sense of *Morrowind*'s size upon him and helped him become immersed within the diegetic space.

Avatar Identification

Shiva seemed consistently to identify strongly with Shi throughout her *Morrowind* gameplay. In keeping with this, when asked what she remembered the most about her time spent playing the game, Shiva replied, "My character. I really liked my character." She went on to explain in greater detail:

> SHIVA: You get so much control over that character. I got to do whatever I wanted. I felt very connected with that character I guess and it was just, I don't know, that's what's with you the whole

time, the character. You kill things, you wander, you're stuck in
the wilderness, and you have to talk to people, but you're always
with your character so that is what stuck out to me.

ZACH: Who was [Shi], in your mind?

SHIVA: I guess mostly an extension of me.

Shiva's point is well taken: in a v–RPG, the avatar is continually present (even in first-person POV), and each decision made by the user contributes to the burgeoning history and projective identity of the user-as-avatar. Shiva demonstrated consistently throughout her gameplay a willingness to "ego-invest," to use Schafer's concept, in her avatar in a substantial way Vishnu never seemed interested in. Whereas Steve! took all the items from the Census and Excise Office's newbie room, Shi only took the dagger and some food, refusing to take the many miscellaneous tableware items. Her explanation demonstrated this ego investment, this fusion, between her real-world and virtual world identity: "I just don't think my Witchhunter would be the type. I was thinking about playing as my Witchhunter, and Witchhunter was the type of character that would take what we needed, but not go overbounds with it." Shiva's usage of the word "we" in this statement is interesting. She clearly sees a strong connection between herself and her avatar and this connection was consistent throughout her ten hours of *Morrowind* gameplay (illustration seven).

Vishnu took a more light-hearted approach to role-playing Steve! and never achieved the depth of identification with his avatar that Shiva did with Shi. Vishnu made diegetic decisions strategically and experimentally, seemingly more interested in learning the *Morrowind* gaming system than ego-investing in Steve! But of course his carefree approach to Steve! did not mean that Vishnu was unable to identify with his avatar; he did so by drawing on his past real-world experiences to create Steve! and make diegetic decisions. Vishnu did become gradually more invested in his virtual identity Steve! Early on in his experience, he mostly made decisions (like attempting to Intimidate Ergalla and giving Fargoth his ring back) that reflected Vishnu's desire to test *Morrowind*'s systemic rules and find out if ethical behavior was going to be rewarded as it is in so many v–RPGs. Once Vishnu decided that the game wasn't going to particularly reward ethical behavior, his gameplay tactics shifted. Having somewhat satisfied his real-world identity's desire to learn the gaming system, he began to make decisions based on what was in his virtual identity's best interest. He explained why he made this change:

VISHNU: I think it changed because I realized that the consequences
weren't very significant and I started to get to the point where I
wanted to start collecting items, things that would give you
bonuses, statistical bonuses or anything like that. I think my

Shi after ten hours of *Morrowind* gameplay.

process there was, they are not really going to punish [unethical behavior] so I might as well fuck up.

ZACH: It sounds like initially that's Vishnu making decisions about what he would do, but the farther you get, it stops being about what Vishnu wants, and starts being about what's in Steve!'s best interests.

VISHNU: Yeah, I think so, I think so. That's pretty accurate.

Vishnu was still able to identify with the avatar despite being much more interested and invested in *Morrowind's* world.

What was the connection between the participants' real-world identities and their virtual identities? Analysis of Vishnu's and Shiva's cumulative *Morrowind* data shows both participants relied heavily on their real-world personalities and experiences to construct their avatars. With very little *Morrowind*-specific diegetic knowledge to go on when creating their avatars, both Vishnu and Shiva turned to their past videogaming experiences and memories and their real-world identities and personalities to make decisions about name, race, gender, class, and birthsign. Real-world influences (from Vishnu's passion for humor, statistical analysis, and systemic rules explo-

Steve! after ten hours of *Morrowind* gameplay.

ration to Shiva's fear of water and of dying) also dictated many of the diegetic choices each participant made during these first ten hours of gameplay. Both the virtual and the real contributed to the participants' identity experiences, "deliciously blended" together. Vishnu described the need for this essential blend of real and virtual identity when discussing *Morrowind*'s visually impressive world, speculating that it's immersive potential was reliant on both:

> [*Morrowind* had] a lot of sort of like dualistic properties, that it is patterned in a sense, that it is large like the scope of the real world; it's unique in that it has different textures, terrains in different areas, different plants that grow; the towns are different. So I think the variety there sets it up in a way that is patterned on our real world if you want to call it that, but also that there is enough distinction in the game and in the gameworld that you know that it's a fantasy world as well. Because it's a fantasy world, it's good to have a world that isn't quite like ours, that is kind of alien. So in a game that is a fantasy game, to have a world with no referents to our world, I think it would lose a little bit of the immersive quality. I think it's realistic enough that you know it's almost like your world only better. Only cooler, you know?

Vishnu's words here seem applicable to how both participants felt about their avatars as well. Vishnu's and Shiva's *Morrowind* experiences reveal that the initial creation of a virtual identity is a complicated process that draws heavily on the user's real-world identities and experiences. The in-game, ongoing creation of the avatar's projective identity is also overdetermined, influenced by identity components both diegetic (virtual) and extra-diegetic (real-world). Exactly where real-world identity ended and virtual identity began was uncertain at best for both participants. The projective liminal space between Vishnu and Steve! and between Shiva and Shi was at times indiscernible as real and virtual identities meshed together.

Of course, both Shiva and Vishnu had long videogaming histories, and had many years of v–RPG experience prior to their participation in this study. That may have enabled them to identify with their avatars much more easily than, say, a person with less interest in videogames in general and less exposure to v–RPGs in particular. How might a casual videogamer identify with their v–RPG avatar? For the next phase of my study, I selected just such a person and a new videogame. This participant's name is Tom, and the videogame is *Morrowind*'s sequel, *Oblivion*. I turn now in chapter four to discussion and analysis of Tom's videogaming proclivities and his avatarial experiences within *Oblivion*.

4

Oblivion

Identity and the Casual Gamer

After spending many hours talking with both Shiva and Vishnu for the *Morrowind* portion of this project, I realized that the better I came to know both participants, the greater my understanding was of the connections between their real-world and virtual identities. This was because the participants' personal histories, personalities, and interests significantly impacted the diegetic choices they made for their avatars. As a result, when selecting the "casual gamer" for the next portion of this study, I opted to choose a close friend: Tom. Tom was a colleague of mine in the English Department at Arizona State University; he was also working on a PhD in Rhetoric and Composition. As a result, we had taken classes together, served on committees together, and socialized with each other as well. During the time this study was conducted Tom, a Caucasian male, was 33 years old. Tom had some videogaming experience, but as his gaming history and preferences reveal, he gamed with much less regularity (and for different reasons) than Shiva and Vishnu.

Tom's Videogaming History

Tom's earliest experiences with videogames were when he was five years old. Even as he couldn't remember exactly which videogaming console system his family had, he distinctly remembered a "Pong sort of system" as a young child. This paved the way for additional videogaming systems as he grew older: "We got the Atari 2600 when I was eight; we got a Colecovision when I was about ten or eleven. We got a Nintendo Entertainment System when I was thirteen, and we also had computers. We had an Atari home computer, and we had a 16 mega-hertz PC and I played games on that too." Most of these early gaming experiences for Tom were social opportunities: he and his brother would play, and occasionally his mom would even join in. Most of the games Tom remembered enjoying during these years were arcade games, like *Pac Man*, *Space Invaders*, *Burger Time*, *Popeye*, *Donkey Kong*, and *Joust* (arguably Tom's favorite arcade game ever). Tom and his brother would visit video arcades whenever possible as well, and would play whatever arcade games were in the local grocery store (where Tom's love of *Joust* was born). Unlike most modern console and PC videogames, arcade games are designed so that the user will fail (usually this means dying) rather quickly. This way, more and more quarters are required to keep playing; that's how arcade games make money. Thus, arcade games have relatively short and challenging levels. The early levels of *Donkey Kong* are a perfect example of this: rolling barrels and jumping fireballs both contribute to regular death for Mario, especially for novice gamers. For most arcade gamers, finishing the game isn't a possibility; the challenge of staying alive as long as possible and accumulating higher and higher scores provides the impetus to keep playing. Tom's love of arcade games fell into this category. He and his brother (and occasionally even his aunt) would try to one-up each other's high scores in games like *Ms. Pac-Man* and *Pitfall*. For Tom, these competitive, social and familial aspects were videogames' greatest appeal through his high school years.

After high school ended, however, Tom's videogame play dropped drastically. When I asked him why, he told me that his family stopped buying the newer console systems and computers as they came out. While this made it more difficult to get excited about the new games that were coming out, an even greater factor was the loss of Tom's social gaming network: going to college meant less time spent with his brother, aunt, and junior high and high school friends. For Tom, these family members and friends were the main reasons why he enjoyed videogames in the first place as they provided social opportunities. Tom was and is extremely introverted and quiet; prior to going to college videogames provided an opportunity to be social in ways Tom was comfortable with. To be sure, Tom found his early videogaming experiences fun, but mostly because they aided in socialization. When the social aspects of videogaming Tom was used to dried up in college, he stopped playing videogames regularly: "I do like to play social games. If I don't have too many friends who play those kinds of games or I can't do it socially, it's harder for me to get into [videogaming]." When Tom did play videogames during his college years, it was mostly on the PC his parents had bought while he was in high school. Tom stressed that the videogames he played during college were all "very heavy on action." The *Mechwarrior* series was one of Tom's personal favorites during these years, but Tom admitted he played videogames sporadically at best during his college years. Since Tom began his graduate school work, he admitted that his videogaming experiences were a little more frequent, as having friends who enjoyed playing allowed Tom to use videogaming to his social benefit. He stressed how fun he found playing Wii

Sports to be with a group of friends periodically, saying that several social gaming sessions had recently lasted two hours or more. Unlike Shiva and Vishnu, who both admitted that they could game alone for hours on end, Tom was adamant that only his social videogaming experiences were ever for very long periods of time (more than an hour). When gaming alone, he usually played for only twenty minutes or so (usually a level or two): "There is no way I'd sit for hours in front of [the computer]. I'd really have to like the game and I haven't found anything that will captivate my attention."

Tom definitely had different gaming preferences than Shiva and Vishnu. Whereas those diehard gamers both stressed how much they loved videogames with interesting narratives and how much they enjoyed figuring out the gaming system and exploring vast gameworlds, Tom expressed none of these interests. Instead, through our interviews, Tom made it clear that he enjoyed dominating videogames rather than learning how to dominate them. In announcing *Joust* as his favorite arcade game, Tom said, "I do love to break out *Joust*. And I'm good at it." Much of his fondness for that particular arcade game stemmed from his perceived mastery of it. This gaming preference was reiterated when Tom discussed why he loved the *Mechwarrior* series:

> ZACH: How did you get turned on to *Mechwarrior*?
> TOM: *Mechwarrior* came to me in high school through people that I knew. So when I got *Mechwarrior*, it was fairly new and fairly advanced videogame technology at the time. It was fun to blow things up. It was fun to win! There is a story that goes with it but I didn't care too much about that. It was all about the levels. It's got different difficulty levels on it. You can start with the easy one and just blow stuff up and be completely invincible and nothing will really hurt you very much.
> ZACH: Is that where you would start?
> TOM: Yeah, then work my way up. Exactly. There were some levels I really like, and I can set those on the hardest setting, and it's challenging, but it's also relaxing for me. Because I know a pattern that works really well with the level, and it is fun to come out victorious. And I know that I will. I would play some of those levels over and over again, because I wanted to win it.
> ZACH: So part of the challenge is in figuring out the pattern on that level? Figuring out the strategy?
> TOM: No, the appeal is **knowing** the strategy. Once I know it, I could play that level over and over again, in a short burst, just to relax.

For Tom, the joy of playing *Joust* and *Mechwarrior* wasn't in the process of figuring out **how** to master the game, as is common for many videogamers (like Shiva and Vishnu). Instead, Tom enjoyed the mastery of the game itself, or in a game like *Mechwarrior*, in particular levels of the game. Once he figured out the strategies necessary to dominate a level, he would play that level over and over again. This domination made Tom feel powerful and gave him the confidence he was good at something.

These videogaming traits were also revealed in Tom's explanation of the only v–RPG he had every played prior to this study. It was called *Alternate Reality*. Released in 1985, *Alternate Reality* was a first-person perspective fantasy/science fiction RPG centered on the human avatar surviving and exploring an alternate reality (having been abducted and sent there by aliens). Tom identified this game as an "anomaly" among his early videogaming experiences: it didn't fit the arcade/action type of games he otherwise played exclusively. I asked Tom why he also didn't enjoy the much more popular *Ultima IV*, released the same year:

> TOM: I think with *Ultima IV*, I don't know, I mean I had *Ultima IV* and I had *Alternate Reality*, and in *Alternate Reality* the view was first person, which seemed more realistic to me. *Ultima IV*, at the time the technology was different, but you had this little almost stick figure on the ground going around. So in a sense, *Alternate Reality* was more realistic because it was first person.
>
> ZACH: That's an interesting point: you consider first-person more realistic than third?
>
> TOM: Yeah. I think I enjoy it more.
>
> ZACH: Interesting. So first person is your preferred gaming viewpoint? You don't crave seeing your avatar? It's not crucial?
>
> TOM: No. It's not crucial. Another thing, I liked the graphics on *Alternate Reality* better. They were done pretty well for the time I think. There was music, and something that was kind of a big deal for me, I knew other people who had played it, and one kid had actually gone and mapped out the entire game on graph paper. I wasn't motivated enough to do that, but if I had the map, it was fun to go find the stuff and play, develop the character. And another reason that I liked *Alternate Reality* better than *Ultima*: with *Alternate Reality*, we had little cheat programs that we could use to resurrect our characters if we wanted to. We could give them money that they needed to buy the equipment they were supposed to have.
>
> ZACH: So you could in a sense hack the game to cheat, give extra life, extra money?
>
> TOM: Yeah, and so that just made it easier for me to go through and find everything I needed on the map.
>
> ZACH: No guilt? No guilt about cheating with extra money? There are purists who would say that's cheating, they would never do that.
>
> TOM: I'm not a purist. [Laughs.] I was happy to get the map for *Alternate Reality*. I probably would not have played it if I didn't have

one because it was very complex. And also, if I was dying off too much, I probably wouldn't have wanted to play it either.

ZACH: So having the cheats in *Alternate Reality* kept you playing the game.

TOM: Yeah. I didn't want to invest the time into the character. I just wanted to enjoy the game, do the stuff I wanted to do, win, not get killed. I wanted to go wherever I wanted and do whatever I wanted.

Tom made it clear here that he didn't have any interest in building up the strength of his avatar or in exploring the gameworld; he simply wanted to dominate the game in the same way he enjoyed dominating levels of arcade and action games. Of course, v–RPGs like *Morrowind* and *Oblivion* require gamers to do exactly the things Tom expressed little interest in: slowly raise the avatar's attributes through exploration of a vast gameworld. *Oblivion* has no real levels, and even completing the main narrative of the game takes many dozen hours; dominating the game in the way Tom prefers is not possible without a cheat code. Tom's gaming preferences convinced me he was a casual videogame player who was not inclined to identify strongly with his avatar or the overall *Oblivion* gaming experience.

Indeed, Tom revealed that with rare exception, he had never really felt any connections between virtual videogame identities and his real-world identity. When I pushed Tom specifically on this point, he stressed that during his younger years when he was gaming regularly, the only way he identified with the videogames he enjoyed was through purchasing merchandise. He admitted that he had a few *Pac-Man* t-shirts that he wanted to wear all the time, so much so that his mom had to sneak them away to wash them. But other than this consumerism, Tom's early videogaming experiences made little impact on him. This was also true of Tom's more recent return to sporadic videogaming as well, but with one notable exception: *Grand Theft Auto III*. This was the one game that Tom admitted he had noticed having a temporary real-world effect. Interestingly enough, it was the same effect that Vishnu had experienced: having difficulty following traffic laws when driving immediately after a *GTA III* gaming session. Tom stressed that this was the only aspect of that game that had affected him, saying that none of the "other types of violence" in the game stayed with him "unless they were related to the car." I asked Tom to speculate on why the car-related mayhem impacted him more:

TOM: Just off the top of my head, I would say that the car is something that I use on a daily basis, I own one. It is an integral part of my life, in a way that gun violence is not.

ZACH: So that stuff is more removed from your daily experience, so it doesn't have the same impact, the same carry over?

TOM: Yeah. I don't own a gun.

Tom is not an imaginative person. His lack of interest in the stories of *Mechwarrior* and *Alternative Reality* attest to this. His identification with the one aspect of *GTA III* that he could tangibly relate to also demonstrates his literalmindedness. For Tom, the potentials of videogames to explore fantasy worlds and play with virtual identities for the sake of these explorations holds little interest. If a videogame can't be dominated and won fairly easily, Tom historically has had little interest or motivation in that game.

Videogame Selection: Oblivion

All of Tom's videogaming proclivities were challenged by *Oblivion*. Like its predecessor *Morrowind*, *Oblivion* offers gamers an enormously open-ended fantasy roleplaying experience. Released in 2006, four years after *Morrowind*, *Oblivion*'s design and gameplay mimics *Morrowind*'s quite closely with a few relatively minor but important changes. In keeping with the history and lore of the Elderscrolls universe, the same ten racial options are available for the avatar as in *Morrowind*: Argonian, Breton, Dark Elf, High Elf, Imperial, Khajiit, Nord, Ord, Redguard, and Wood Elf. The gamer may choose to play as a male or female in any race as well and is free to select the name of the avatar. However, whereas *Morrowind* allowed only a small sampling of preconstructed facial options for each race, *Oblivion* takes full advantage of technological improvements to offer an incredibly deep facial construction system. All parts of the face can be manipulated individually, from the shape of the brow ridge to the ears, eyes, nose, cheekbones, and chin. The coloring of hair, eyes and skin can be manipulated as well. As a result, each gamer's *Oblivion* avatar has the potential to be truly unique in appearance, given the thousands of choice combinations possible. I was curious to see if these options would have any impact on Tom's identification with his avatar.

Oblivion also offers the same eight avatar Attributes as *Morrowind*: Strength, Intelligence, Willpower, Agility, Speed, Endurance, Personality, and Luck. These Attributes range from 0–100, initially dependent on the race and sex of the avatar. Over the course of the gaming experience, the gamer can choose which of these Attributes to improve when leveling up; it is these decisions that help make each invested gamer's roleplaying experience unique, immersive, and personalized. Leveling up occurs just as it did in *Morrowind*: the avatar must improve ten points of their preselected Major Skills and then rest and meditate. However, whereas *Morrowind* offered 27 Skills from which to choose the Major Skills, *Oblivion* offers only 21.[1] *Oblivion*'s creators also made certain actions more simulatory than they had been in *Morrowind*. For example, attempts to pick the locks of doors and chests in *Morrowind* were handled by the game's preprogrammed AI; the avatar attempted to pick the lock by pushing a button, and the game calculated the percentage chance of success based on the avatar's rating in the Lockpick skill and the lock level of the door in question. The AI then conducted an automatic "dice-roll" to determine whether or not the attempt was successful. The gamer simply awaited the instantaneous pronouncement of success or failure. *Oblivion* gives the gamer an active role in the success or failure of their lockpicking attempts by simulating the manipulation of a lock's tumblers with a lockpick. The *Oblivion* gaming manual describes this process specifically:

> Locks are crafted in five grades of quality. The better a lock's quality, the more tumblers it has, and the harder it is to pick. To pick a lock, use the lockpick to test each tumbler and loft it into its set point. Springs of varying tensions are used to restrain tumblers from their set points. Press [the appropriate button] to attempt to lock each tumbler into place when it is at its set point. The slightest error may cause other tumblers already lodged at their set points to drop, requiring them to be picked all over again. The higher your Security skill, the easier it is to lodge a tumbler in its set point [41].

If the gamer prefers not to spend time manually attempting to pick a lock, *Oblivion* does offer the same "Auto Attempt" option as *Morrowind*. *Oblivion* also allows for more strategic hand-to-hand melee combat by making the Block skill active. In *Morrowind*, Block was a passive skill like Lockpicking: the game's AI calculated whether or not the avatar successfully blocked a

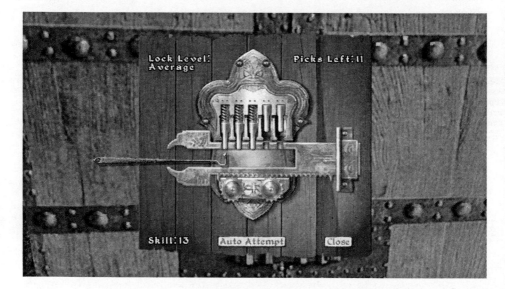

Oblivion's simulatory Lockpicking feature.

melee attack based on the Block skill level. *Oblivion* gives the gamer more control over when or if to attempt to Block a melee attack:

> To block, push and hold the [appropriate button]. A shield or weapon block reduces the damage you take. Shields are much more effective at Blocking than weapons. An effective combat strategy is to block an enemy's blow, then quickly follow up with your own attack to catch the enemy before he can ready his block. Establishing this block-and-counter rhythm in melee combat can greatly improve your combat effectiveness [28].

The inclusion of the strategic Lockpicking and Blocking active skills allows interested gamers additional opportunities to identify with their avatar in simulatory ways and become further immersed in the gameworld.

Oblivion also continues in the fantasy role-playing tradition with a typically epic storyline that places the gamer's avatar as the pivotal player in a struggle of good vs. evil. In similar fashion to *Morrowind*, the gamer's avatar begins the game in prison: this time in the Imperial City in Cyrodiil. Predictably, the avatar doesn't remain imprisoned for long:

> *Oblivion* begins with the arrival of Emperor Uriel Septim VII accompanied by a troupe of Blades bodyguards, at the Imperial City prison, seeking to flee from a group of assassins—later revealed to be members of the Mythic Dawn—through a secret underground exit in the city sewers. By chance, the exit is located in the cell occupied by the [avatar]. The Emperor frees the player as he believes that he saw the character in his dreams, and sets off into the catacombs as the avatar follows. At the end of the catacombs, the group is ambushed, and quickly overwhelmed by assassins, which results in the protagonist taking on the task of guarding the Emperor while the surviving bodyguards engage the enemy. While awaiting the result, Uriel entrusts the protagonist with the Amulet of Kings, a special amulet that can only be worn by those of the Septim bloodline. He orders the player to take it to a man known as Jauffre. Immediately afterwards, an assassin ambushes and kills the emperor before he is, in turn, defeated. The sole surviving guard, Baurus, questions the [gamer's avatar], and explains that Jauffre is the Grandmaster of the Blades, and can be found at Weynon Priory. As the game progresses, it is revealed that the prolonged lack of an Emperor has broken an old covenant, allowing multiple gates to Oblivion to open, and a Daedric invasion is to begin as a result. The only way to close down the gates permanently is to find someone of the Septim bloodline to retake the throne and re-light the Dragonfires in the Imperial City [Wikipedia, "Oblivion plot"].

Of course, the responsibility of finding a Septim heir and closing all the Oblivion gates ultimately falls to the gamer's avatar. But the gamer can choose not to pursue this central storyline and simply wander in Cyrodiil, discovering other adventures. Thus, *Oblivion* offers both types of temporality (kairos and

Cyrodiil, *Oblivion*'s setting.

chronos) just as *Morrowind* does. The gameworld of *Oblivion* is expansive, offering approximately sixteen square miles of terrain for the avatar to explore. If the gamer wants to learn about Cyrodiil lore, there are approximately 250 different books that can be located and read; some of these are the same as the books in *Morrowind*. Ultimately, *Oblivion* is a worthy descendant of the massively open-ended roleplaying experience offered in *Morrowind*: it offers the same core gameplay experience while offering improved AI, physics, and graphics. But would any of these factors impact Tom, whose gaming history showed no tangible interest in avatar creation, development, or traditional roleplaying?

Choosing the Avatar's Name, Race, and Sex

Even though Tom had no history of v–RPG avatar identification, he still took the initial creation of his avatar's appearance at least as seriously as

Shiva and Vishnu had. Tom is a dark-haired Caucasian male of Scandinavian descent. In *Oblivion*, the initial avatar creation of name, sex, race, and facial appearance happens immediately after a brief cinematic. Tom spent almost 25 minutes creating his avatar, a dark-haired male Nord named "Tom." Tom spent most of this time carefully adjusting the facial creation options, ultimately creating an avatar that looked remarkably like real-world Tom (from this point forward, to distinguish between Tom and his avatar "Tom," I'll refer to the avatar as "virtual Tom"). Tom confirmed he was trying to create a likeness of himself in our post–*Oblivion* gaming interview:

> ZACH: I'm watching you create your avatar, you chose a Caucasian Nord, which is a dark haired, fair skinned race, and you named him "Tom." Were you trying to create yourself?
>
> TOM: I was trying to do that the best I could.
>
> ZACH: Why?
>
> TOM: I didn't find the other options appealing.
>
> ZACH: But you didn't really look at the other options, you only looked at one other race! You looked at the lizard Argonian, and then

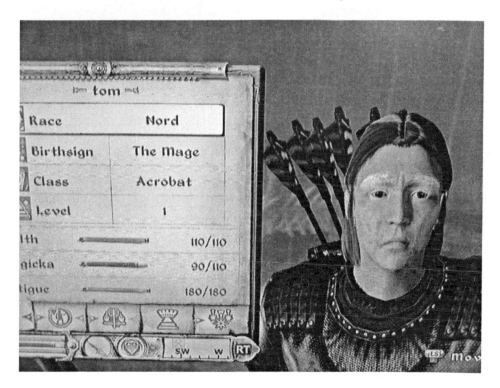

Virtual Tom, initial creation.

just scanned a couple more. You didn't even really look at all the
racial options. Why not?

TOM: Because the ones that I saw as I was kind of scrolling through
them, there were lots of animals and stuff like that, and I didn't
think that was representative of me.

ZACH: So it was in some ways chance that the Nord male, the dark
haired fair skinned race, happened to be the first one that came
up? That just kind of stuck in your mind and you said, "Oh, this
is one I can kind of make look like me"?

TOM: I'd say that's part of it, I'd also say just the idea that he seemed
Scandinavian. That's where a lot of my ethnic roots are.

ZACH: Were you thinking the name itself, "Nord," was kind of Nordic?

TOM: Exactly. And that's what my, not my first name, Tom, but my last
name, is Nordic — Scandinavian.

ZACH: So why did you want to play as a Nordic, Scandinavian, white
Caucasian named Tom?

TOM: I just wanted to be me.

ZACH: You wanted your avatar to be as much like you in appearance
and name as possible?

TOM: Exactly.

ZACH: Was that going to enhance your gameplay experience? Or would
it have detracted from your gaming experience if you were a
lizard named [a series of clicking sounds]. Or whatever. Would
that have negatively impacted your gameplay?

TOM: I think for me it would have been harder to take the game seriously. If I hadn't I don't think I would have been able to get into
it as much.

Here, Tom's lack of a strong imagination prevented him from seriously
considering any of the less human racial options. He clearly didn't want to
roleplay in the way Shiva enthusiastically did with her Dark Elf Witchhunter.
However, Tom's decisions here resulted in an avatar that he could identify
quite closely with right from the beginning of the game. Whereas there was
a gendered, racial, and name discrepancy between Vishnu and Steve! The
Dark Elf female, Tom and virtual Tom were as closely aligned as was possible at this point of Tom's gaming experience. Tom's only regret about this
initial avatar creation process was that he didn't realize he could change the
hairstyle of his avatar. As a result, virtual Tom's hairstyle, long and braided,
didn't mirror Tom's own hair style (shorter and curlier) during his gameplay. Tom admitted he had overlooked the option to change the avatar's
hairstyle, saying he didn't realize it was possible until later in the game (when
it was too late to go back and make any changes). Otherwise, virtual Tom
and Tom were very similar in terms of name and appearance. In these identificatory aspects, Tom's literalmindedness lead him to construct an avatar he
could closely relate to.

Birthsign, Class, and Skills Selection

Whereas *Morrowind* allowed the gamer to select the avatar's Class and Major Skills almost immediately (in the Census and Excise office), *Oblivion* takes a different approach, allowing the gamer to act in the gameworld for a longer period of time before making these choices. After King Uriel Septim is killed in the catacombs under the prison and gives the avatar the Amulet of Kings and instructions to take it to Jauffre, the gamer must explore the remainder of the sewer system to discover the way out. This takes some time, with many opportunities for the avatar to experiment with various skills: fighting with goblins (with both melee and ranged weapons), picking locks, sneaking in the darkness, and casting magical spells. When the avatar finally makes his way to the exit out of the sewers, the game displays the Class and Major Skills it has preselected for the avatar, based on how the gamer has chosen to play up to this point. For example, if the avatar repeatedly cast Fireball spells in combat, Destruction Magic would be selected as a Major Skill. But the gamer is not obligated to keep the Class and Major skills recommended by the game; any class and/or any Major Skills can be changed at this point. When virtual Tom reached this point, the game informed Tom that he was an Acrobat (a class that specialized in stealthy behavior) with the following Major Skills: Blade, Block, Acrobatics, Marksman, Security, Sneak, and Speechcraft. Tom spent time here (approximately five minutes) considering all the other classes that were possible, but ultimately chose to remain an Acrobat. I asked him why:

> TOM: Ultimately, as I went through all of those [Class choices], there were so many options, that I felt ill equipped. And so I thought the game was giving me the best advice.
> ZACH: That's in essence what they are trying to do there, saying that based on the way you've played this tutorial section of the game, these are the skills you're using, maybe you like these skills, so here is the class that would go with those Major Skills. You trusted that, and you didn't want to branch out.
> TOM: Right. I think in terms of the magic, I felt like maybe that would be balanced out by the Mage a little bit. As I was looking through those, I was trying to play out in my mind because of all of the different options, if there were any other good fits that might give me an advantage, and I was just overwhelmed.
> ZACH: So trust the game to give you the class that best represents what you've done?
> TOM: Right.

Two factors played a role in Tom's decision here. First, his lack of experience with this type of open-ended fantasy RPG meant he didn't know which

Skills would be most beneficial to virtual Tom. Second, Tom's gaming preferences have shown that he has little patience for setting up his videogaming experiences and learning how to play preferring instead to play (and dominate) immediately. Tom lacked the patience to slowly and systematically look at each Class and the related Major Skills. He admitted when originally creating virtual Tom that the special skills and traits available to Nords (each Race has different perks and abilities) were not a factor at all. In fact, Tom didn't even know what they were. He had been solely focused on virtual Tom's appearance. As a result, Tom was relieved to have *Oblivion*'s artificial intelligence select his Class and Major Skills for him.

In Tom's explanation here, he mentions that the "Mage" was his attempt to incorporate magic into his avatar's skill set. This refers to virtual Tom's Birthsign. Avatar Birthsign selection had occurred earlier, while the avatar was escorting the Emperor through the catacombs. At one point prior to his fatal attack, the Emperor asks the avatar what sign he was born under, triggering the Birthsign selection screen. Tom spent about five minutes examining the possibilities before deciding on the Mage, which according to the in-screen description, "confers a permanent bonus of 50 points to your Magicka." I found this choice interesting, given that Tom had not yet shown any interest in casting spells in his gameplay to that point. I had assumed he wasn't interested in the amount of strategic thinking that would be necessary to wield magic successfully, but his answer to my query surprised me:

> ZACH: Can you tell me why [the Mage] was your choice, given that at that point, you hadn't really used your magicka much at all?
>
> TOM: I enjoy magic in games. I really enjoy it. I played *Baldur's Gate*.[2] It's not as involved as this, but in those I really enjoyed being able to step back away from people and destroy them from a distance.
>
> ZACH: And so your anticipation was that you'd increase the magicka with the birthsign, and even though you haven't got to it yet, down the road you'll look forward to getting in and using magicka to kill people from afar.
>
> TOM: Yes. And I also thought that maybe, because of the way the game was going, I knew that I was developing more of my corporal, physical skills, like the Sneaking and some of those other things, and I had done hand to hand combat, and so I think my character was getting better with the blade, and so I didn't know how the game was going to go, what opportunities I'd have to develop magic.

Tom's past videogaming experiences (a combination of diegetic and extra-diegetic knowledge, similar to that displayed by Vishnu and Shiva) dictated his decision to opt for a Birthsign that would help his magical abilities later in the game.

Learning the Gaming Interface and Selecting POV

At this point, Tom had established a clear videogaming identity: he had little interest in or patience for figuring out **how** to play videogames, preferring instead to dominate the game itself. Predictably, then, Tom expressed some frustration in having to learn the fairly complex *Oblivion* inventory system. In the inventory, there are several different "tabbed" menus that can be scrolled through. These show maps of the gameworld, current quests, and the avatar's inventory of weapons, armor, clothing, potions, and other miscellaneous items. Figuring out where items are located and learning how to interpret all the symbols within each menu[3] takes time. Tom admitted that this was difficult for him to do; even after several hours of gameplay he said he struggled to remember where different items in his inventory were and what the various iconic symbols meant. When I suggested that some of his difficulties understanding and negotiating the inventory system could have been made easier if he had read the forty-seven-page *Oblivion* gaming manual ahead of time or at least referenced it while playing, Tom replied, "I don't want to sit there and read it. I want to play it. I consider myself a tech-savvy person, and so I felt like I could figure it out. I would rather be in the game than reading about it." I found this surprising, given Tom's desire to dominate games; wouldn't being as well-prepared for the gaming experience as possible make it easier to dominate more quickly? In this case Tom's lack of initiative won out over his wish to dominate. As a result, Tom continued to struggle with *Oblivion*'s complicated interface after several hours of gaming.

As Shiva had done with Shi, Tom chose to play virtual Tom through the first-person POV almost exclusively. Only on one occasion did he switch to third-person POV: when crossing a high bridge between two towers. Tom said this was strictly a pragmatic decision: he wanted to make sure virtual Tom didn't fall off and plummet to this death on the rocks below. As result, it was easier for Tom to see if his feet were "lined up" with the bridge by switching to third-person POV and rotating the camera angle directly above virtual Tom. Except for this careful bridge navigation, Tom remained in first-person POV for the remainder of his gameplay. However, this was also a practical decision for Tom, one unrelated to identifying with his avatar. Tom explained that he found combat in third-person perspective difficult, saying that he felt the avatar "got in the way" and that it was "harder to know what is going on" when fighting in this perspective. So, this was a purely tactical decision. Even as Tom had spent a great deal of time making sure virtual Tom looked as much like him as possible, he had no great need to be able to view his avatar continually while exploring Cyrodiil. Of course, the avatar is immediately viewable upon entry into the inventory system, thus allowing ample opportunities for the gamer to visually connect and identify with the avatar. Tom entered the inventory 89 times during his gaming sessions for this project. This is much less than either Shiva or Vishnu, who both cared a great deal about making sure their avatars were using the best weapons and armor. Shiva also spent a great deal of time in the inventory examining the medicinal and magical properties of herbs and other ingredients so that she could create new potions. Tom expressed none of these interests. His trips into the inventory menus were more perfunctory: he studied the maps to help orient virtual Tom in the gameworld and only occasionally equipped new weapons and armor as he came across them.

In fact, on several occasions virtual Tom was carrying armor and weapons in his inventory that were better than the items he was currently using. However, Tom rarely bothered to look at his inventory items, only doing so when the items he was using became broken or when virtual Tom was struggling to stay alive. On these occasions, Tom looked through his inventory for foods and ingredients to eat to improve his health and for better weapons and armor. When I asked him why he didn't take advantage of his inventory items more frequently, it became clear that Tom's previous videogaming experiences hadn't prepared him for this level of avatar control:

> ZACH: Lots of decisions are possible in *Oblivion*: what armor you wear, what clothes you wear, what weapon you use, all the ingredients that you can pick up, and eat, or not eat. And a lot of those things impact how efficient the play is. Have you chosen the best armor? The strongest weapon? When do you take your potions? Did you like having to negotiate all those things to play?
>
> TOM: There was a lot there. I wasn't used to making as many decisions as that. I was trying to learn the menus. I mean, there is a real learning curve with this game. I was aware of what dungeons and dragons is, and so I was familiar with how those things worked, but there was a real learning curve with learning the menu, with learning the environment; things like armor were fairly frustrating. I didn't want to spend a lot of time on those. I tried to pick the best weapon, and I knew that armor would be coming to me that would be better, the farther in I got.
>
> ZACH: You knew that how? What made you think that would be true?
>
> TOM: Just based on experience from previous games. Because I know that the weapons and armor and things, the grade goes up as you go along. So there was a lot of that. With the food, I was aware of that, that that was a way to get health, but it took me a little

while. I remember with *Alternate Reality*, it does that too. When you eat, health goes up. One that surprised me, a little bit, I thought that the rats would be a great way to stock up on food, and it took me a little while to figure out that it would hurt me to eat rat meat. So it was something that I had to learn.

ZACH: Was having to distinguish between healthy and poisonous food items particularly bad? Was it frustrating?

TOM: Actually, I just thought, "Okay, that makes sense." You eat the good food, and you get rid of the bad food. Now that I think about it, I wasn't thinking about this at the time, I do have previous experience with this, having played *Gauntlet*.

ZACH: "Warrior needs food."

TOM: Exactly! You can either get poison or you can get food.

It is clear here that Tom initially tried to draw on his previous experiences with *Alternate Reality* and *Gauntlet* (both games have dungeons and dragons-like fantasy settings) to inform his *Oblivion* choices. It is also clear that this didn't work very well as *Oblivion* offers a much more complex interface and much greater freedom of choice than either of those older, less technologically-sophisticated games. Tom had no experiences with any more recent v–RPGs than *Alternate Reality*, which meant it had been more than twenty years since Tom had played a true roleplaying game. As a result, Tom wasn't prepared for the high number of avatar choices required to succeed and "dominate" in *Oblivion*.

These combat-influenced situations weren't the only times virtual Tom's actions were dictated by Tom's *Alternate Reality* experiences. Shortly after escaping from the sewers underneath the Imperial City's prison, virtual Tom entered the Imperial City Market District, populated with shops where various goods can be bought and sold. There, Tom chose to enter the Merchants Inn, where he rented a room so that virtual Tom could rest. As the game had not prompted Tom to do this, I was curious as to why he felt compelled to allow virtual Tom to sleep in a bed for eight hours. Tom revealed that his *Alternate Reality* experience had influenced this decision:

TOM: I had no idea what the time sequence was or how many days I had been awake in the gameworld.

ZACH: But you still chose to go in and rest for eight hours. Why did you do that?

TOM: I thought well, my character probably needs some rest, I can't remember for sure at that point if there were any indicators on the character's health or status that would tell me that I needed to. I just thought, "Well, I probably should."

ZACH: You knew you'd been wandering in those caverns for awhile, and so getting some rest for the avatar may replenish...

TOM: Whatever. Yeah. And that, once again, is reminiscent of the *Alter-*

nate Reality game, because you could do that, there was a specific inn you could go to, and you had to do that.

ZACH: What would that resting accomplish? What would it improve on your avatar?

TOM: It would improve all sorts of stuff. It could improve health, if health was low. It could improve the ability to do the melee combat, because there were melee combat sequences you could do. And if you get too tired, you have trouble fighting and also have trouble with health and other things.

ZACH: That is kind of similar to how *Oblivion* does it. Health will replenish, fatigue will replenish, magicka will replenish. Yet you didn't specifically know that those were going to happen when you rested.

TOM: No!

Here, Tom's decision to rest actually did aid his *Oblivion* gameplay, as virtual Tom had been wounded in battles with goblins and rats in the sewers. Of course, Tom didn't know resting would help heal his wounds, since he hadn't bothered to read the game manual at all and the in-game tutorial messages never mention it. Tom's lack of relevant videogaming experiences certainly seemed to hinder his identificatory *Oblivion* experience at times.

Avatar Ethics: Killing, Stealing, and Dying

Like Vishnu and Shiva, Tom looted corpses continually throughout virtual Tom's wanderings in Cyrodiil. Both of those more experienced v–RPGamers had clear rationales for this behavior; they believed it was expected of their avatars as a means to obtain "loot." They also both made it clear that in this regard, their avatar's ethics was different than their real-world ethics. I was curious to see if Tom had these same rationales for virtual Tom's continual corpse looting:

ZACH: In your gameplay, you looted corpses freely. You had no qualms about taking items from dead bodies. Looting corpses! Did you have any ethical qualms about doing so?

TOM: No.

ZACH: Why? Is that something you would do in non-virtual Tom's life? Would you be a corpse or grave robber?

TOM: Um, no. I think I did that just to be able to advance my character.

ZACH: No qualm about whether this was unethical behavior?

TOM: Right. Give me an advantage in the game. And not only that, I felt like, especially those first bodies if I remember right, they were these assassins who had been sent to kill the emperor, and it seemed like they were the bad guys.

ZACH: So, it is okay to loot bad guys? But now Tom, you also looted the body of the guards who had been killed by those assassins. In the very same battle. Explain to me the difference, the distinction.

TOM: Um...

ZACH: They are there protecting the emperor, at least one guard is killed there, and you end up looting him, taking some armor and weapon off of him.

TOM: There, I felt like I had to gain advantage, and I felt like that at some point, it seemed to me in the gameplay there was an opportunity to follow the emperor and his guards and to participate with them. They obviously weren't going to kill me.

ZACH: Why not?

TOM: I felt like the emperor had already looked upon me favorably in some way, and so I felt like, well, if I'm going to follow them, I might as well be equipped to do so.

ZACH: So that justified taking the items off of the guard.

TOM: If the emperor liked me and his guard's stuff is sitting there uselessly, I might as well use it. I identified more with the emperor than the guards.

ZACH: So the guards were discardable pieces you could take from freely.

TOM: Yes.

ZACH: Would that be the way non-virtual Tom would handle it? Would non-virtual Tom take items off of bodies if he thought that they were going to be helpful? Because you created a virtual Tom that looked like the non-virtual Tom and named him "Tom." I guess I want to see where the distinction is between the avatar's behavior and your behavior in this world. Were you playing it as "I would do this" if I was in the gameworld? Or was there a distinction between the ethics?

TOM: I feel like non-virtual Tom has never been confronted with that option. And so, I don't have any previous experience to draw on in order to do that.

ZACH: So if it was an experience in the game that you'd had previous experience with outside of the game, you'd be more likely to respond in the game based on how you responded here (the non-virtual world)?

TOM: I might. I think that's my understanding of how I would be. But I had no parallel experience [here], because I haven't actually killed anybody or looted anybody.

Tom's statement here about not having "any previous experience" reminds me of his explanation for why the driving experiences of *Grand Theft Auto III* had such an enduring impact on him. He drives often in real life, and therefore can relate to the virtual experience of driving more intimately. If *Oblivion*'s gameworld and gameplay had more features and activities that Tom felt like he had experience with, would his identification with this type of videogame increase? Of course, a fantasy setting and an epic, good-vs-evil plot are standard v–RPG conventions. It would be interesting to see how a casual gamer like Tom would identify with a v–RPG set in a more real-world setting that allowed for more simulatory, familiar experiences.

Even as Tom had no compunction about looting corpses in the wilderness, he displayed a very different ethical sensibility about stealing in the Imperial City. Prior to visiting the Merchants Inn, Tom wandered in the bazaar, opening various crates and boxes that were stacked there. Several of these containers held items of food and clothing, but Tom chose not to take any of these items, even though virtual Tom could have benefited from many of them by selling or ingesting them. When I asked Tom why he would loot freely from the corpses he encountered or created in the sewers but not from these containers, he responded, "There are different rules in the city." This was a fascinating response: why did Tom think this? Nothing in Tom's gameplay had informed Tom of this. Although the game's manual explained the difference between the icons indicating which items, if taken, would be considered theft (a red hand) and which would not (a clear hand), Tom of course had not read the manual, and indicated later he had no idea at this time what those icons meant. Yet for some reason he thought taking items from these bazaar chests would be considered stealing (which was not true in this case). Where did Tom get this idea? He explained why he had this belief:

> TOM: What made me think that was the context. Because there, in the city, and I was just learning what was going on, and all of this stuff was just sitting out there in the open, and if I'm not mistaken, it was right there by the shops that would have been selling it. And so, I wasn't familiar yet with the way the game indicates that something is going to be stealing. And at the beginning I just thought, "Oh, this is all just sitting out here in the open," and then it dawned on me, that those shops are nearby, and it might belong to the people in the shops.
>
> ZACH: So you're applying a kind of logic to the gameworld. These are near the shops, so therefore they belong to the people who own the shops, so therefore it would be stealing.
>
> TOM: Yeah. And also it kind of reminded me, I have spent time in Europe, it reminded me of some of the markets and stuff that they have there, sitting outside. If stuff is sitting right outside the shop, usually it belongs to the shop.

Here, Tom is directly applying his non-virtual experiences (extra-diegetic knowledge) to his diegetic decision. This is a clear example of how real-world experience informs virtual action.

Tom viewed the death of virtual Tom differently than either Shiva or

Vishnu had for their avatars. Shiva took her avatar's death very seriously, and as a result Shi never died once during the *Morrowind* gameplay for this study. Vishnu merely saw his avatar's death as a learning opportunity and remained fairly indifferent to Steve!'s death. Steve! died 26 times as a result of Vishnu's diegetic experimentations. Virtual Tom died 23 times during Tom's recorded gameplay. Perhaps predictably, the main emotion Tom felt when his avatar died was frustration:

> ZACH: How did you view the death of your avatar when that would happen?
>
> TOM: I thought, well the first thing I thought was, "Did I save the game?" And where did I save it, and did I have to go through all of that stuff again to get to where I was. And it took me awhile to start to save it again and again, after every single thing that happened. Because especially at the beginning there, with the training part (in the Imperial sewers), the tutorial, that was really easy. The rats would bite me and stuff but it didn't hurt and when I got out there (through the Oblivion gate in Kvatch), I think the first ones I fought were those little gremlin guys (scamps). Those killed me after a couple of strikes. And so, those scamps come up on me, and they were shooting fireballs at me. I don't remember having fireballs shot at me before that point, and so I've got all this stuff going on. It took me awhile to adjust to the difficulty level I think.
>
> ZACH: Inside the Oblivion gate, where things were tougher?
>
> TOM: Yeah. Inside my mind, I thought about how I was not as invincible as I was in the tutorial.
>
> ZACH: And was that frustrating, was that a challenge you enjoyed, that you didn't enjoy? Was it traumatic, the death of Tom, the avatar who looks as much like you as possible?
>
> TOM: I think it was just frustrating. Because I thought, this Tom is supposed to be able to just kill those guys and he's not supposed to have this (getting killed) happen to him.
>
> ZACH: Is he supposed to be able to just kill those guys? Or you wanted him to be able to just kill those guys?
>
> TOM: I wanted him to be able to kill those guys. So, You know when Tom died I didn't really care because I knew it was a game, and I could just fall back on the previous save and do it again, but what was frustrating was just the fact that I knew I was dying. I wasn't winning in the way I wanted to be.

Tom likes to dominate videogames; he likes to win them. His repeated death at the hands of fireball-wielding scamps through the Kvatch Oblivion gate frustrated him enormously, as these deaths were a continual reminder that he was "failing" at the game. At least, this was Tom's perception of what virtual Tom's deaths meant. Tom didn't like the fact that virtual Tom wasn't "invincible" in battle, even though he had been playing *Oblivion* for only a few hours at this point. If Tom had more experience with this type of v–RPG, his expectations might have been tempered. He would have known that his avatar was going to be relatively weak and vulnerable in combat early in the game. Of course, videogames like *Mechwarrior* had conditioned Tom to expect to be able to dominate right out of the gate, with different levels and difficulty settings. That he couldn't do this in *Oblivion* bothered him. Once he realized how vulnerable virtual Tom was through the Oblivion gate, he began to save his game progress every few minutes (after almost any encounter of note).

Tom had no problem killing *Oblivion*'s "bad guys": the assassins who killed the emperor and the scamps and other monsters through the Oblivion gates. But Tom revealed different diegetic ethics when it came to killing other, more innocent characters in Cyrodiil. I pressed Tom specifically on this point to determine the connection between his diegetic and extra-diegetic ethical decisions. On several occasions, Tom had encountered NPCs who had weapons, armor, and items that were better than what virtual Tom was currently carrying. I asked Tom why he hadn't killed those NPCs so that he could improve virtual Tom's status:

> ZACH: Would you kill an innocent in a game, to give yourself an advantage?
>
> TOM: I think I would have qualms.
>
> ZACH: Tell me why.
>
> TOM: This would kind of go back to the beggar woman, and choosing the forces of light or darkness. I would think that based on the choice I made before I would want to choose the light side. I might try to barter with the person.
>
> ZACH: Let's say that's not an option. But they've got just the perfect piece of armor you want. What would keep you from killing them? Would it be your expectation that the gaming system will reward you for that decision? Or your fear that it will punish you? Or just your own personal moral code?
>
> TOM: I think it would have to do with my moral code.
>
> ZACH: Tom the avatar, he could be just a vicious murdering villain. What would stop you from playing it that way?
>
> TOM: I think like the beggar woman, I think I would feel bad about if I just killed someone for their stuff.
>
> ZACH: It sounds to me like you're saying it's a moral thing, that you would feel bad. That doesn't sound like very much separation between Tom, and virtual Tom, in terms of morals. They're the same.
>
> TOM: I would agree with that.

Here is a fascinating instance where Tom either can't or won't make a distinction between himself and virtual Tom: neither of them is willing to kill someone who doesn't seem to deserve it. The "beggar woman" in this passage refers to a woman Tom encountered just after he escaped from the sewers under the Imperial Prison and entered the Imperial City Market District. At this very early stage of his gameplay, virtual Tom hadn't yet acquired much money. And yet when the old beggar woman asked him for some coins, Tom gave her some gold. When I asked him why, he explained that he had been once again influenced by *Alternate Reality*:

> TOM: based on some of my past experience, I told you about *Alternate Reality*, I know that you've got choices you can make, in that game, and the choices that you make determine whether you head toward the forces of light or darkness. That determines what sorts of guilds you can join, what sorts of spells you can get. And so, for me, that was a choice that was reminiscent of that old game.
>
> ZACH: Your thought process being, you're going the "light" route by giving her coins, and that is going to unlock possibilities for your avatar that might be different than if you...
>
> TOM: ...killed her.
>
> ZACH: So it's the old light Jedi, dark Jedi, opportunities down those different paths. So you wanted to be the light Jedi? Why? Where is the fun in that?
>
> TOM: [Laughs.] You know, I have to be honest, I probably didn't think about that too horribly much. It was kind of a reaction. I think I might have felt bad if I had killed her.
>
> ZACH: She's not real.
>
> TOM: I know.
>
> ZACH: Or is she? Is that real-world Tom, unconsciously making that decision? Rather than thinking that virtual Tom can do whatever the hell he wants and it will be okay?
>
> TOM: Yeah, I think it was something of an emotional reaction.

Tom begins by attributing his decision to his past *Alternate Reality* experiences, but it quickly became apparent that he simply didn't find it ethical to kill the beggar woman. Tom reacted emotionally, instinctively following his real-world moral code. There was no distinction between his ethics and his avatar's ethics in this situation.

Diegetic Experimentation, Gameworld Exploration, and Narrative Immersion

Even as he expressed little interest in figuring out how to be successful in Cyrodiil, Tom still did show evidence of experimentation through virtual Tom's actions. One example of this diegetic experimentation came in the Imperial City's Market District just after virtual Tom had emerged from his slumber in the Merchants Inn. Upon entering Jensine's "Good as New" Merchandise (a shop selling exactly what its name suggests), virtual Tom spoke briefly to the proprietor Jensine about her wares. The avatar's next actions were intriguing: virtual Tom went up the stairs in Jensine's shop, where Jensine's personal living quarters were. As Jensine's shop was open for business, the door to her private quarters was locked. Nevertheless, virtual Tom picked the lock on this door and entered her living quarters. Jensine promptly called for the city watch, and a guardsman arrived. Virtual Tom was summarily arrested for breaking and entering. I asked Tom to explain why he wasn't willing to take items out of the bazaar chests (because of the "different rules" in the city) but had no problem breaking into a woman's home:

> ZACH: So tell me about the discrepancy between "there are rules in the city for me to not take the stuff out of the boxes" in the bazaar but you're going to go upstairs and pick a lock in someone's private residence. How is that okay?
>
> TOM: Um... [at a loss for words]
>
> ZACH: Because the picking of the lock seems more egregious to me than taking an item out of a chest in a plaza when there is no one around. Whereas, Jensine's right downstairs, it's clear she doesn't want you to go in there, and you do it anyway. And it did say on the screen, "Pick the lock." So that implies that it's not open, that you're going to have to use a thief's tool to get in. Explain!
>
> TOM: Right. I think I would say that, I could go anywhere, and she doesn't stop me from going upstairs or anything like that, and when I got there, there wasn't any indication that I would be doing something wrong. I don't think. No sort of overt indication.
>
> ZACH: Nor was there any overt indication that anything would be wrong if you took stuff out of those boxes [in the bazaar].
>
> TOM: Right. But to me that's wrong. That's stealing.
>
> ZACH: Okay. But is breaking and entering a lesser crime? Or you didn't consider that breaking and entering when you did it?
>
> TOM: I didn't necessarily consider that breaking and entering, and then I didn't steal anything. I felt like it was clear to me that if I'd taken something [it would be a crime]. I was surprised when I was arrested!
>
> ZACH: I see. You weren't aware that you'd done anything wrong.
>
> TOM: Right. I wasn't aware. I just didn't think about it in those terms. I'm trying to think of any, are there any examples I can draw from previous gameplay.
>
> ZACH: Where just entering a location would be a criminal activity?
>
> TOM: It's possible, yeah.
>
> ZACH: So you were thinking if you can enter, they must want you to go in there.
>
> TOM: Yeah. It must be okay to go in. There is something about being

able to go where you want to, despite her [Jensine]. And it's kind
of funny, because it does feel like private space, and I thought it
was a way to tease a character, push her buttons or whatever.

ZACH: But you didn't think there would be legal ramifications from
doing so.

TOM: Right. There is something about, how far can I push her. A little
test. How far can I push her?

It is interesting that Tom describes this diegetic experimentation not in terms
of testing the gameworld, but of testing "her," meaning Jensine. As I'm sure
you've noticed, Tom also refers to virtual Tom's actions and decisions in the
first person: "How far can I push her?" This shows close identification between
Tom and his avatar — even as this identification seems to often be unconscious on Tom's part. Both Shiva and Vishnu also seemed to at times be
unaware of the connections between their extra-diegetic selves and the decisions they made for their virtual selves.

Another instance where Tom showed enjoyment of diegetic experimentation came early in his gameplay while virtual Tom was still in the sewers
under the Imperial City prison. In order to give the avatar as many different
experiences as possible during this tutorial portion of the game, several different weapons can be found and used. Soon enough in his explorations, virtual Tom found a bow and arrows near a well. There is a bucket hanging from
a rope over the well, and a tutorial message appears on the screen, explaining how to target and fire with the bow. The game instructs the user to practice firing arrows at the bucket. Tom did so, carefully lining up his first shot
and hitting the bucket squarely with his arrows. This sent the bucket wildly
swinging back and forth on the rope it hung from. When this happened, Tom
laughed out loud: a rare display of emotion from a man not known for many
demonstrative emotional reactions. I asked Tom what it was about this experience that caused such a (for him) strong reaction. He replied that he had
found it "satisfying to know that I could actually control the bow well enough
to actually hit something. It was the first shot! It felt like a weapon that would
be useful and easy to use." Tom reacted favorably to his first bow-and-arrows
experience because he was able to succeed at it immediately and easily. This
reaction is completely in keeping with Tom's preestablished gaming preferences, and this was really the first time in his *Oblivion* gameplay where Tom
perceived he had "mastered" a skill immediately. It was also one of the last
times, as the type of gameplay *Oblivion* offers isn't set up to allow for the avatar
to dominate in the way Tom would have liked. After all, this is no *Mechwarrior*. Tom never laughed like this again during his gaming sessions for this
project. Too many Scamps throwing fireballs, most likely.

One other aspect of Tom's gaming experience for this project that was interesting was his complete disinterest in the game's narrative. Even as neither Vishnu nor Shiva had closely followed the *Morrowind* central narrative plot during their gameplay, both gamers had remained adamant that a good story was essential to their favorite videogaming experiences. Those experienced v–RPGamers had been able to create ongoing narratives for their avatars as they explored Vvardenfell. Both gamers also admitted that they were ultimately interested in uncovering *Morrowind*'s main plot; they just wanted to do some exploring first. Tom expressed none of these narrative interests. Like *Morrowind*, *Oblivion* begins with an opening cinematic, with voice-over narration from Emperor Uriel Septim (voice acted by Patrick Stewart of *Star Trek: the Next Generation* fame). This cinematic runs for approximately thirty seconds, but Tom only watched for three seconds before pushing the button on his gamepad that skipped the rest of this introductory cinematic. I asked why he did this: did the game's story not matter to him?

> TOM: I wanted to play the game. I don't have a lot of patience for the cutscenes and stuff like that.
> ZACH: Even though, didn't you suspect that the opening cutscene would try to establish some sort of narrative story or mood? Would that have been your expectation?
> TOM: I thought that it would, but I also had the expectation that the game itself would, in little cutscenes as I would complete levels.
> ZACH: So you didn't feel like watching the cutscene was going to enhance your gameplay experience at all.
> TOM: No.

It is easy to see here that Tom's previous gaming experiences lead to false assumptions about what his *Oblivion* experience is going to be like. He clearly is expecting definitive levels or stages as is typical of many action and FPS games, and he assumes there will be additional cinematics between these levels. Both assumptions are wrong. *Oblivion* has no levels to speak of. To be sure, entering new locations like forts, caves, and cities requires a few seconds of a wait-while-the-game-loads screen, but no cinematics occur. The plot is relayed in dialogue with crucial NPCs in-game. Later in this interview, Tom went on to admit that he really didn't care about the game's story anyway. His goal in playing, he said, was to "advance the game." In my own videogaming experiences, "advancing the game" is closely tied to furthering the game's narrative arc. I asked Tom what he meant by this advancement. He stressed that he wanted to "advance the quest. Not necessarily the story, to draw that distinction. I would want to get to the next level, and I wouldn't care about the story." Tom went on to explain that he was only interested in the quests related to the main narrative because he knew that these quests would give him specific things to do: that there would be items to locate or bad guys to fight. Tom wanted exciting quests to be as easy as possible to find; he didn't want to have to wander in Cyrodiil looking for important locations.

In my opinion, that was Tom's loss: Cyrodiil is vast, and is rendered in gorgeous visual detail. There are mountains to climb, lakes to swim in, forests to hunt deer in, and many dozens of caves, Elven ruins, forts, and cities to explore. Gameworld exploration and discovering secret locations is one of the great draws for most v–RPG fans; wandering on foot can really aid immersion and gaming identification as I discussed in earlier chapters. But I discovered that Tom just didn't care about exploring the gameworld. This was immediately illustrated by the very first quest given to virtual Tom by the dying Emperor: deliver the Amulet of Kings to Jauffre in Weynon Priory. After his rest at the Merchants Inn and his brief diegetic experimentation in the Market District of the Imperial City, Tom accessed his inventory to examine the world map to locate Weynon Priory. When Tom located the priory and moved the cursor over it, he was given the option of "Fast Travelling" to Weynon Priory. In *Oblivion*, the avatar has two means of traveling through Cyrodiil. One is to simply walk/run through the world on foot (or on a horse). This takes time, but offers the advantage of really seeing the virtual gameworld with the possibility of discovering new locations that don't yet appear on the avatar's map. Initially, the avatar's map only shows the major cities of Cyrodiil (the Imperial City, Kvatch, Anvil, Bravil, Bruma, Cheydinhal, Chorral, Skingrad, and Leyawiin) and a few locations the avatar has been told about by NPC conversations, like Weynon Priory. All of the rest of the numerous ruins, caves, forts, mines, and Oblivion gates must be discovered by the avatar through exploration of the world. However, Tom immediately chose the Fast Travel option from the Imperial City to Weynon Priory. In effect, this "teleports" the avatar immediately to the desired location, allowing the user to skip the travel time. No random encounters with bandits or monsters will occur along the way, but neither will additional locations on the map be discovered. From Weynon Priory, the avatar is instructed by Jauffre to travel to the city of Kvatch to locate Brother Martin. Tom again selected the Fast Travel option from the priory to Kvatch. I asked Tom why he didn't want to experience moving through Cyrodiil to arrive at these locations:

> TOM: I didn't have patience with the map. I didn't want to have to figure out where I was in relation to the map, and then find the path. I know there is that little indicator on the compass, but I figured I don't want to spend all this time meandering on some path when I could advance the story.
>
> ZACH: So that's what it was all about? Advancing the story? Getting the quest, then moving to the next quest location after that?

TOM: Yes.

ZACH: But at the same time, when talking to those quest characters, like Martin in the chapel in Kvatch and Jauffre in Weynon Priory, and other characters that you had to talk to to get the new quests, you were always impatient it seemed to me going through the conversations with them. You skipped through lots of narrative exposition.

TOM: Yes.

ZACH: That makes me think it wasn't really about the story at all, but rather the quest. Is that accurate?

TOM: I would say that probably just to be able to see what comes next. I know in the story, it's a narrative that has a structure to it, but as you say I didn't really care about that.

ZACH: It sure didn't seem like it, after skipping that opening cutscene, jumping through the dialogues quickly to get to "what's the quest I have to do."

TOM: Right. That would give me opportunities to get some action. At least in my mind, that's where the action was. And I wanted the game to give that to me, I didn't want to spend a lot of time meandering on the paths to see what other things were there. I wanted there to be something there, and I knew the quests would give that to me.

It should be clear by now that Tom doesn't want to struggle with his video-gaming experiences, and the gameworld-exploration-for-the-sake-of-the-exploration that intrigues so many videogamers only frustrates Tom. He wants clear tasks to do (preferably tasks that virtual Tom can complete easily). Remember, most of Tom's gaming history is with action-oriented videogames with distinctive levels that begin and end — and more importantly, that can be learned and mastered. *Oblivion* resists this paradigm, offering instead a virtual space to inhabit and explore. Tom resisted this opportunity. Instead, he chose to Fast Travel from one Important Quest Location to another eschewing Cyrodiil exploration:

TOM: I did not like to have to navigate!

ZACH: You would want to go from one quest spot to another. So you didn't really care about the world, the big open-ended world: if you can see it in the environment, you can get there. That exploration meant nothing?

TOM: I didn't want to do that. Even in the town, where you've got all these little shops, you know there are all of these things that you can do, I thought about going to some of those because I wanted to upgrade my armor, I knew that I had some gold and maybe I can sell some things, but I didn't want to have to find it. And there were names on some of the shops that didn't necessarily tell you what was in each shop. And that to me was frustrating. That's where I decided to just leave the city.

In traditional action games (such as Tom's favorite *Mechwarrior*), there is very little down time between action spots in levels. The excitement remains consistently high throughout a level; the adrenaline often does as well. *Oblivion* exploration offers many quiet, more sedate moments where there are no monsters to fight. For Tom, wandering to the top of a mountain, picking the mushrooms found there, and gazing down at the panoramic view of Cyrodiil isn't an exciting or immersive videogaming experience. Tom wanted action, and the satisfaction of completing/dominating/winning specific quests.

Avatar Identification

Ultimately, how did Tom's gaming predilections and personality affect his identification with virtual Tom? After he completed the required hours of *Oblivion* gameplay for this project, I asked Tom if he would continue to play the game on his own time. He said that he would, but likely only as long as the main quest kept giving him specific tasks to do. After that, he would probably stop playing, not being proactive enough to want to find other interesting things to do and places to visit. Tom (both virtual and non-virtual) lacked the initiative and imagination to undergo this exploration if given the choice. Indeed, this wasn't the only area where Tom's identity overlapped with virtual Tom's. I've already discussed Tom's explanations for how he justified looting corpses but not containers in civilization along with his moral qualms about killing NPCs he believed to be "innocent." These were clearly instances where Tom was reacting to the virtual world just as he would to similar situations in the non-virtual world. And many of Tom's diegetic decisions (deciding to Fast Travel, to sleep in a bed at the Merchants Inn, to assume the items in the Market District bazaar were owned by the shopkeepers) were unquestionably influenced by his extra-diegetic experiences. Was virtual Tom as "real" to Tom as Shi was to Shiva? No. Not even close. But there were areas where the distinctions between Tom and virtual Tom were deliciously blended. This was revealed by the final questions I asked Tom in our post–*Oblivion* gaming interview:

> ZACH: Who did you want Tom to be? When I say Tom, I mean [virtual] Tom. What was your goal for Tom?
>
> TOM: As I was creating Tom, I was trying to create me. You know, I didn't think that I could create my own face. [Laughs.]
>
> ZACH: You came pretty close, actually. I was pretty impressed.
>
> TOM: I took it as far as I could go. If I had knew that the hair [customization] was there, I would have tried to at least match the texture of my hair. But I would say for that I was at least trying to replicate my race, my northern European roots. And so, when I was doing that I was thinking about how I imagine northern

Europeans to be. I've got a lot of northern European blood in my veins. I tried to make it look more like me and my people, I guess.

ZACH: So that's in the creation. What about when the game starts? Did you have any thoughts about who you wanted Tom to be or was that never a factor? Or was it all about quest advancement?

TOM: I would say it was about quest advancement.

ZACH: But you didn't want Tom to be a murderer, it doesn't sound like, killing innocent people.

TOM: No, you're right. I didn't want to do that.

ZACH: So you did have a sense of something beyond just quests.

TOM: Possibly. I didn't necessarily want Tom to do things that I wouldn't do. Maybe it depends on what you mean by, "to be."

ZACH: To be a law abiding citizen, to be a grave robber, to be somebody who would fight for justice, or the opposite, none of those types of things were in your head as you were playing.

TOM: Not necessarily. No. I mean, just the moral part. If I was faced with those choices, I wouldn't want to kill somebody.

ZACH: Except scamps.

TOM: Except scamps. In the real world, if I make a distinction between my avatar and real-world Tom, I think the choices are different, and when I think about what I want my person, my character in the world to be versus what I want myself to be, I've got real-life goals that can't be realized in the game. And so I wasn't thinking about my identity in that sense. But it does make sense when you remind me that I was acting morally.

Even as there were many obvious distinctions between Tom and his avatar, they still shared much commonality. They shared a name. Their appearances and ethnicities were similar (as much as was possible). They shared certain moral codes, with neither wishing to openly steal or kill. On several occasions when trying to explain the distinction between virtual Tom's behavior and his own, Tom stressed that he had no experiences like the ones virtual Tom was having (deciding to loot corpses, kill a person in self defense, or break into a woman's home) and therefore didn't know how closely he was identifying with his avatar. This excuse seems a bit of a cop-out to me, a perhaps unconscious resistance to admitting to identifying with the virtual avatar. Both Shiva and Vishnu were also occasionally unaware of how some of their diegetic choices revealed their connectedness to their avatars. With those two diehard gamers, my questions during the post-gaming interviews usually made them aware of these connections. Shiva in particular seemed comfortable admitting her significant identification with Shi. Vishnu was slightly less willing, but still acknowledged how closely tied to his non-virtual identity his diegetic decisions for Steve! were. Tom was much more resistant to the notion that virtual Tom and Tom shared many traits. This resistance remained even when our post-gaming interview/discussion revealed these commonalities. It seems to me that for many videogamers, a large portion of their identification with their virtual avatars happens unconsciously: Tom wasn't even aware why he didn't take items from the bazaar chests until I asked him about it and forced him to consciously explain his decision. Similarly, Vishnu initially wasn't even aware that he was accumulating *Morrowind* books without reading them until I asked him about it. Each of these participants had to make diegetic decisions continually when gaming: some of these decisions seemed willful and performative while others seemed unconscious and automatic. In terms of identity, this makes perfect sense. Each of us is motivated to act by tangible external and internal stimuli, but also by unconscious conditioning driven by our desires and past experiences.

Diehard gamers Vishnu and Shiva both identified more strongly with their avatars than casual videogamer Tom. They were also more willing to consciously take ownership of the connections between their diegetic and extra-diegetic actions, decisions, and morals. Tom continually used the fantasy setting of *Oblivion* as an excuse not to willfully identify with virtual Tom's actions. I was curious to see if a v–RPG that had a more realistic setting might make it easier for a user to identify with the gameworld and the avatar's options. I was also curious to see how a non-gamer (someone who not only didn't enjoy roleplaying games, but who didn't play videogames as a rule at all) would identify with her avatar. Would there be more merger or division if the gamer in question had even fewer videogaming experiences to draw on to aid in avatar identification? Fortunately, an epic v–RPG had recently been released that wasn't set in a fantasy world. This game is *Fallout 3*, set in Washington, D.C., in the year 2277. *Fallout 3* offers a future dystopian vision of a post-apocalyptic wasteland of America's capital city and the surrounding countryside. Familiar national landmarks like the Jefferson Memorial and the Washington Monument are surrounded by the bombed-out ruins of the city's neighborhoods. Mutated humans and animals wander the wastes. Would this familiar yet futuristic setting aid the identification of a non-gamer? To find out, I turned to my fiancée Bianca (a decidedly non-videogamer) to see how her lack of videogaming experiences and disinterest in virtual identities and worlds would impact the diegetic choices she made for her avatar in the Capital Wasteland of *Fallout 3*.

5

Fallout 3

Identity and the Non-Gamer

My fiancée Bianca, 32 years old at the time of this study, is a child psychiatrist. She is a non-videogamer, as you'll soon discover. However, this doesn't mean that she has never played videogames. Like so many of us who were children growing up in the early eighties, Bianca was exposed to Atari and Nintendo as a child. The youngest of four children, Bianca has two older sisters between her and her eldest sibling, a brother ten years older than Bianca. When I asked her about her childhood videogaming experiences, she explained that she was first exposed to Atari when she was six or seven. Her brother was still living at home at that time, and he had an Atari then. As was the case with Shiva and her older brother, Bianca watched her brother play on the Atari first, which made her want to play. Indeed, Vishnu as well had been drawn to videogames as a result of his older brother. How often, I wonder, are our own childhood interests dictated by the interests of a big brother or big sister? Certainly, all the participants in this study were first introduced to videogames by siblings.

Bianca's Videogaming History

Bianca couldn't remember which Atari system her brother had, but in all likelihood it was the Atari 2600, as the games she remembers playing on it are *Adventure* and *Pitfall*. Of course, Bianca couldn't remember the names of either of these games, describing *Adventure* as "the one where you went through different castles, with the keys and the dragons" and *Pitfall* as "the one where he goes over crocodiles and everything." Other than these two games, Bianca couldn't remember playing any other Atari games at all. When I asked her what it was about these two games that made them enjoyable (and therefore memorable), her first response was that she had been playing them with her cousins (who were near her own age). Like Tom, Bianca remembered the social aspect of her childhood videogaming as most important to the fun of playing videogames. Bianca remembered that a Nintendo system (certainly the NES) came into her home when she was around ten. Her brother was still living at home then as well, saving money while attending college, but Bianca stressed that he didn't really have time to play videogames then as a pre–Med major. Instead, her friends at school had spurred her interest in the Nintendo: "I think we had it because our friends had it. I don't remember specifically asking for it." As with the Atari, Bianca only remembers playing on the Nintendo when her friends or cousins were over; she couldn't remember ever playing alone, with no one watching. The two games she remembered playing on the NES were *Super Mario Bros.* and *The Legend of Zelda*. Without the social benefits of bonding with friends and family, Bianca likely would have never played videogames during these early years.

Bianca stopped playing videogames when she entered high school; in fact, she claims to have no memories of ever playing videogames during high school, college, or medical school. When I asked her why, she replied that she "had other things that were more interesting for me to do, like go to the mall with my friends or study." That Bianca found studying "more interesting" than playing videogames says a lot about her she viewed videogames at this point in her life. Since I've entered Bianca's life, she's had a little more exposure to videogaming, which has resulted in a three trips to the local video arcade in the past four years. Despite the advances in videogame technology since Bianca was in middle school, most of her time in the arcade when we have gone is spent in the "classic" gaming section, playing *Pac-Man* and *Frogger* for approximately ten minutes each. The only "modern" videogames Bianca shows any interest in are simulatory racing games that have a steering wheel and foot pedals. Yet after twenty minutes or so, Bianca grows bored even with racing games, and we leave the arcade.

What keeps Bianca from playing videogames now? There is plenty of opportunity. I play videogames as often as I can, owning an Xbox 360, a Playstation 2, and a Nintendo Wii. Why doesn't some of my videogaming passion rub off on Bianca? In the pre-gaming interview discussing her childhood gaming experiences, Bianca revealed several different preferences that explain why videogames hold no interest for her anymore. Here, she describes why *The Legend of Zelda* was her favorite videogame:

> BIANCA: I had the most fun playing it.
> ZACH: Why?
> BIANCA: Because it was interesting and I had a really positive association with that game. It was new, it was novel at the time to me, and I liked the different platforms that you played on.
> ZACH: What does that mean?

BIANCA: Just the different screens, and how cool they were. I thought the character, what they were able to do, was exciting at the time in the sense of the places they went.

ZACH: So there is some exploration of the kingdom, the land?

BIANCA: Yes. I liked that. But I think there was also a sense of mastery. I was able to master the game and do well. Me and my cousin were both good at it. Once I really got into it, we could spend hours playing. I remember I played a lot of it with my cousin there, and I got to the end and I finished the game with my cousin watching.

ZACH: But you didn't start out being a master of *Zelda*; it took awhile to get the hang of it. So how did you get through those first few hours?

BIANCA: Hanging out with my cousins and friends.

ZACH: The social aspect.

BIANCA: Yes. And learning their skills too.

ZACH: Watching them play, and learning from that, was helpful too?

BIANCA: Yeah. And I think I was just more stimulated with videogames back then. They just interested me more.

ZACH: So, I'm hearing that several things were a factor in you liking *Zelda* the best: the exploration of the different types of the world, the different screens and sections, were interesting to you.

BIANCA: Uh-huh.

ZACH: That you were able to master the game, that was important, and that it was a good social bonding experience with your cousin.

BIANCA: Yes.

ZACH: All three of those things equally contributing to that being your most memorable videogaming experience?

BIANCA: What were the three again?

ZACH: The exploration of the different parts of the gameworld, that you had good mastery of the game, and that you were also socializing.

BIANCA: Yeah. All of those equally. But probably mastery being the most important.

ZACH: That was important to you? You like to master things?

BIANCA: Yeah, I'm a perfectionist.

Bianca makes it clear here that she enjoys mastering things with videogames being no exception. She's similar to Tom in this regard: neither of them derives any joy out of learning **how** to play a videogame. In fact, both of them find this learning curve frustrating. For Bianca part of the appeal of classic video arcade games is the simple joystick-and-button control mechanism. She explained her preference for the Atari 2600 joystick over even the NES' simple gamepad:

BIANCA: I think it [the Atari joystick] is easier to play. I feel like I'm more in control.

ZACH: The Xbox 360 has multiple buttons, for example.

BIANCA: I guess I don't feel comfortable because I don't know the controls.

ZACH: There was a time when you didn't know the Atari either.

BIANCA: It is easier to learn. Even the Nintendo was easy to learn.

ZACH: So you feel that modern games require you to deal with too many buttons?

BIANCA: They take longer. I don't have the patience to learn it.

ZACH: You don't have the patience? You have enormous patience. You have a medical degree, which indicates you have incredible patience to study and focus your mind on something that you want to learn.

BIANCA: The incentive is different! [In videogames] I have no incentive beyond hitting one button to play a game.

Bianca isn't interested in learning a complex gaming interface, claiming she lacks the patience to learn sophisticated control schemes. This is one of the reasons why her enjoyment of videogames today begins and ends with twenty-minute bursts of classic arcade gaming. These are games with simple joysticks and usually no more than a button or two. Ironically, most arcade videogames cannot be mastered or completed; they're designed so that the player will lose/die sooner rather than later. For Bianca, "mastery" in this case means mastery of the gaming controls along with mastery of how the game is to be played. *Frogger* is a good example of the type of arcade game Bianca likes to play: only the joystick is used to navigate the frogs through the obstacles into the safe zones at the top of the screen. No new gameplay aspects need to be learned after the very first level. Certainly, the difficulty of the levels increase, but the basic gameplay mechanic does not. In *Frogger* (and most other arcade games), learning how to play the game takes no more than a minute. For Bianca, this is essential to her enjoyment of videogames. I asked her what variables would stop her from playing a videogame (other than an arcade game) that she had started. After all, she had completed both *Zelda* and *Super Mario Bros.*:

ZACH: What would stop you playing a videogame?

BIANCA: Unable to master.

ZACH: Meaning, the skills needed?

BIANCA: Yes. Lack of patience in learning the complexity of the joystick.

ZACH: Is there another aspect that you'd be worried you couldn't master other than just what buttons to push when?

BIANCA: Maybe, the storyline. Like how complex it is.

ZACH: Being able to follow the storyline?

BIANCA: Yes.

ZACH: What about being able to care about the storyline?

BIANCA: Exactly. More that.

Bianca not only confirms here her lack of interest in complicated gaming interfaces but also reveals another reason why she is a non-gamer: she has almost no interest in stories or fictional narratives. As I soon found out, this led to her disinterest in not only videogames, but also movies and novels:

> ZACH: Do you have any interest in videogames that have a narrative arc or story, something like a movie has, with ups and downs, twists and turns, surprising developments? Would that interest you in a videogame?
>
> BIANCA: No.
>
> ZACH: Why not?
>
> BIANCA: It bores me.
>
> ZACH: What? You don't like interesting stories?
>
> BIANCA: Correct.
>
> ZACH: You don't like a narrative in a good book?
>
> BIANCA: Nope.
>
> ZACH: What about in a movie?
>
> BIANCA: Yeah, I like it in a movie.
>
> ZACH: What is the difference between the narratives you like in movies and not liking them in books or not having any interest in trying them in a videogame?
>
> BIANCA: My time and enjoyment. I'd rather enjoy it in a movie form, and I think part of it is the time it takes. And the time to read a book, too. A movie is an hour and a half. And I honestly don't do movies that often either.
>
> ZACH: No, you don't. That's true. So these types of entertainment media, you're not interested in investing much time in any of those. Why is that?
>
> BIANCA: Because there are other things that I'd rather do.
>
> ZACH: Such as?
>
> BIANCA: Exercise, shop, work, hang out with my friends, talk on the phone.

Ever since beginning medical school more than a decade ago, Bianca has been heavily invested in her career, spending long days and nights studying for comprehensive exams and medical certifications, working in hospital emergency rooms while on call, and now, writing and editing documents and attending meetings for her work as a state administrator in the field of child psychiatry. She has much less leisure time than I do in academia, and less leisure time than Vishnu, Shiva, or Tom. Rather than actively concentrating her mind in the way required to follow the plot of a novel or an elaborate videogame, Bianca prefers leisure activities that allow her to take a mental break, like shopping and surfing reality TV shows and talk shows.

Despite her long-standing disinterest in videogames, I was pleasantly surprised when Bianca admitted that she believed her childhood gaming experiences had a substantial effect on her at that time. I asked her to clarify her belief:

> ZACH: Have you ever been affected or influenced through playing videogames?
> BIANCA: I think so.
> ZACH: In what sense?
> BIANCA: I think like when I played *Super Mario Bros.*, I think it made me think of an underworld. You know how *Super Mario Bros.* had that underwater world?
> ZACH: Yes.
> BIANCA: It just made me think of life on a different dimension when I was playing.
> ZACH: Is that any different than being affected by watching a movie that makes you think about a fantasy world, or reading a book that makes you think about a fantasy world?
> BIANCA: I think somehow it is qualitatively different. The effect that it has on you, 'cause you're part of the videogame versus the movie you're once removed. So it does affect you differently.
> ZACH: In what sense? It stayed with you longer?
> BIANCA: No, I wouldn't say that it stayed with me longer. I wouldn't say that.
> ZACH: You thought about it more deeply as a result of playing?
> BIANCA: Yes! Uh-huh.

So, Bianca believed that the interactivity that came from playing *Super Mario Bros.* allowed her to think more deeply about the themes and subject matter than she would have from watching a movie or reading a book about the same themes. This is an interesting and important recognition. But even with this recognition, it is clear that Bianca has never really identified with the videogame agents (like Mario) or avatars (like *Zelda*'s Link) she's controlled in the past. If you recall, Vishnu, Shiva, and Tom all referred to their avatars' exploits in the first-person: I threw for 30 touchdowns in Madden; I was afraid to get near the water; I killed the goblin with my sword, etc. However, Bianca, when describing what she liked about *The Legend of Zelda*, used the third person to describe Link: "I thought the character, what they were able to do, was exciting at the time in the sense of the places they went." This shows that Bianca did not identify very closely with the avatar. Bianca seems here to make a clear distinction between herself as the game player and the diegetic avatar; she believes that it is her who must master the gaming controls, but that it is *Zelda*'s Link who is exploring the gameworld. Bianca has no history of any blurring of her real-world identity and her virtual identities.

Perhaps this is because she has yet to experience any modern roleplaying games that truly allow for vast avatar customization. Part of the problem might also be Bianca's disinterest in fantasy or other fictional settings. As I mentioned earlier, Bianca has expressed an interest in car racing videogames, but only the most simulatory ones in arcades that have cockpits with a steering wheel and foot pedals. I asked Bianca why this was currently the only type of videogame she had any interest in:

> ZACH: What is it about car racing games?
>
> BIANCA: Because I like to drive. I always have. It has always just stimulated my mind. Even before I could drive, I liked going fast in cars.
>
> ZACH: So there is an immediate relationship between something you like to do in the real world and in the videogame? There is a direct correlation?
>
> BIANCA: Yes.
>
> ZACH: So, you don't for example like guns, and so you don't like games where you have to shoot people.
>
> BIANCA: Correct.
>
> ZACH: You're saying that you want games that mimic the real world as closely as possible, or you can't get interested? You aren't interested in playing games that are about things that you don't do in the real world or that you can never have the opportunity to do?
>
> BIANCA: Correct.
>
> ZACH: Why is that, do you think? Many people play videogames to escape. It's leisure time which is often not about things that people have to do in the real world. Why do you think you're the opposite in this regard?
>
> BIANCA: Because I think, why waste time on something that you can't really do?

Bianca might be even more literal-minded than Tom. For her, leisure time escape comes from voyeuristically peeking into the lives of pseudo-celebrities on reality-TV shows like *Keeping up with the Kardashians, The Hills, The Girls Next Door* and *The Real World*. Bianca also regularly watches the E! Channel to keep caught up on the latest Hollywood scandals, divorces, and celebrity adoptions. The bizarre lifestyles of celebrities as shown on TV are fantastical enough for Bianca and most of these stories can be absorbed in less than thirty minutes. Who needs Lara Croft or goblins when one has Kim Kardashian and Hugh Hefner? Not Bianca; she's content to let her mind unwind with the trivial absurdities of reality television. Fantastical worlds with complex narratives and sophisticated gaming interfaces require more mental work than Bianca has ever been willing to give to videogames in the past.

There is another important factor that has kept Bianca from playing videogames for most of the last twenty years: her belief that videogames are the trivial pursuits of children. Despite her toleration of my own love of videogames and videogame scholarship, deep down, Bianca thinks adults should grow out of this affection. When I asked her how and why she had begun playing Atari at the age of six or seven, she admitted that she had been influenced by her brother: he played, she watched him play, and then wanted to play herself. When I asked her if this sibling mimicry was the only reason, she replied, "Partly. Just like, I was a kid. It was something that interested me." This is a telling statement: Bianca suggests that she wanted to play videogames in part simply because she was a child. And of course, children will like videogames. It's true, many children do like videogames. But Bianca has set up a binary in her mind: children play videogames, adults do not. I strongly believe this mindset contributes heavily to Bianca's disinterest in videogames. She revealed this mindset again when, in trying to prepare her to play *Fallout 3* for this study, I asked her if she might not enjoy playing as a hero:

> ZACH: Most videogames place you as the central character, the protag-
> onist. You don't have any interest in being the hero, saving the
> world?
> BIANCA: I don't believe it.
> ZACH: What don't you believe?
> BIANCA: I don't believe in a videogame you're the hero and you're sav-
> ing the world.
> ZACH: Why not?
> BIANCA: Because it is just a videogame.

Perhaps to Bianca, this is true, but try telling that to Shiva, whose real-world fear of water kept Shi out of Vvardenfell's lakes and rivers. Or to Vishnu, who exhibited such pride at compiling gaudy quarterbacking statistics in *Madden*. Or Tom, who laughed out loud with satisfied pleasure the first time virtual Tom fired an arrow into the hanging bucket. Bianca clearly believes that videogames are not "real" in any sense of the word, tangible or intangible. How would this mindset affect the connections between her real-world and virtual world identities for this project?

Videogame Selection. *Fallout 3*

Little in Bianca's brief videogaming history prepared her to experience *Fallout 3*. As I briefly mentioned at the end of the last chapter, *Fallout 3* is not set in a fantasy world with mythical creatures or magical spellcasting as so many v–RPGs are. Instead, the Fallout universe draws inspiration from a popular science fiction genre: future dystopia. Mel Gibson's *Mad Max* films, Ridley Scott's *Blade Runner*, and C.M. Stirling's *Dies the Fire* and its sequels in the Emberverse series are among the many popular texts of this genre.[1] Typically, future dystopian works depicts a bleak vision of Earth in the future, when much has gone wrong (usually as a result of human greed, ignorance, and/or global warfare). The first *Fallout* videogame, released in 1997, envisioned our world ravaged by nuclear war. In this future dystopia diplomatic relations between the United States and China deteriorate, leading in 2077 to nuclear war. Even though the war lasted less than two hours, most of humanity was obliterated in the maelstrom of fire and radiation. Most who survived the war did so underground, in community-sized bomb shelters called vaults. Well stocked with provisions and amenities, hundreds of people could live in each vault indefinitely. A generation passed, and still the vaults remained closed to the outside world. The plot of *Fallout* takes place in 2161 in Vault 13 (located in southern California). Due to the failure of a computer chip essential to the vault's water purification and recycling system, the gamer's avatar is sent out from the vault to try to find a replacement. The plot unfolds from there; the avatar must not only find a suitable water chip, but also eventually defeat an army of super mutants led by a mysterious mutant called "The Master."

Fallout received much critical accolade, and in 1998 *Fallout 2* was released. Here, the story takes place in the year 2241, eighty years after *Fallout*. The gamer's avatar is a direct descendent of the *Fallout* avatar, who founded a tribal community named Arroyo in northern California after saving Vault 13. Once again, the gamer's avatar is charged with saving the community he/she has grown up in. This time the avatar must venture into the wastes to find a Garden of Eden Creation Kit (GECK), a technological device reputed to be able to turn the radiation-ravaged wasteland back into a green, healthy ecosystem. As with *Fallout*, *Fallout 2*'s plot ends up being much more complicated than this simple find-and-retrieve mission. Ultimately, the avatar must confront the Enclave, the last corrupted remnants of United States government, on an offshore oil rig. To complete the main narrative and end the game, the avatar must free both Arroyo's villagers and members of Vault 13 from this Enclave base and destroy the oil rig, ending the Enclave's evil experimentations with mutagenic airborne viruses.

Both *Fallout* and *Fallout 2* are much beloved by v–RPG aficionados for the many freedoms they afford the gamer in terms of avatarial creation and development and also gameworld exploration. Male or female avatars were possible, even though technological limitations didn't allow the faces of the avatars to be customized. Both games' isometric, third-person gameworld perspectives, although standard at the time, are predictably antiquated by current technological standards. Nevertheless, both games have incredibly deep customization options available for avatar creation. Whereas *Morrowind*

Fallout 2's isometic, third-person POV.

and *Oblivion* use eight primary avatar attributes (Strength, Intelligence, Willpower, Agility, Speed, Endurance, Personality, and Luck) the Fallout games created an attribute roleplaying system known by the acronym SPE-CIAL. In order, these attributes are Strength, Perception, Endurance, Charisma, Intelligence, Agility, and Luck. In typical v–RPG fashion, the gamer must choose which of these attributes the avatar is initially stronger in and which weaker. These choices affect the avatar's actions in the game-world. For example, an avatar with a high Intelligence may receive additional conversation options when talking to NPCs. An avatar with a higher Luck score may have a greater chance of scoring a critical strike on an enemy in combat. A higher Endurance score may mean the avatar won't become poisoned when stung by a radscorpion, and so on. Do you want to play as a tough, strong, simpleton? How about a charismatic, slick-talking physical weakling? Each gamer can use the SPECIAL attribute system to create the type of avatar they want to play, thus increasing their identification potential with the avatar.

Once decided upon, SPECIAL attributes are fairly immutable; only in rare circumstances can they be altered during gameplay. To allow avatars to continue to develop during the course of the gaming experience, both games offer eighteen different Skills: learned abilities that can be strategically improved when the avatar levels up.[2] During initial avatar creation, the user is also allowed to select up to two Traits for their avatar (none need be selected if the gamer so chooses). The *Fallout 2* game manual (known as the "Vault-Tec Lab Journal") describes Traits in the following way: "Traits are characteristics that better define just exactly who your character is. They don't really fit into a single statistic or location. They all have a good and bad impact on your character. If you want the good side of a Trait, you must take the bad with it" (26). Sixteen different Traits are possible.[3] If the user envisions an avatar that relies on speech and non-violent problem-solving, the description of the Good Natured trait might be enticing: "Your combat skills start lower than normal, but your skills in First Aid, Doctor, Speech, and Barter start higher" (27). If the gamer intends to craft an avatar that relies on her fists to solve problems, the Heavy Handed trait would be a better choice: "You do more damage in melee- or hand-to-hand combat. And while you have the same chance to cause a critical hit, your critical hits are not as good as the next fellow" (27). Finally, both Fallout games also allow the user to select Perks every three levels. Perks are similar to Traits but only have positive effects on the avatar. A whopping seventy-six Perks are available for selection, ranging from Cult of Personality (all NPCs react positively to the avatar regardless of the avatar's Karma rating) to Night Vision (reduces the combat penalties for attacks at night or in low-light conditions). So, eighteen Skills, sixteen Traits, and seventy-six Perks are available in addition to the SPECIAL attributes. These options offer users the ability to craft highly personalized and fairly unique avatars. These features, combined with a compelling main narrative, interesting locations, and strategic turn-based combat, garnered *Fallout* a place of honor on many critics "Best Videogames of All Time" lists.[4]

Fans of *Fallout* and *Fallout 2* had to wait a decade for 2008's *Fallout 3*. During this time, Black Isle Studios (the developer of the first two games) closed down and original publisher Interplay sold the Fallout license to Bethesda Softworks, who began working on *Fallout 3* in 2004. Of course, Bethesda Softworks is also responsible for *Morrowind* and *Oblivion*, so there was much speculation that *Fallout 3* would be designed in a similar manner. Many fans of the original two Fallout games worried that this new design team would lead to *Fallout 3* being more an "*Oblivion* with guns" experience than a true spiritual successor to the earlier games in the series. To a certain extent, those fears had real merit: *Fallout 3*'s gameplay does closely resemble *Oblivion*'s in many ways, from the optional first or third-person POVs to the lushly rendered and open-ended gameworld exploration. Yet Bethesda Softworks did an excellent job of blending the *Oblivion* gaming mechanics that allow for incredible immersion and avatarial identification into a world, story, and mood that embody the existing *Fallout* universe.

As I briefly mentioned at the end of the last chapter, *Fallout 3* is set in the same future dystopia as *Fallout* and *Fallout 2*. Set thirty-six years after *Fallout 2*, *Fallout 3* shifts the setting from the West coast to the wastelands on America's East coast, specifically those of Washington, D.C. This time, the gamer's avatar is a resident of Vault 101, located near the ruins of the capital city. When the avatar's father mysteriously leaves the vault, the avatar leaves the vault in an attempt to find him in the wasteland. From this narrative beginning, the avatar is free to explore the vast gameworld, searching for Dad or not as she see fit. The usual suspects of the Fallout universe are present: encounters with the Enclave, the Brotherhood of Steel, and super mutants all play a role in the game's central plotline. But in keeping with the open-ended experiences of *Morrowind* and *Oblivion*, the avatar need not follow the main narrative, choosing instead to explore leisurely. If the gamer wants to thoroughly explore the entire world map, this is advisable, since completion of the *Fallout 3* main narrative will result in the end of the game. While this is in keeping with *Fallout* and *Fallout 2*, it marks a departure from *Morrowind* and *Oblivion*: both of those Bethesda Softworks v–RPGs allowed the user to keep playing after the completion of the main storyline indefinitely. As with *Fallout* and *Fallout 2*, the cinematic that ends *Fallout 3* varies depending on the avatar's previous gameplay actions. Obviously, the town of Megaton cannot be shown to be a thriving community in this cinematic if the avatar had previously destroyed the community with a small nuclear bomb (one distinct possibility). Through the variability in the ending cinematic, the gamer can tangibly trace the consequences of their diegetic actions on *Fallout 3*'s gameworld.

Fallout 3 allows the user to choose either a male or female avatar just as its predecessors did, but also takes advantage of the deep facial customization options of *Oblivion*: all the different parts of the face can be manipulated, allowing for incredible diversity. When I created my *Fallout 3* avatar Zachary, I spent twenty-five minutes on facial construction, making my avatar's face and hair as much like my own as possible. How much time would Bianca spend customizing her avatar, I wondered? *Fallout 3* also offers the SPECIAL attribute system. Each attribute begins with a base rating of five (out of a maximum of ten); the user can choose where to place the five additional points available at the beginning however she wants. *Fallout 3* also offers Skills and Perks but eliminates the Traits available in *Fallout* and *Fallout 2*. The number of Skills has been reduced from eighteen to thirteen[5], and the number of Perks from seventy-six to fifty-eight. Despite these reductions, the user still has an impressively large number of customization options available. Leveling up in *Fallout 3* occurs through the accumulation of experience points: completing different tasks and quests garner the avatar points, and when a certain number of points are accumulated, the avatar levels up and is allowed to improve their Skills and select new Perks. *Fallout 3* offers an explorable gamespace larger than its predecessors but slightly smaller than *Oblivion*'s Cyrodiil. Dozens of locations can be discovered, from a slaver base called Paradise Falls to the thriving Rivet City, located on a wrecked aircraft carrier. Like temporality in *Oblivion*, *Fallout 3* displays chronos as the avatar explores the Wastes in real-time. Kairotic moments are also available as the avatar discovers quests and locations at their own pace in whatever order they choose.

One of the most popular aspects of *Fallout* and *Fallout 2* was the turn-based combat system, which allowed the avatar to target specific parts of the opposition's body. Depending on the avatar's proficiency with the weapon they were using and their proximity to the enemy target, each game would display a chance-to-successfully-hit percentage for each enemy body part. This allowed for strategic combat depth: successfully crippling the left leg of a radscorpion with a sniper rifle shot slowed the rush of its attack, allowing the avatar extra shot opportunities before the radscorpion closed to attack range. A successful shot to the eyes of an enemy could blind them, reducing the likelihood of them being able to hit the avatar with a fist or bullet. As a result of these options, combat in *Fallout* and *Fallout 2* could be incredibly tactical, adding a highly strategic element to the combat. Neither *Morrowind* nor *Oblivion* offered turn-based combat, but Bethesda Softworks, heeding the pleadings of rabid *Fallout* fans, wisely included a turn-based combat option in *Fallout 3*. The game does offer real-time combat like *Oblivion* in either first or third person POV, but also allows the avatar to use the Vault-Tec Assisted Targeting System, known by the acronym VATS. This turn-based combat option pays tribute to *Fallout* and *Fallout 2* by allowing the avatar to target specific body parts on the enemy. However, not all combat can be done in VATS: each VATS attack costs a certain number of Action Points. The number of action points available depends on the avatar's Agility and any relevant Skills and Perks. The smaller the weapon, the fewer the Action Points are expended in VATS to use it. When the avatar has used all their available Action Points, they must exit VATS and continue any remaining combat in chronos time. Action Points slowly replenish in real-time as well. As a fan of the turn-based combat in the original *Fallout*, I was definitely relieved to see turn-based combat in *Fallout 3*. It is incredibly satisfying to strategically target a super mutant's left arm with a shotgun and cripple that limb with a successful shot, preventing the mutant from using the heavy two-handed sledgehammer it had been carrying. *Fallout 3* brilliantly weds the fast-paced combat of *Oblivion* with the thoughtful tactical combat of *Fallout*; having both combat options available is ideal, and I hope future v–RPGs follow Bethesda's lead.

Fallout 3 is also more simulatory than *Oblivion*. After all, this is our world, America, the avatar is exploring. Even with the futuristic setting, the ruined houses and communities of the wasteland are dotted with familiar objects. Teddy bears, wooden blocks and toy cars heartbreakingly indicate what had once been a child's bedroom. Burned and ruined books are strewn haphazardly on shelves and on floors. Rusted carcasses of cars and trucks dot the landscape, indicating where roads and highways once were. It's all very familiar, even though this is clearly a world that has moved on from our own. All the best works of future dystopia excel at creating this mixture of the familiar and the strange and foreign and *Fallout 3* has captured this blend. The game also offers simulatory mini-games. The avatar can attempt to pick locks on containers and doors using a bobby pin and a screwdriver. By rotating the bobby pin and applying pressure with the screwdriver, the user can "feel" how much pressure is being placed on the bobby pin. With too much pressure, the bobby pin will snap, causing the avatar to begin the process again with a new bobby pin. In this way the user's skill and patience in rotating the bobby pin to find the pressure points of the lock can directly impact their success lockpicking. *Fallout 3*'s world also has many computer terminals (all with glowing green CRT monitors) that the avatar can attempt to hack into by correctly guessing the login password from a screen full of potential passwords. *Fallout 3*'s game manual (entitled the "Vault Dweller's Survival Guide") describes the hacking process: "Each incorrect guess will tell you the number of letters that are in the right location for the actual password. Using the process of elimination you should be able to determine what the correct password is before you run out of tries" (35). The user has four tries to guess the password before the computer locks her out of the system. Both the lockpicking and computer hacking mini-games increase the potential for simulatory immersion in the *Fallout 3* gameworld. Whereas *Oblivion* and *Morrowind* offered many dozens of books filled with Elderscrolls lore, *Fallout 3* avatars can discover analog tapes that can be listened to. Some of these audiologs provide insights into quests and some of them recount the last words of people obliterated in the nuclear war of 2077. These audiotapes help to flesh out the gameworld and provide a tangible history of the radiated land the avatar is exploring. Similarly, several radio broadcasts can be listened to, including an Enclave station and a CNN-like Galaxy News Radio station. Listening to these stations can also provide insights into both the history and political climate of the gameworld. So, *Fallout 3* offers an incredibly immersive experience with avatar construction options that have the potential for deep identification between the virtual and real-world identities of the user. But would Bianca be able to find these connections? Would she be willing to care enough to identify with her avatar in any meaningful way? I turn now to an examination of Bianca's *Fallout 3* gaming experience.

Choosing the Avatar's Sex and Name

Fallout 3 begins with a cinematic, narrated by Ron Perlman. It recounts the history of the Fallout world, describing the nuclear war, humanity's retreat into vaults, and the still-sequestered status of Vault 101. Even as other vaults have cautiously opened their doors to allow their denizens to return to the surface now that the lethal doses of radiation have retreated, Vault 101 has remained closed. No one enters, no one leaves. Are Vault 101 citizens kept safe, protected from the horrors of the wastes, or are they prisoners of the outdated traditions of their ancestors? It is into this situation that the gamer's avatar is born — literally. The game begins with the birth of the avatar, delivered by the avatar's father (voiced by Liam Neeson). As if speaking to himself, Dad asks if the new baby is a boy or a girl; a prompt then appears asking the gamer to choose the sex of her avatar. Bianca chose to play as a female avatar. I asked her why: "Because I'm female! I wanted to be the sex that I am, I wanted to represent more who I am." The first avatarial identification Bianca is able to make demonstrates merger with her real-world identity. Next, Dad asks his wife what a good name for the little girl would be. This triggers the name creation screen; the user is free to input any name they wish. Bianca chose the name "Joojee." Bianca is second-generation Persian-American; both of her parents' first language is Farsi. As a result, Bianca speaks broken Farsi as well as her first language English. In Farsi, "joojee" is a term of affection, usually given to a beloved younger relative (like one's own child, a niece, or a cousin). When I asked her to explain why she chose this name for her avatar, Bianca replied, "It's a term of endearment, and I wanted to see how they would use it in the videogame and also how it would sound in the automated computer feature." This statement not only reveals that Bianca thought on her infant avatar self with affection (as a "joojee") but also her vast inexperience with videogames. Bianca thought that NPCs in the game would say the avatar's name; she clearly expected Dad to say "Joojee." This is a naïve assumption: *Fallout 3*'s programmers cannot predict what English names will be given to the avatar, let alone user choices in other languages like Farsi. That Bianca expected to hear her avatar's name spoken in the gameworld reveals an unrealistic expectation. Nevertheless, it is clear that

Bianca is drawing on her real-world identity to make the initial decisions on sex and name for her virtual identity.

Racial, Facial, and Hair Selections

After seeing that Bianca had chosen a name that had personal meaning to her, I expected her to try to make Joojee's face and hair mimic her real-world appearance as closely as possible. She didn't, even though at first it seemed as if she was going to. Bianca began manipulating the deep facial customization options, experimenting with how far apart Joojee's eyes were from each other and how long her nose sellion was. But after three minutes of playing around with the individual components of the facial construction system, Bianca returned to the initial facial creation screen and selected one of the pre-established facial templates available for a Hispanic woman. I asked her why.

> ZACH: You tried to customize the face for awhile, but then you gave up, went back, and let the game randomly assign one. Tell me how you made this decision.
>
> BIANCA: I liked the original face better. When I got into it, there was so much detail in going into putting a face together. I didn't have the patience to do it. I just wanted to create a face fast and that's why I went back.
>
> ZACH: And you decided on a face that you liked the appearance of in what way?
>
> BIANCA: I thought she looked cool and pretty.

If it had been quick and easy to do, Bianca likely would have tried to have Joojee mirror her real-world face. When it became clear that accomplishing this was going to take quite a bit of time, Bianca lost interest, opting instead for the first "pretty" face she had seen earlier. Bianca also gave Joojee electric orange hair. I was curious: why not select one of the pre-established faces and hairstyles that were more like Bianca's own?

Bianca's avatar Joojee, initial creation.

ZACH: Explain to me why you didn't select face and hair that were more
representative of how you look.

BIANCA: Because it is more fun to do a hair style to make you look different than you actually look.

ZACH: Then why not make Joojee a man? That would be even more different.

BIANCA: Because I don't associate ... it's not as fun to create a character
for a man, there are not as many options for a man as for a woman.

ZACH: What do you mean there aren't as many options? There are exactly
the same number of options for a male as for a female in there!

BIANCA: But, not all the options look as good on a male as they do on
a female.

ZACH: How do you know? You didn't go through any of the male
options so how can you say?

BIANCA: Because I've seen through Wii games how to create hairstyles
and other stuff for men.

ZACH: What Wii games are you talking about?

BIANCA: I'm talking about the little stylistic person that you are.

ZACH: You're talking about the mii people?[6]

BIANCA: Yep!

ZACH: So you like the way the women look better in the mii people?

BIANCA: Yeah. They are more fun.

ZACH: And so you used that to project that you wouldn't like the way
the male avatar looked in *Fallout 3*?

BIANCA: Yes.

Even as Bianca seems willing to experiment with Joojee's appearance, she isn't willing to roleplay a male avatar. Notice here that she begins her explanation of why a male avatar wasn't a consideration by saying that she doesn't "associate" with male avatars. Too much identificatory division, perhaps? It is interesting here that even a non-gamer like Bianca tried to draw on her past videogaming experiences to explain her diegetic choice here in *Fallout 3*. Bianca had watched me create a personalized mii in Wii *Sports*; I had also created a mii avatar for Bianca to try to encourage her to play with me. Apparently she found the hairstyle options for female mii avatars much more appealing. Vishnu, Shiva, and Tom also drew on past videogaming experiences to help inform their gameplay for this study; Vishnu and Shiva did so with much greater success than Tom or Bianca, as these latter two lacked relevant v–RPG experience to help accurately prepare them for their *Oblivion* and *Fallout 3* experiences respectively.

How SPECIAL: Attribute Selection

Once Bianca made the final decisions about Joojee's appearance a cutscene ensues: complications from the delivery of Joojee lead to the death of the avatar's mother. The game then resumes after one year has passed, with the toddler Joojee in her playroom. It is here that the game's tutorial begins, offering instructions for how to move the avatar around, look around, and interact with and pick up items. The user is instructed to pick up and read the SPECIAL book on the ground. This triggers the Attribute selection process. How would Bianca decide which attributes to raise and which to lower, given that she hadn't read the gaming manual at all and therefore knew nothing about how the Attributes would affect gameplay? Each SPECIAL attribute starts with a base of five points (out of a maximum of ten); five additional points can be added to any of the Attributes here at the beginning of the game. After looking at each of the seven Attributes briefly, Bianca decided on the following values: a Strength of seven, a Perception of four, an Endurance of six, a Charisma of five, an Intelligence of eight, an Agility of five, and a Luck rating of five. I asked Bianca why she had privileged Intelligence, Strength, and Endurance as her preferred Attributes:

ZACH: Can you tell me about the ones you raised the highest? Why was Intelligence the highest?

BIANCA: The reason why I chose why I did, it was points that I value in real life.

ZACH: Intelligence, Strength, physical strength, was the next highest, and Endurance. So those are the three you value?

BIANCA: I think it's a combination of what I think you'll need in a videogame to do well versus what I value in real life.

ZACH: Tell me about that combination. Why did you think you'd need a high intelligence?

BIANCA: To figure out the different levels and how to get places, and what to do next.

ZACH: And Strength?

BIANCA: Because usually you have to kill things, and defend yourself in videogames.

ZACH: You know that how?

BIANCA: Because of my past experiences with videogames.

ZACH: And then you chose Endurance. Why? That's kind of a strange choice.

BIANCA: I don't think it is!

ZACH: Why not Perception? Or Charisma? Or Agility? Or to be Lucky?

BIANCA: Maybe because I don't feel like Charisma is necessary in a videogame.

ZACH: Why not?

BIANCA: Charisma?

ZACH: How is Endurance necessary?

BIANCA: Because you want to be able to get through the game!

ZACH: I see. But it was hard to fathom how Charisma might be something you would need to get through the game.

> BIANCA: Yeah. Or even Agility. I guess Agility might come in handy to get through complex courses but I thought Endurance was more important. I felt Endurance trumped Agility.
>
> ZACH: Okay. And your lowest one was Perception. Why that one?
>
> BIANCA: I had to give up some. I would have liked to raise all of them but I couldn't.

I find it interesting here that Bianca the non-gamer admits that she makes her Attribute decisions drawing on both her real-world identity ("the points that I value in real life") and her beliefs about what her avatar will need to be successful in this virtual world. Bianca views herself both as intelligent and strong and wanted Joojee to have these attributes as well. She was clearly able to convince herself that they would be beneficial within the gameworld as well, even though Bianca's past videogaming experiences with *Super Mario Bros.*, *Pitfall*, and *The Legend of Zelda* didn't prepare her for attributes like these impacting gameplay at all. I suspect that Bianca made these decisions drawing almost exclusively on her perceptions of her real-world identity's own skills. I believe during her post-gaming interview she felt obligated to justify these decisions in relationship to the avatar's needs, even though Bianca was really selecting Attributes she felt she herself embodied. All of the participants have demonstrated in some capacity or another that some of the avatarial identifications made are unconscious; I'm pretty sure Bianca hadn't consciously made the connection between her Attribute selections and her views of her own self-identity when selecting her SPECIAL attributes.

This unconscious blurring between real-world and virtual identity was also revealed when the avatar's Dad entered the playpen room and said hello to Joojee. Bianca responded with an enthusiastic "Hi, Daddy!" However, when I asked her why she had felt compelled to speak to the TV screen, Bianca didn't at first remember that she had spoken out loud:

> ZACH: Do you remember that you said "Hi, Daddy!" when your father was talking to you when you were one-year-old?
>
> BIANCA: Yes, I remember. Wait, I said that myself?
>
> ZACH: Why did you say that?
>
> BIANCA: Because that was developmentally appropriate.
>
> ZACH: What do you mean?
>
> BIANCA: I wanted to see what I could say! Didn't I say it with my character? I didn't say it myself out loud, did I?
>
> ZACH: Yes, you said it out loud.
>
> BIANCA: I think he [Dad] said something out loud.
>
> ZACH: Yes, he was talking to you. But your avatar doesn't have language yet, just sounds.
>
> BIANCA: I thought in the playpen room she does have language.
>
> ZACH: No, just gurgling and bubbling. But you said, "Hi, Daddy!" Explain that.

BIANCA: I don't know if I can. Um, I was trying to get into character?
ZACH: And so you were responding as Joojee?
BIANCA: Yes.

It is fascinating that in her mind, Bianca had mistakenly believed that her avatar had responded to Dad, even though it had been her real-world identity that had spoken the words aloud. This seems to demonstrate a clear merger between the real-world and virtual identity in the projective identity: Bianca and Joojee were the same in Bianca's mind in this moment of spontaneous verbal response to diegetic Dad. And it was clearly an unconscious identification, as Bianca initially believed the words had been spoken by the avatar Joojee. How often does liminal space get crossed unconsciously in videogaming moments like this? Even Bianca the non-gamer is susceptible to this blurring of identity.

Diegetic Experimentation and Avatar Ethics

After Bianca made her final SPECIAL choices, the game once again moves forward in time: this time to Joojee's tenth birthday party. This phase of the tutorial is designed to allow the avatar to practice choosing conversation choices when talking to NPCs, moving around the gaming environment, using the PIP Boy menu and inventory screens, and to get her feet wet in combat. Dad invites Joojee to spend time to talking to the other guests at the birthday party, who include other ten-year-olds like Amata and Butch along with adults like the Overseer (Amata's father) and some of Dad's co-workers. When conversing with NPCs, the avatar is usually given at least three dialogue choices: one is respectful, one is neutral, and one is mean, disrespectful, and rude. Bianca quickly demonstrated in conversations with Amata and Old Lady Palmer a willingness to choose the rudest possible conversation choices. I asked her why:

ZACH: At your tenth birthday party, you started to have dialogue options: you could talk to Amata, the other little boys, etc. Your first choice, you chose to be friendly to Amata, but then you quickly chose kind of a mean conversation option, and then you chose other mean conversation options too. Tell me how you made those decisions.
BIANCA: I just was curious to see where that would take you, take me. If I clicked on the nice ones, that seemed a little bit boring, it seemed like I wasn't getting enough information.
ZACH: So you're saying you thought you would get more information if you were mean as opposed to if you were nice? Explain that.

> BIANCA: First I chose the nice route, and I wasn't getting the informa-
> tion I needed, so I tried the opposite route.
> ZACH: And so do you feel like you got the information better by being
> mean?
> BIANCA: Um, different information.
> ZACH: That's true. Did you not have any moral qualms about being rude
> or mean or impolite? Especially Old Lady Palmer, for heaven's
> sake? You were immediately disrespectful to her.
> BIANCA: None. It's a videogame, for god's sake! It's not life.

Bianca clearly demonstrates here that she never considered Joojee's ethics when making diegetic decisions. Why would she? After all, Bianca believes there is nothing "real" about the action taking place in *Fallout 3*. She was willing to say or do anything if she thought it would help Joojee progress through the vault. This was further evidenced by Joojee's willingness to try to pickpocket all of the guests at the birthday party. Playing with a Xbox 360 gamepad, Bianca had unwittingly pushed in the left thumbstick; doing so causes the avatar to crouch down, entering Sneak mode. In this mode, the avatar's option to converse with NPCs changes to an opportunity to pickpocket them instead. It was clear that Bianca didn't even know that the left thumbstick could be depressed as a button; she had accidentally pushed in on it when moving around the party room. But when the opportunity to pickpocket Dad (and Amata, and the Overseer, and the other party guests) presented itself, she never hesitated, gleefully searching each NPC. When I asked why she was so willing to steal from her dad and friends, she replied, "I wanted to see if I could have an advantage. In the videogame, I might need what they have. That's why." Once again, there was no connection between Bianca's real-world ethics and Joojee's virtual ethics. To confirm this fact, I asked Bianca if she had any ethical qualms about stealing from Joojee's loved ones. She replied, "Not at all! Not in a videogame. I don't think there is any direct correlation between my ethics in real life and my ethics in a videogame." Consciously, Bianca makes a clear distinction between herself and Joojee. Soon enough, Dad instructs Joojee to leave the party and go down to the reactor room, where Jonas has a special birthday present waiting. This present turns out to be a BB gun, scrounged and repaired by Dad and Jonas. This is the avatar's first opportunity to use a weapon, and Dad instructs Joojee to practice shooting at the metal targets in the room. Instead, Bianca had Joojee shoot Dad and Jonas in the face with the BB gun several times first, giggling hysterically all the while. When I asked Bianca about this choice later, she laughed again before giving her explanation:

> BIANCA: Here's the thing. I figured I might as well amuse myself while
> I'm playing since I don't usually play.

ZACH: Why was shooting them with the BB gun more amusing to you than doing what he asked you to do right away (fire at the targets)?

BIANCA: I wanted to see their responses!

Once again, Bianca's desire to experiment diegetically outweighed any ethical considerations. Bianca didn't even seem to consider the fact that there might be repercussions from shooting her father in the face with a BB gun; what if Dad had taken away the gun as punishment? Then the avatar would have no ranged combat option available. It was clear that Bianca never considered that immoral diegetic actions might have repercussions for Joojee.

The Avatar at Sixteen: Taking the GOAT

Once the avatar demonstrates she can hit the metal BB targets and kill a radroach that appears near them, Dad instructs Jonas to take a picture of Joojee and himself. This triggers the next flash-forward in time: the avatar is now sixteen, the age at which all Vault 101 citizens take the Generalized Occupational Aptitude Test (or GOAT, for short). The GOAT consists of ten questions, each with four answers. In a manner reminiscent of *Morrowind*'s character generation (the ten questions asked by Socuscius Ergalla in Seyda Neen's Census and Excise Office), how the avatar responds to the GOAT questions will determine which three skills will be tagged. The avatar will begin with a higher rating in these three skills as a result. The GOAT questions are predictably open-ended, with opportunities for the user to choose answers that relate to the different skills available in the game. For example, Question Seven on the GOAT is as follows: "Oh no! You've been exposed to radiation, and a mutated hand has grown out of your stomach! Whats the best course of treatment?" The four answers possible are 1) a bullet to the brain, 2) large doses of anti-mutagen agent, 3) prayer, maybe God will spare you in exchange for a life of pious devotion?, and 4) removal of the mutated tissue with a precision laser. These responses show an interest in the Small Guns, Medicine, Barter, and Energy Weapons skills, respectively. Once the avatar finishes the text, the proctor, Mr. Brotch, let's the user know what skills have been favored. Based on her answers, the game recommended Joojee tag Barter, Explosives, and Medicine. I asked Bianca about the GOAT test and how she felt about these recommended Skills:

ZACH: How did you feel answering those ten GOAT questions?

BIANCA: Some of them were funny and others were just, like the first question, I didn't understand that first question.[7]

ZACH: You chose the technical, gobbledegook answer.

BIANCA: Yes. Because I didn't understand any of the answers.

ZACH: Do you remember the gist of the other questions?

BIANCA: Yes, I do.

ZACH: Think about how you answered them.

BIANCA: I think I answered them morally correct. How I would answer questions in my own life.

ZACH: So you are saying you are answering as Bianca would respond rather than any roleplaying that Joojee might be different that Bianca?

BIANCA: Yes. And also, the other thing was, when pickpocketing, and all those types of things, those characters wouldn't necessarily know it, because you were being sneaky, but the results of the GOAT exam would be available for everyone to see, and that would determine who you would become.

ZACH: Did you know that's what would happen with the GOAT ahead of time?

BIANCA: They said that. I knew it was significant.

ZACH: So you took the GOAT kind of seriously, and answered them as Bianca would answer them.

BIANCA: Yes.

ZACH: And so, he then tells you the results, and basically what that did was tag three of those skills based on how you answered, that you would be proficient in. And those three were Barter, Explosives, and Medicine. How did you feel about those three?

BIANCA: Initially I wasn't sure, but when I looked at the other options I was happy with the three.

ZACH: Why?

BIANCA: It just seemed like my options were just as good as any of the others.

ZACH: Barter? Is it clear what that means?

BIANCA: Yes—be able to trade.

ZACH: Explosives?

BIANCA: Be able to blow things up.

ZACH: How did you feel about that one as something that you would want to do based on how you had answered?

BIANCA: Good. Because I think it had said if you were going to play a trick on your dad, I chose to put a cherry bomb in the toilet.

ZACH: That sounds like fun, but not too harmful at the same time.

BIANCA: Maybe.

ZACH: Some of the options (to play a trick on dad) would have been dangerous to his health.

BIANCA: Yeah. I didn't want to do any of those.

ZACH: And the third one was Medicine. How'd you feel about that one?

BIANCA: Good!

ZACH: Why so?

BIANCA: Because that relates to my real life.

While taking the GOAT, Bianca clearly answered for her real-world identity rather than for Joojee. This was one of the few times when Bianca's real-world ethics and morals carried over into *Fallout 3*. I suspect this was because Bianca had no clear plan for how she wanted to roleplay Joojee; she didn't care about creating a particular type of avatar. As a result, how could Bianca answer the GOAT questions but through her extra-diegetic identity? Certainly, she could have just randomly answered each question without really reading them carefully. Yet she didn't. She admits here that she knew the GOAT was significant to who her avatar was going to become, and perhaps more significantly, that all the other vault citizens would know the results ("the results of the GOAT exam would be available for everyone to see, and that would determine who you would become"). Why should Bianca care what the other vault dwellers thought about Joojee? She made it clear that the *Fallout 3* world wasn't real to her. And yet her response here indicates that some part of her did care about not only who Joojee was, but also who Joojee was perceived to be by others in the gameworld. Once again, unconscious identification seems to be taking place between Bianca and Joojee.

Obstacles to Immersion

After completing the GOAT, this tutorial portion of the game again moves forward in time another three years. The avatar is now nineteen, and is awoken in her quarters by a panicked Amata. Amata tells the avatar that Dad has left the vault! The Overseer is furious, Jonas has been killed (as he likely aided Dad in his escape from the vault), and the vault's guards are on their way to arrest the avatar. Amata begs the avatar to flee the vault via a secret hatch connected to the Overseer's office. To survive, the avatar must follow Amata's advice. This desperate flight through the vault allows the avatar to really test the skills introduced earlier in the game: combat with radroaches and the vault's guards ensue, and there are opportunities to pick locks and hack computers. Once the avatar successfully escapes from the hatch (after a tearful goodbye from Amata), she emerges for the first time into the fresh air of the Capital Wasteland. At this point, the game announces that the tutorial portion of *Fallout 3* has come to an end; the user has one final chance here to make changes to their avatar's name, appearance, attributes, or tagged skills. This is similar to the completion of the *Oblivion* tutorial. From this point forward, the avatar can wander anywhere in the Wastes they want, looking for Dad or not. From this Vault 101 exit, the ruined skyline of Washington, D.C., can be seen in the distance, with the Washington Monument and the Capitol Building clearly visible. Likely some *Fallout 3* gamers are immediately enticed to make their way to these familiar landmarks; others may choose to faithfully travel to Megaton, a nearby settlement where the game has prompted the avatar to look for information

Fallout 3's skyline, post Vault 101.

about Dad. It's up to the user to decide where to go once escaping from Vault 101.

Bianca completed this tutorial section of *Fallout 3* after one hour and fifty-four minutes of gameplay. After Joojee emerged from the vault, Bianca spent less than one minute looking at the wasted skyline of D.C. before asking if she could finally stop playing. During the course of her *Fallout 3* gaming, she repeatedly made it clear that if not for her agreeing to play for this project, she wouldn't have played at all. Bianca: the very picture of a non-gamer. When Bianca began playing *Fallout 3*, I thought it was conceivable that she might come to enjoy playing once she got used to it. This never happened: Bianca stressed that her two hours of gameplay felt "like working a full day, like writing a paper" and that she was exhausted by the experience. Several factors contributed to Bianca's frustrations playing *Fallout 3*. Among them was the complicated control scheme/gaming interface. In fact, Bianca identified "trying to learn the controls" as her least favorite part of her *Fallout 3* experience:

> BIANCA: I think the most frustrating for me was just the angle, and walking.

ZACH: What do you mean by the angle?

BIANCA: You could change where you're looking, up, down, left, right. And then also the direction that you're pointing. I feel like since I'm not a videogame player, I get more frustrated with that.

ZACH: Did you feel like it got easier, more intuitive, or did you still struggle as much as the end as at the beginning?

BIANCA: I still struggled.

ZACH: A lot of the time I noticed you would be moving sideway, not facing the direction you were walking.

BIANCA: I was impatient, so I wasn't pushing the button. I hated trying to learn all the controls. And I'm not committed to learning them either. So there is that combination of that they are complex, and if I want to learn them, what is the outcome for me? I'm not interested in playing the game.

ZACH: So, no motivation to learn the controls, but you have to be motivated to learn the controls because they are complex.

BIANCA: Yes.

Bianca has articulated why she struggled with the gaming interface here: in order to learn to use the interface well, one has to be interested and motivated to do so. As Gee has pointed out in several of his works, learning happens best when the learner is enjoying the process of learning. Bianca hated playing *Fallout 3*; it drained her energy and didn't hold her attention. As a result, she had a terrible time paying attention to the on-screen instructions for controlling the avatar, using the Pip-Boy menus, and opening doors. As result, Joojce wandered aimlessly in the bowels of Vault 101 for several minutes before finding the stairwell that led to the higher levels of the vault and ultimately freedom.

Nor did Bianca enjoy wandering in Vault 101: she made it perfectly clear that the richly rendered gameworld of *Fallout 3* held little interest for her, even the newly-discovered land outside of the vault:

ZACH: When you finally got outside of Vault 101, you got to look out at the wastelands. Did you find any interest in exploring that gameworld space, this new open territory where you can go anywhere? Did you have any interest in exploring it?

BIANCA: I think it was exciting at first to see the light of day but when I looked around it looked depressing, so no.

ZACH: When you were down in the vault, how did you find the environment, the space you were navigating?

BIANCA: Claustrophobic, depressing.

ZACH: And so you weren't interested in the way the game designers had put this futuristic yet retro vault together?

BIANCA: I liked when the vault opened up, that type of thing. I liked the sound it made. I liked being able to go and do something different.

ZACH: What would be an example of different things that you got to
    do?

BIANCA: Like when I opened the vault door and got to go up into a dif-
    ferent area. Or when I got to move on to the next level.

ZACH: So it wasn't about the spaces themselves, it was about moving
    through the spaces, knowing you were getting one step closer to
    your goal.

BIANCA: Yes.

ZACH: So the gameworld was just space you were moving through to
    get from A to B without the space being particularly interesting.

BIANCA: Yes. Except I thought it was interesting the way they designed
    the vault and everything.

ZACH: What do you mean?

BIANCA: Like how it opened up, when you put the code in correctly [in
    the Overseer's office computer] I wasn't expecting the floor to
    open up.

ZACH: Now that you are out in the wastes, how interested would you
    be in going to try and find dad? What would you do in theory?

BIANCA: I would probably just go search for my dad.

ZACH: Why?

BIANCA: That would be the goal. I would be kind of upset: why didn't
    he tell me ahead of time? I would want to know the answer as to
    why he left.

ZACH: What happens after you find him? What would you do?

BIANCA: I would ask him why he left. And then hopefully his answer
    would help clue me in to what I would do next.

ZACH: That sounds like you would be following the main plotline.

BIANCA: Yeah. I'm not interested in other stuff.

ZACH: You would want to get through that main storyline, even though
    there are dozens of other places you can go, people you can talk
    to. No interest?

BIANCA: No.

ZACH: Why?

BIANCA: Cause I'm all about getting from point A to point B.

ZACH: And that's in completing the story?

BIANCA: Completing the game.

Bianca's words here reveal two key factors that helped prevent her from
becoming immersed in *Fallout 3*. First, the world of the game didn't interest
her; she had no desire to explore in the Capital Wasteland, let along the different rooms in Vault 101. The future dystopia presented was too depressing
for her. To Bianca, the environment of *Fallout 3* existed not to be explored
with interest in discovering new locations, but to help her move from "point
A to point B." Her statements here highlight another component that no
doubt hurt her investment in the game: Bianca had no real interest in *Fallout 3*'s main narrative. To be sure, when I asked her to speculate on what she

would do next if she kept playing, she said she would try to find Dad, to ask him why he had left the vault and hope that Dad would "clue me in to what I would do next." But Bianca's willingness here to follow the main storyline of *Fallout 3* does not really convey serious interest in the narrative for the sake of the narrative. Rather, she is following this plot for the same reason Tom followed the *Oblivion* main plotline: the assurance that there would be something to do, some tasks to "complete." Both Bianca and Tom approached their gameplay with very linear mindsets, and with little interest in or patience for exploring and discovering locations and side quests. Bianca in particular made it clear that she would only continue playing *Fallout 3* if she was forced, and that she would try to finish the game as quickly as possible. She knew that completing the main storyline would accomplish this. Bianca also stressed that point of view made no difference to her level of immersion or identification with Joojee. She played the first half of her *Fallout 3* gameplay in the default first-person POV before accidentally figuring out how to switch to third-person POV; she then played the final hour in third-person perspective. When I asked her why, she replied that it was simply to make her experience less frustrating:

> ZACH: Once you discovered the third-person POV, you seemed to prefer that. Can you tell me why?
> BIANCA: Because you could see more of the surroundings.
> ZACH: And why was that better for you?
> BIANCA: I was fearful of people coming up from behind me and kicking my butt.
> ZACH: You didn't like the first-person POV?
> BIANCA: I liked it, but when people started attacking me, I preferred being able to see what was around me. I think it was easier for me to navigate too.

Bianca's POV preferences had nothing to do with her identification with Joojee at all. She liked both perspectives equally, but found it easier to navigate and see when she was being attacked in third-person POV. Bianca had similar ambivalence about the game's combat options, saying that while it was easier for her as a beginner to use the VATS system due to its slower pace, she thought that it was more impressive to use the quicker real-time combat. Bianca believed this demonstrated a higher level of videogaming skill (even as the real-time combat frustrated her given her difficulties controlling the movement of Joojee and aiming her weapon effectively). She also stressed she would ultimately prefer the real-time combat because it took less time than the VATS combat. Once again, Bianca's lack of patience for a component of videogame play that I find endlessly fascinating (turn-based tactical combat) hurt her immersion within the diegetic world of *Fallout 3*.

Avatar Identification?

As you can see, Bianca did not have a pleasurable *Fallout 3* experience. Playing for a scant two hours exhausted and frustrated her. When I asked her to sum up her experience playing *Fallout 3* for this project, she replied, "I just think that I've been provided the opportunity to realize something I already knew: I don't like playing videogames!" A truer statement has never been uttered, to be sure. But did the fact that Bianca disliked her experience necessarily mean that there was no connection between her real-world identity and her virtual identity? Bianca, at least, was adamant in her belief that there was no connection between her and Joojee:

> ZACH: Who did you want Joojee to be?
> BIANCA: I would say I really didn't care. I just wanted to create a character so I could get the play going. Just get through it.
> ZACH: So you didn't care who Joojee was or what Joojee did.
> BIANCA: No.
> ZACH: Why not?
> BIANCA: Because I'm not invested in this!
> ZACH: And you don't see any way you could be invested in an avatar like this in a videogame?
> BIANCA: No!
> ZACH: Who was Joojee?
> BIANCA: The person she had to be in order to play this game.
> ZACH: Which was who?
> BIANCA: No one particular.
> ZACH: No one you cared about, no one you were invested in?
> BIANCA: Not at all!

So, Bianca claims that she made no investment in Joojee at all. I don't agree. I believe Bianca did invest parts of her real-world self into the creation of Joojee. After all, the name "Joojee" itself has personal and cultural meaning to Bianca. And her refusal to select a male avatar also spoke to Bianca's wish to play an avatar that shared her sex. Remember also Bianca's confusion about whether it had been her or Joojee who had spoken the words "Hi, Daddy!" Bianca also admitted earlier that she had answered the GOAT questions "morally correct, how I would answer the questions in my own life." No investment? No connections between Bianca and Joojee? I beg to differ. During Joojee's flee out of Vault 101 she encountered several guards who attack her on sight. The first of these, Officer Kendall, beat Joojee severely with a police baton. Bianca had no weapon equipped at the time, and struggled mightily with real-time combat as a result. While Office Kendall was hitting Joojee over and over with his night stick, Bianca said, "This is traumatic for me!" Later, I asked her why she felt compelled to say this:

> BIANCA: I think when you don't know how to play the game, and you
> have someone coming after you like that, it is not very much
> fun.
> ZACH: But "not much fun" is different word choice than "it's traumatic
> for me."
> BIANCA: Well, I don't like getting beat up!
> ZACH: Well, you weren't getting beat up. Joojee was getting beat up.
> BIANCA: Well, I mean, it is your character, and so, you don't want to
> be destroyed.

It seems to me that Bianca is identifying with her avatar Joojee more than she is willing to admit here. Note that she also refers to the avatar with the first person "I" in this passage. Bianca is experiencing merger identification with Joojee, even if identification is unconscious.

Why can't Bianca see that she has indeed invested aspects of her real-world identity into her virtual identity? For the most part, I think it is because Bianca does not want to see these connections, since she has a pre-established binary about what types of experiences are "real" and which are not. This is evidenced by the following statement she made when explaining why she had no ethical qualms about being rude to Old Lady Palmer or killing vault guards when escaping: "I think I am able to separate out what is real and what isn't. Obviously, I know this videogame isn't real, so certain things it is fun to continue with the same things I am like, and certain parts it is interesting or fun to do something that I wouldn't do in real life." Bianca is convinced that videogame experiences are not real. Therefore, her avatar Joojee isn't real either (even though Bianca admits here that some of her decisions are the result of "the same things I am like" in her non-virtual identity). Bianca's viewpoints here, when compared with the opinions of the other participants in this study, suggest that the gamer's mindset can greatly influence how conscious the gamer is of the identifications taking place with her diegetic avatar. Hardcore gamers Vishnu and Shiva willfully and consciously identified with their Morrwowind avatars continually, whereas non-gamer Bianca never consciously identified with Joojee at all. Casual gamer Tom demonstrated a mix of both conscious and unconscious identification with virtual Tom. However, regardless of whether or not the identification was conscious or unconscious, all four participants demonstrated tangible connections between their real-world identities and their virtual identities via projective identities. But why is this discovery significant, and why does it problematize new media terminology? In the next and last chapter, I answer these questions and make recommendations for future studies on videogame faces, spaces, and places.

6

Virtual and Non-Virtual Identities

Connections and Terminological Implications

Virtual identities are real and productive interventions into our cultural belief that the unmarked social unit is a single self in a single body.
— Allecquere Roseanne Stone, feminist technology theorist, 1995

The human-technical interface occurring at the personalized computer terminal requires a reassessment of questions of human perception and the body.... Where the real becomes highly unstable as a result of the ability to remake it over and over in a manner both comprehensive and spontaneous, we are compelled to turn our attention away from this reality.
— David Holmes, identity & technology theorist, 1997

A video game [avatar] is no more virtual than the images of real movie or pop stars: they too are representations which are carefully managed.
— Helen Kennedy, video game theorist, 2004

What does this project reveal about identity construction in video role-playing games? First and foremost, it is complicated, with many factors contributing to whether or not users identify consciously or unconsciously with their avatars. Vishnu's and Shiva's *Morrowind* data demonstrates a complex relationship between real-world identity, virtual identity, and projective identity. Each participant's real-world identities heavily and consciously influenced the decisions made for their avatars both during the initial creation of the avatar and throughout their gameplay for this study. Neither of these hardcore gamers saw their avatar as a distinct, separate identity. Instead, Vishnu and Shiva admitted that the predilections of their real-world identities often determined the diegetic choices of their avatars, even as they were aware that *Morrowind*'s Vvardenfell was decidedly not the "real" world. Casual gamer Tom and non-gamer Bianca were less willing to admit many similarities between themselves and their avatars. This did not mean that these connections did not exist, however. Tom and Bianca were simply more close-minded about being willing to acknowledge them. In this study the projective, liminal identity representing the theoretical space between real-world identity and virtual identity was easily and often traversed by Vishnu and Shiva (and occasionally and unconsciously by Tom and Bianca). At times, all four participants moved from their real-world identities to their virtual identities via the transitionary passage through the projective identity seemingly instantaneously. Shiva's ethical switching related to stealing (her willingness to loot corpses and take potions and herbs but never a person's books) is one clear example of this. This near-instantaneous passage is significant because it reveals just how closely related the real-world and virtual identities were for the hardcore gamer participants. Both Vishnu and Shiva chose to role-play their avatars in ways that were closely related to their real-world identities. Vishnu's selection of his avatar's name and gender reflected his penchant for humor; many of his other gameplay decisions were motivated by his desire to learn the limits of the gaming system and figure out the diegetic rewards for ethical and unethical actions. His cavalier attitudes toward avatar death demonstrated this greater interest in figuring out how to beat the gameworld and gaming system than in truly ego-investing in his avatar Steve! Shiva took her investment in her avatar Shi more seriously, avoiding dangers (such as entering the water) when possible and fleeing when Shi's life was threatened. Shiva also consistently followed a code of ethics (albeit a slightly different code than she follows with her real-world identities) with Shi, only taking items that she needed to survive such as food, potions, and weapon and armor upgrades. In addition to these conscious identifications with their avatar, both Vishnu and Shiva also made unconscious identifications with their avatars as well. Vishnu's hoarding of books that he never read is one such example. Until I asked him about it in the follow-up interview, he wasn't aware that he was even doing this book collecting. Tom and Bianca also made unconscious diegetic decisions that connected their real-world and virtual identities. Bianca's spontaneous "Hi, Daddy!" and Tom's belief that he couldn't take items from bazaar chests in the streets of the Market District reflect these unconscious identifications. To a certain degree, each participant's real-world personalities and identities were continually present in the diegetic decisions made by their avatars (whether the users were conscious of their presence or not). These connections allowed for easy identification between the users and their avatars as the avatars were continually imbued with the real-world identities' characteristics, values, and preferences.

Kennedy argues that this identification common in v–RPGs actually blurs the distinction between user and avatar: "Interaction with and immersion in the game affords users the narcissistic satisfaction of relating to a technological second self. [The avatar becomes] an extension of the player and the separateness of the avatar's body is obliterated" (6). Kennedy's argument here seems to ring true for the participants in this study. Both Vishnu and Shiva viewed their avatars as extensions of themselves. Each described the actions of their avatars in the first-person "I." Tom did as well. All four participants also gave their avatars names that were meaningful to their real-world identities. Indeed, most of Vishnu's and Shiva's avataristic choices reflected the desires and interests of their real-world identities (described in greater detail in chapter four). This was less true for Tom and Bianca, but even these less enthusiastic gamers still imbued their avatars with traits that reflected their extra-diegetic interests.

This notion of users and their avatars as being separate-yet-the-same is crucial to the significance of this study to identity and videogame theory. As noted in chapter two, Fuss accurately reflects the complicated nature of identity: "Identity has multiple and sometimes contradictory meanings. A full awareness of the complicated processes of identity formation, both psychical and social, [is needed].... Fictions of identity are no less powerful for being fictions" (98–99). The identity of a *Morrowind, Oblivion,* or *Fallout 3* user's avatar is certainly in many ways a fiction: it is constructed in a virtual fantasy world that is external to the physical body and the pre-established social world of the user. But I believe Fuss is accurate in pointing out that fictional identities are potentially no less powerful psychically than non-fictional ones (socially as well as in gaming worlds). Certainly, the experiences of Dante Nerevar, Bloom, and the other *Morrowind* enthusiasts I met on Elderscrolls. com (discussed in chapter one) show that these users identify powerfully with their avatars. Both Vishnu and Shiva seem to as well (Tom and Bianca much less so). However, my analysis of all four participants' data for this project supports both Kennedy's and Fuss' views on identity: even as the participants' "separateness" from their avatars disappeared for some diegetic decisions, at other times the distinctions between real-world and virtual-world identities were clearly demarcated. However, exactly when these distinctions might occur was unpredictable and/or unconscious, as Shiva's willingness to kill and loot corpses but not steal books exemplifies. The connections between the participants' identities (real-world, virtual, and projective) while playing these v–RPGs were indeed multiple and contradictory. This multiplicity of Vishnu's, Shiva's, Tom's, and Bianca's identities and the blurring that took place between them while gaming leads me to the following question, one with larger implications for identity and videogame studies: are virtual identities necessarily any less "real" than non-virtual identities to the users who create and maintain them?

Obviously this is a difficult question to answer. Yet all participants demonstrated in this study that at times their avatarial identities were deeply intertwined with their real-world identities and interests. The avatars' identities were also influenced and shaped by the videogame world and the game's programming; users don't have complete freedom to shape the virtual identity. Yet these diegetic constraints provide a type of social identity construction. Our real-world identities are also molded by social pressures and limitations: we live in a world not entirely of our own creation, bending to laws and ethical conventions that were discursively established long before we ever entered the conversation. So too are our virtual identities bound by discursive conventions. Bethesda Softworks' programmers and designers have created a world, a system, which users must learn in order to be successful within that world. All participants in this study admitted that learning (or not being able to learn) these systemic rules played a large role in their immersion in and identification with the games' virtual worlds (Vishnu in particular). Is this really all that different from the creation and evolution of our non-virtual identities in our non-virtual world? No. Both virtual and non-virtual identities are discursive in nature.

The data collected from Vishnu, Shiva, Tom, and Bianca demonstrates that all four users brought not only their extra-diegetic identities into this project with them (Shiva's inability to play a cruel, unethical character and the tongue-in-cheek name of Vishnu's avatar come to mind) but also that these users brought their past experiences within other v–RPGs with them as well. Both Vishnu and Shiva justified their diegetic decisions to loot corpses in *Morrowind* by saying that it was both ethical and expected behavior despite no direct evidence to support these claims within the gameworld. Both participants cited their past experiences within the genre of video role-playing games, arguing that through these earlier experiences they learned that this behavior was essential to having success in these types of virtual worlds. Both participants were able to apply their earlier virtual experiences to their *Morrowind* gameplay. Tom rested in the Merchants Inn because resting had been crucial to his success in *Alternate Reality*. Bianca chose a high Strength score because she expected to have to kill other creatures in *Fallout 3* and thought being stronger would make this easier. All of these decisions demonstrate that virtual identities and experiences can be transported outside of the virtual space they were created in and can influence a person's future behaviors as well. Certainly, once a user quits a gaming session, these virtual experiences may fade into the background of the user's mind as other aspects of their identities come forward. But does this make these virtual identities and experiences any less "real"? Do my non-virtual experiences become "unreal" when I leave them behind? No, just as the non-virtual aspects of Shiva's identity do not cease to exist when Shi is exploring Vvardenfell but rather inform the decisions made there. These memories of past virtual experiences are thus part of both the user's virtual identities and their real-world identities.

Fuss' notion of identity as multiple and protean, complicated by a cease-less combination of psychic and social factors, is a typically postmodern one. Data collected from Vishnu and Shiva (and Tom and Bianca to a lesser extent) for this project shows that the virtual identities created and maintained by these participants (via a delicious blend of psychic and social variables) can be as "real" as the real-world identities of some users. That is, they are con-structed purposefully in ways that are meaningful to their creators and have the ability to influence their creators' future interactions with and reflections on external stimuli (whether these stimuli be virtual or non-virtual). It seems clear that the term "real-world identity" used by Gee is problematic: the word "real" sets up a binary with the term "virtual" implying that virtual identi-ties are not and cannot be real. Using these terms, projective identity must then be a bridge between reality and unreality. Gee's discussion of multiple identities in *What Video Games Have to Teach Us About Learning and Liter-acy* clearly demonstrates that he does not consider his virtual identity Bead Bead in *Arcanum* nor the projective identity (James Gee *as* Bead Bead) that aids in Bead Bead's creation to be "unreal" at all. Why then has Gee chosen identity terminology that seems to misrepresent the very relationships he is explicating?

In 1989, Dr. Marvin Minsky wrote the following words when theoreti-cal awareness of and interest in virtual worlds and virtual identity was in their infancy: "Our connection to the real world is very thin, and our connection with the artificial world is going to be more intimate and satisfying than any-thing that's come before" (161). At that time, too little was understood about the impact of virtual identity construction in virtual game spaces—indeed, too little is understood about virtual identities now. Minsky was likely not the first person to separate virtual and non-virtual spaces and identities but his influential words certainly helped create a terminological binary, a lim-iting binary, that can be traced through the writings of video game and iden-tity theorists to this day.

Real-World and Virtual: A Problematic Terminological Binary

Murray (perhaps inadvertently) demonstrated just how problematic using the terms "real" and "virtual" as opposites was in *Hamlet on the Holodeck* when she provided her own definition for the word "liminal." Lim-inal, she says, refers to "the threshold between the world we think of as exter-nal and real and the thoughts in our mind that we take for fantasies. When we are in a threshold state [we are] filled with real sensations and emotions for imaginary objects" (292). It is interesting to note that Murray here uses the word "real" to refer alternately to external stimuli (real-world) and to imaginary stimuli. If both types of stimuli are "real" and it is the human mind processing and reflecting on stimuli that makes them real for that individual's identities, and if a fantasy identity (such as a *Morrowind* avatar) triggers real emotions and sensations, then the binary "real" vs. "virtual" that sets up fantasy identities as "not-real" is inaccurate and in need of adjustment.

However, once terminology is established, it is often used without being challenged. The antagonistic pairing of "real" and "virtual" is found throughout video game theory. In attempting to explain the concept "cyberbeing" (essentially another way to describe liminal space and projective identity), Nicholls and Ryan define it as "an indeterminate space that hovers between the actual and the virtual, the real and the imagined" (1,4). In describing identity construction in v–RPGs, Filiciak says "[Avatars provide] an opportunity to painlessly manipulate our identity, to create situations that we could never experience in the real world" (90). These two statements, written in 2005 and 2003, respectively, show the field's willingness to uncritically accept the term "real" even as scholars continually recognize the enduring impact of virtual experiences. Nicholls, Ryan, and Filiciak all use the word "real" in opposition to virtuality while at the same time admitting that the experiences that happen in virtual space may be significant to identity formation. Bolter and Grusin acknowledge the non-virtual impact of video role-playing games in *Remediation*, describing the thoughts and emotions experienced in these spaces as "authentic": "[Role-playing games] provide a new and authentic experience while at the same time divorcing us from the physical world. If virtual realities can evoke emotions, how can our culture deny that the experience is authentic? Like other media, virtual reality can provide its own, self-authenticating experience" (103, 165). "Authentic" means something that is substantially true, something that is real. I believe the data collected from the participants for this project make it is clear that "real" experiences impact the identity formations that can take place in virtual settings. Therefore, I recommend that it is time to eliminate usage of the term "real-world" to describe identificatory experiences that take place outside of virtual spaces. The term "non-virtual" is more accurate and sets up a more appropriate contrast to "virtual." This substitution would create a continuum that focuses on the technological and physical differences between virtual and non-virtual identities and experiences rather than on the authenticity or "realness" of those experiences. I believe other videogame scholars would find this term more accurate. Indeed, Gee himself acknowledged the problems with the term "real-world" in a question-and-answer session following his keynote address on videogames and literacy at an academic symposium in February 2006. When questioned about his usage of the terminology real-world identity, virtual identity, and projective identity in *What Video Games Have to Teach Us About Learning and Literacy*, he admitted that real-world identity was "a lousy choice" terminologically because of his belief that the experiences and emotions felt in video games were in fact quite real. Gee is willing to acknowledge the inaccuracy of a term he himself featured prominently in his important treatise on videogames and literacy; it is time "real-world" is eliminated from videogame and identity scholarship and replaced with the more accurate and less problematic term "non-virtual." With this new terminological continuum perhaps Vishnu wouldn't be as quick to sheepishly discount his sense of accomplishment compiling gaudy statistics quarterbacking in *Madden* as discussed in chapter three. Instead of using terminology that forces him to consider these accomplishments as "not-real," he could instead take satisfaction in relating how his projective identity in *Madden* excelled at figuring out and learning how to beat the gaming system.

There also remains confusion within videogame studies about how exactly to characterize the experiences taking place within the virtual worlds of videogames. Like reading books and watching movies, videogames have the capacity to trigger real human emotions as this study demonstrates. Yet the much greater levels of interaction and user freedom to choose their course of action make videogames unique from these other entertainment media. The following statement from leading videogame theorist Berger demonstrates not only problematic usage of the word "real" but also this difficulty in characterization as he speculates on the effects of videogaming experiences: "What is difficult to know is how being immersed into such a real-life simulation will affect players.... Will video games become a kind of opiate for people who can find an outlet in simulations that seem better than those offered by their real-life experiences?" (107–108). Berger refers to all videogames as "simulations" here. Yet this blanket statement does not effectively cover all the different genres of videogames. Certainly, many genres of videogames do not seek to faithfully represent the non-virtual world. In chapter two I discussed the differences between simulations and simulacra. Simulations seek to be as realistic and as true-to-life as possible whether or not the simulation is recreating the experience of flying an airplane or trying to recreate the battle for Stalingrad. They try to copy the original experience as much as possible. Simulacra on the other hand are copies without any original (Baudrillard). How should we characterize v–RPGs like *Morrowind*, *Oblivion*, and *Fallout 3*? Rilstone states that when playing role-playing games "we are creating a fiction, not a simulation: dealing not with reality but with the impression of fictional reality. What type of reality we are talking about is a matter of taste, of artistic temperament. Whatever it is, we should be allowed to become engrossed in it: to accept it as real, to want to spend some time there" (Mackay 28). Rilstone is right to suggest that v–RPGs are simulacra rather than simulations (or at least are much closer to the simulacra end of the continuum than the simulation end).

Morrowind represents this distinction well, as the box that contains *Morrowind* on CD-ROM also contains a glossy map of Vvardenfell, containing topographical information (mountains, rivers) and also marking locations of towns, cities, and other points of interest (ruins, shrines, strongholds). It may seem strange to novice videogame users that *Morrowind* supplies a non-virtual map for a terrain that only exists virtually. However, the mental exercise of creating simulacra is not as uncommon or as difficult as one might think. For example, I have never been to Iceland. I know where it is, geographically, I have viewed its location on a globe, and I have seen a few snapshots taken there, but that is the extent of my knowledge about Iceland. What happens when I view a topographical map of Iceland? I can look at a map of the country and "read" it based on my past exposure to geographical maps. Based on my past experiences with maps, my travels in other parts of the world, and my limited knowledge about Iceland, I can (and do) create mental images and impressions about Iceland that may or may not accurately reflect the physicality of the country. Unless I visit Iceland and create new impressions, my pre-constructed images of Iceland generated from looking at a map are "real" for me; they are all I have, and they influence the way I think and feel about Iceland. We create virtual mental representations every time we look at a map of a place we haven't physically traveled to and in, drawing on past experiences, things we've heard, images we might have seen, and other places we've been. In the Baudrillardian sense, mental imaginings of these places may very well be simulacra. I might have created a version of Iceland in my head that in quite unlike the physical non-virtual Iceland, which exists at a particular longitude and latitude on planet Earth. My mental representation of Iceland may be a copy that does not accurately model the original non-virtual Iceland at all. I may have created a mental copy of a place that doesn't exist in the form I have created. Similarly, if a gamer chooses to view the *Morrowind* map before they begin playing, they begin to imagine what the land is like. Playing the game itself may prove or disprove those imaginings, just as visiting Iceland may prove or disprove my pre-established notions of the island nation. Of course Iceland exists non-virtually; Vvardenfell does not. Visiting Iceland would create new mental impressions of the country replacing the potentially simulacra-ish pre-existing thoughts and images. In virtual worlds like Vvardenfell and Cyrodiil, users know that the world exists nowhere else. Traversing the gameworld provides continual reminders of this fact. Sentient aliens continually speak to the avatar (who in both Shiva's and Vishnu's case was alien herself). Strange and fantastical flora and fauna dot the landscape. Magical clothing, items, and spells allow for actions impossible in the non-virtual world. *Morrowind* is clearly not a simulation of any non-virtual space.

Verisimulacratude

How is it then that users like Vishnu, Shiva, Dante Nerevar, and Bloom become so immersed in video role-playing games and the avatars they control there? What would be the best way to characterize this phenomenon terminologically? A new terminological continuum is needed. Simulations immerse users by recreating the non-virtual world and experience as faithfully as possible: verisimilitude. The *Oxford English Dictionary* defines verisimilitude as the appearance of being real, with as much likeness to reality as possible; literally as "true to the substance" of the original as possible. The verisimilitude of simulations is an essential component of simulations' immersive appeal for many users. Yet v–RPGs like *Morrowind* and *Oblivion* offer a different immersive experience because of the many opportunities for identification with the avatar and the gameworld. Users like Vishnu and Bloom spend many dozens of hours within *Morrowind* immersed in a world that only exists virtually. This world is decidedly unlike the non-virtual world in many ways: casting Fire Bite spells from one's fingertips, riding within the hollowed-out exoskeletons of giant insects (silt striders), and levitating through Velothian wizard towers are actions that have no non-virtual world equivalents. How then does a simulacra v–RPG become immersive for so many users?

The statement made by Vishnu I provided at the beginning of chapter three provides a clue: "[*Morrowind* is] realistic enough that you know it's almost like your world only better. Only cooler, you know?" Vishnu astutely points out that *Morrowind*'s Vvardenfell has many properties that are like non-virtual spaces. These similarities are essential because without some kind of connection to the non-virtual people would not be able to identify at all. Thus, the gameworld mimics many of the spatial properties of the non-virtual world: gravity, a geographical land mass with urban centers and diverse rural terrain, and opportunities to interact both with other sentients (*Morrowind*'s many NPCs) and with lower life forms (plants and animals). In this way *Morrowind* is "realistic enough" (to use Vishnu's words) that users can identify with the physics and design of the world fairly easily (since these physical laws mirror the non-virtual world's properties). These game design elements are simulatory and aid identification. *Morrowind*'s many fantastical elements like magic, sentient alien races, and monsters also contribute to identification as the user encounters all of these through the avatar. This identification does not happen through verisimilitude but rather through the user's familiarity with and interest in the generic conventions the v–RPG draws inspiration from. I discussed in chapter two how *Morrowind* borrows from the established generic canons of fantasy, role-playing games, and videogames. Videogame users like Vishnu and Shiva with a high level of literacy within the v–RPG genre are likely aware of these conventions and expect them to be present in some form. Certainly Shiva and Vishnu demonstrated that they relied on their past experiences with other v–RPGs to aid their understanding of *Morrowind*'s world. This in turn allowed both participants to be invested in their avatars and immersed in the gaming world. Tom and Bianca also tried to draw on their past videogaming experiences but with much less success, as neither of them had exposure to modern v–RPGs prior to this study.

V–RPGs like *Morrowind* and *Oblivion* strive to be "realistic" and immersive in their depiction of a world that exists nowhere else but in virtual space. This world must follow certain established conventions of the genres it draws inspiration from and from the non-virtual world while at the same time being enough unlike other worlds (both virtual and non-virtual) to feel original. Identification in a v–RPG is in this way similar to Gee's tripartite concept of identity: identificatory immersion depends on a "delicious blend" of non-virtual, virtual, and projective aspects. Analysis of the data collected for this study reveals that the term verisimilitude does not accurately characterize the phenomenon by which many video role-playing games offer immersion and identification. I do not believe an adequate term yet exists in videogame theory to describe this phenomenon and I therefore propose a new term of my own: verisimulacratude. Rather than being true to the substance of a non-virtual experience, place, or object (verisimilitude), verisimulacratude describes the process by which a v–RPG like *Morrowind* strives to be true to what videogamers have come to expect from the simulacra they play. If a v–RPG follows established generic conventions yet also feels fresh and original, then literate v–RPG users have a greater chance of identifying with and becoming immersed within the role-playing world. Of course, there are many variables in play here: the gaming interface, the main narrative, the combat system, the appearance and customization of the avatar, and the appeal and diversity of the gameworld all impact individual users' identification and immersion. I offer the term "verisimulacratude" as a way to describe the general phenomenon and process of becoming immersed in a v–RPG and avatarial identification within those virtual settings. I believe verisimulacratude, when paired with verisimilitude, creates the terminological range of a continuum that would enable videogame scholars to more accurately articulate, categorize, and investigate the phenomenon of identity construction in videogames.

Scope, Time, and Data: My Study's Limitations

I acknowledge a few significant limitations in this study on video role-playing games and identity construction. The first is the small number of participants. The experiences of four participants are a very limited sampling; many more user experiences need to be studied to ascertain more definitively how identity is constructed through user interactions with video role-playing games. Four participants may seem like an insignificant number to fully understand a complex phenomenon like videogame identity construction given the many variables that may impact its formation. Vishnu and Shiva both relied heavily on their non-virtual identities to create Steve! and Shi, respectively. Yet their motivations and decisions were quite different, just as the levels of investment in their avatars were quite different. Shiva seemed to exhibit greater identification with her avatar, yet Vishnu ultimately seemed more immersed in his *Morrowind* experience, logging more than twice as many hours in the gameworld than Shiva did after this study. Tom and Bianca also displayed complex and nuanced identifications with their avatars with these identifications often happening unconsciously. Tom played *Oblivion* for six hours for this study; Bianca played *Fallout 3* for only two hours before quitting in frustration. Studying additional users in each of these v–RPGs would obviously provide more data to help analyze the connections between avataristic identification and immersion in greater detail.

A second and related limitation of this study was the number of gameplay hours recorded and analyzed for each participant. Ten hours of videogame play is indeed enough time to "finish" games in some videogame genres such as adventure games and first-person shooters. Yet in an open-ended role-playing game like *Morrowind*, this actually constitutes a fairly small of time. Most v–RPG users spend dozens of hours exploring the virtual world, leveling up their avatars, and completing the large number of errands and missions that can be undertaken. Vishnu estimated that he played between 100 and 120 hours of *Morrowind*; Shiva estimated that she played the game for approximately 50 hours. Neither participant came close to finishing the game's main narrative during that time. Of course, Tom only played *Oblivion* for six hours for this study. Even though he said he was interested in the game, he has not played a single hour of *Oblivion* since his participation in this project ended. Bianca only played two hours of *Fallout 3* and will never play it again. In contrast, I estimate that I personally have spent over two hundred hours playing *Morrowind*, over one hundred playing *Oblivion*, and sixty hours so far playing *Fallout 3* (I will easily double this amount before I leave the Capital Wastes). It seems likely that the longer the amount of time one spends in the gameworld of a vast v–RPG the greater the potential for identification with the avatar would be just as the potential for immersion within the gaming world would increase with increased exposure in that world. The few hours recorded from each participant in this study represent a small sampling of at least Vishnu's and Shiva's overall *Morrowind* experience. In the recorded ten hours, Steve! only leveled up three times; Shi twice. Each leveling up process allows the user to make choices about strengthening the avatar, which aid in identification. *Morrowind* and *Oblivion* offer users the opportunity to level up their avatar dozens of times. *Fallout 3* avatars can level up twenty times. There are hundreds of other gameplay decisions possible in the quests and sub-quests within these games as well. The choices made by the participants in each of these situations would provide valuable data on the connections between the users' virtual and non-virtual identities. Too few of these quests are revealed in the recorded hours of gaming for this project. This is evidenced by the illustration below which displays the amount of Vvardenfell explored by Vishnu and Shiva during their gameplay for this project. As you can see, it is a small amount of the available terrain. Recording a participant's entire gameplay experience within a v–RPG would be ideal to fully understand what identifications take place. However, the time-consuming nature of the data recording and gameplay transcription make this a difficult endeavor. In v–RPGs users make decisions continually and often unconsciously ("Hi, Daddy!") — or at least they aren't consciously articulating their avatarial decisions to themselves as they are playing. Their rationales for diegetic decisions may quickly fade from memory. For a study that analyzes the diegetic decisions of users, a think-aloud protocol that records the user's extra-diegetic rationale for their diegetic decisions in the

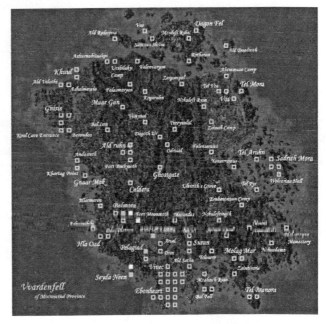

Morrowind **locations visited by Vishnu and Shiva.**

exact moment those decisions were made would be helpful. Yet the thought of a researcher needing to be present for potentially one hundred to one hundred and fifty hours of gameplay, audio recorder and notebook in hand is daunting. But how else might we be able to fully understand all of the conscious and unconscious avatarial identifications taking place?

Recommendations for Future Studies

Despite these limitations this study creates a greater understanding of what form future videogame studies might take. More comprehensive studies of identity formation in video role-playing games are needed. Due to the heavy temporal and logistical demands of data collection, compression, and analysis, these studies might best be undertaken by scholars working in pairs or in groups. Studies with as many participants and as many recorded hours of gameplay as possible would provide the most comprehensive data on avatarial identity construction. As mentioned previously, to record all the *Morrowind* gameplay for one participant, transcribe the data, analyze it, and interview the participant would require hundreds of hours of scholarly work — yet these are the types of studies needed if we hope to better understand the connections between virtual and non-virtual identities.

The v–RPG data I collected from this study's participants reveals additional avenues for research and analysis. In this project I have not explored how gender (of both the user and of the avatar) impacted diegetic decisions and identity formation; two male and two female participants are too few to draw substantial conclusions about the impacts of gender. Yet statements from all participants suggest that gender might have played a significant role in the creation of their virtual identities. Shiva's strong desire to select a female avatar and her rejection of the Nord facial options as not being "pretty enough" hint at the influences of Shiva's gendered identity. Bianca also selected an avatar she considered "pretty." Vishnu's desire to employ strong-armed Persuasion tactics and to problem-solve violently may reveal the influences of a masculine gendered identity. Additional studies with larger numbers of participants that focus directly on the influences of gender on virtual identity formation are needed to explore the connections between the gendered aspects of non-virtual identities and diegetic decisions made for avatars.

The work done for this project also suggests that videogame literacy plays an important role in identificatory immersion. Both Vishnu and Shiva began their *Morrowind* experiences with high levels of videogame literacy honed over many years of playing videogames. Having played other v–RPGs in the past both participants learned how to manipulate *Morrowind*'s gaming interface quickly: Vishnu only needed to adjust the Y-axis and Shiva made no changes to the control interface at all. Having read the gaming manual before beginning to play, both participants were also well prepared for *Morrowind*'s diegetic space. Each participant entered the avatar inventory screens many times over the course of their recorded gameplay for a variety of reasons: to examine items the avatar was carrying, to examine the local and world maps, to examine the avatar's attributes and skills, and to equip spells. The length of time spent in the inventory screen varied greatly, from several minutes (examining all the items in a full inventory) to less than one second (checking the avatar's geographical location on the local map). Did the participants' visits to the inventory screens aid or hinder their identificatory immersion within *Morrowind*? What role did the participants' high levels of videogame literacy play in their diegetic immersion? In contrast, Tom and Bianca both struggled mightily with the complex control pads and diegetic inventories of *Oblivion* and *Fallout 3*. How much did these struggles impact these participants' enjoyment and immersion? Answers to these questions need to be explored to help us understand the connections between technological literacy, diegetic learning, and immersion. The videogame transcriptions produced for this study (appendix) help to highlight the types of diegetic decisions that might be analyzed to ascertain how videogame literacy impacts virtual identity construction and immersion. This study demonstrates how diegetic data might be effectively collected for videogame literacy and identity studies as well.

Additional scholarship needs to explore identity and immersion in other genres of videogames besides v–RPGs. Both Vishnu and Shiva in their initial interviews stressed the importance of narrative to immersive videogaming experiences. Yet both participants admitted that they were more interested in exploring Vvardenfell than furthering the game's main narrative. Vishnu indicated that the lack of a narrative history for Steve! kept him from caring about the avatar as much as he otherwise might have. Neither Tom nor Bianca cared about the main narratives of their games at all, seeking instead to move from "point A to point B" because "that's where the action was." When asked what he liked best about *Morrowind*, Vishnu emphatically answered "the gameworld." Shiva also stressed how important navigating Vvardenfell's terrain was to her immersion. It seems clear that the space of a v–RPG plays an important role in the identificatory experience. *Morrowind*'s diegetic space offers both verisimilitude and verisimulacratude. It can be navigated slowly on foot or quickly via silt strider or magical teleportation, and it contains a large variety of diverse locations to explore. It is likely all of these spatial variables play an important role in the game's immersive potential. The point of view through which the terrain is navigated may also be important. Certainly, the rhetoric of videogame spaces remains undertheorized. This is true not just in v–RPGs but all other genres of videogames as well. Does spatial immersion happen differently in first-person shooter videogames than it does in v–RPGs? How, and why? This study demonstrates the need for additional analyses of videogame spaces and how data in future studies might be collected.

All of the participants in this study demonstrated that the body of their avatars was significant. Each participant clearly put thought and effort into the appearance of their avatar bodies; being able to view the virtual body seemed to aid in identification. As I discussed in chapter two, several scholars (including Haraway and Stone) have theorized about the connections between body and identity. Giddens also believed that the mind's perception of the body mattered in self-identity: "Regularized control of the body is a fundamental means whereby a biography of self-identity is maintained" (57). This connection is problematized in interesting ways in videogame avatars, which are controlled in the way Giddens describes: is a physical body necessarily essential to identity? In *Why Videogames are Good for Your Soul* Gee describes the connections between identity and the body in the following way: "Identity [is] a state of mind, a value system. Seeing and action are deeply connected for human beings.... We see the world differently as we change our needs and desires for action. [A] mismatch between body and world is all too common for us humans in the real world. We don't always feel a perfect match between the world and our body" (51, 54–55). Gee's words here, when considered with the writings of the other identity theorists mentioned above and the data collected for this study, suggest to me that a physical, corporeal body may not be as essential to one's identity as we might think. What may be essential instead are our mental perceptions about our bodies (or bodies in general). As long as a body is viewable in one's own mind, might it not have the potential to impact one's own self-identification and thus one's identity? This is certainly an area in need of further study as well.

It is also important that future scholarship in videogame and identity theory continue to establish new terminology and adjust existing terms as necessary. This is a pivotal time for the burgeoning field of videogame studies: virtual spaces, places, and faces continue to demonstrate increasing sophistication of verisimilitude and verisimulacratude (and everywhere in between on the continuum) with each new generation of videogame technology. *Second Life* (a virtual online space where virtual employment can be paid in non-virtual currency), *Tiger Woods 2009* (close-to-photorealistic facial creation and customization options) and *Spore* (evolutionary control over a species from its single-celled inception through sentient space travel) are but a few of the diegetic spaces and games that currently test existing notions of identification and immersion. This continual evolution of the medium offers exciting potential for new media scholars to discover new phenomena in relation to videogame immersion and virtual identity construction and play. The creation and application of accurate terminology will help unify the field of study, providing a critical vocabulary through which videogame theorists can participate in the important conversations about how videogame experiences shape identity and are shaped by identity in turn.

It seems likely that debates about identity between modern and postmodern theorists will continue for some time. Yet the participant data analyzed in this study on *Morrowind*, *Oblivion*, and *Fallout 3* fits smoothly into postmodern notions of identity. I reproduce here a statement from Fuss to demonstrate this fact:

> We tend to experience our identities as part of our public personas — the most exposed part of our self's surface collisions with a world of other selves — we experience our identifications as more private, guarded, evasive ... every identity is actually an identification come to light.... Identity is the Self that identifies itself. Identification is the psychical mechanism that produces self-recognition ... the detour through the other that defines a self [*Identification Papers* 2].

Can a v–RPG user's avatar become this "other" through which the player can produce self-recognition? As Vishnu and Shiva demonstrated in this study when creating avatars, users select attributes they want to see embodied in the avatar. Metaphorically (Fuss reminds us that "metaphor" comes from the Greek word meaning "to transport" and that metaphor is the substitution of the one for the other) in identifying with the avatar the gamer acts transferentially in what Fuss calls a "rhetorical process of figuration" (*Identification Papers* 6). And a *Morrowind* user cannot help but identify with the avatar as they have created it and made decisions through and for the avatar throughout the gaming experience: when to fight, when to flee, when to talk, how to talk, and where to go. These continual decisions made by each user allow for the many psychic self-reflections needed for identification as described by Fuss — particularly if the outcome of a decision is not desirable. At the same time, the user remains aware that the *Morrowind* gameworld is not of their own creation — it exists outside of themselves, the virtual creation of others (game designers and programmers). This social awareness is coupled with the user's non-virtual identity becoming increasingly aware of who their avatar is (the virtual identity). It is also coupled with who the user wants the avatar to be (the projective identity). These connections lead to a consistency in the actions of the avatar over time, forging a "delicious blend" of identities. New theoretical spaces and terminologies need to be created to describe and study the processes by which users interact with videogames to blur the already tenuous boundaries between virtual, non-virtual, and projective identities. When we're our avatars, we're still our selves. Still real. Or virtually real. Or really virtual. You decide.

Appendix

Transcription of Vishnu's First Two Hours of Morrowind Gameplay

I include the full transcription of Vishnu's first two hours of recorded gameplay for this study here to illustrate how essential (and time-consuming) it is to be able to look at every diegetic decision made by a user's avatar. Ideally, a researcher would record, transcribe, and analyze the entire length of a user's gaming experience

Data Disc 1, Participant One (Vishnu)

Morrowind's intro movie takes 1.40 to complete. The game then opens in 1st person POV in the hold of an Imperial prison ship, anchored in Seyda Neen. Upon "waking up," a fellow prisoner asks the avatar's name, and the gameplay begins.

1.51: names avatar "Srevel"
2.10: enters the game settings, examines key controls
2.20: returns to gameworld
2.30: enters game settings, inverts axis, examines key controls
3.17: returns to gameworld; experiments with axis
3.56: enters game settings; reconfigures key controls
5.01: returns to gameworld; follows guard up to middle ship deck
5.30: enters game settings; reconfigures key controls
5.37: returns to gameworld; experiments with axis

6.03: enters game settings; resets key controls
7.22: returns to gameworld; follows guard to ladder
7.38: enters game settings; resets axis controls
7.42: returns to gameworld; climbs ladder, exits to ship's main deck, explores deck
8.39: enters game settings; reconfigures key controls
9.03: returns to gameworld; continues to explore deck
9.51: exits ship and talks to waiting guard, triggering avatar sex and racial selection screens (Dark Elf male is default selection)
10.11: highlights Breton
10.12: highlights Argonian
10.19: highlights Breton
10.25: highlights Dark Elf
10.31: highlights High Elf
10.36: highlights Dark Elf
10.39: highlights Breton
10.41: highlights Imperial
10.47: highlights Khajiit

10.56: highlights Nord
11.09: highlights Orc
11.16: highlights Redguard
11.29: highlights Wood Elf
11.46: highlights Dark Elf
11.54: changes sex to female and back to male
11.59: changes sex back to female; scrolls through facial possibilities
12.11: scrolls through hair possibilities
12.43: highlights Argonian; scrolls hair possibilities
12.53: scrolls facial possibilities
12.59: highlights Breton; changes sex to male
13.08: scrolls facial possibilities
13.11: changes sex to female; scrolls facial possibilities
13.24: scrolls hair possibilities
13.36: changes sex to male; scrolls hair possibilities
13.42: highlights High Elf; scrolls facial possibilities
13.53: changes sex to female; scrolls facial possibilities
13.58: highlights Imperial; scrolls facial possibilities
14.06: changes sex to male; scrolls facial possibilities
14.11: scrolls hair possibilities
14.14: highlights Khajiit; changes sex to female; scrolls facial possibilities
14.36: changes sex to male; scrolls facial possibilities
14.46: scrolls hair possibilities
14.51: changes sex to female; scrolls facial possibilities
14.55: scrolls hair possibilities
15.07: highlights Nord
15.12: highlights Orc
15.14: highlights Redguard; changes sex to male; scrolls facial possibilities
15.22: scrolls hair possibilities
15.35: highlights Dark Elf
15.43: highlights Khajiit
15.46: highlights Dark Elf

15.49: changes sex to female; scrolls facial possibilities
15.57: selects "ok" thus creating Dark Elf female avatar; follows guard to land, explores courtyard.
16.24 dataset ends.

.13: enters game settings; examines game controls
.29 dataset ends. [16 minutes 53 seconds overall]

.05: begins Character Generation Q & A (ten questions with three choices for each)
1.09: after finishing Q & A, it is revealed that the avatar's class will be Spellsword; chooses "back" and returns to class generation options
1.12: selects "Pick from Class Line"; examines Spellsword favored attributes, major skills, minor skills
1.27: selects "back"; selects "Create Custom Class"; examines attributes and skills again
1.41: returns to gameworld; talks to Socucius Ergalla in Census and Excise Office, triggering birthsign selection screen. Presented in alphabetic order, the Apprentice is the default highlight.
1.55: selects the Atronach
2.05: selects the Lady
2.10: selects the Apprentice
2.11: selects the Lady
2.15: selects the Lord
2.27: selects the Lover
2.28: selects the Lord
2.30: selects the Lover
2.36: selects the Mage
2.39: selects the Ritual
2.49: selects the Serpent
2.57: selects the Shadow
3.01: selects the Steed
3.04: selects the Thief
3.07: selects the Tower
3.12: selects the Warrior
3.17: selects the Apprentice

3.18: selects the Atronach

3.20: selects the Lady

3.22: selects the Lord

3.28: selects the Shadow

3.30: selects the Serpent

3.32: selects the Ritual

3.43: selects the Shadow

3.52: selects the Ritual (Spells: Turn Undead 100 pts for 30 seconds on target; Turn Undead 100 pts for 30 seconds on touch. Powers: Restore Health 100 pts for 30 seconds on self)

3.54: selects "ok" and returns to gameworld

4.04: enters screen to review customized avatar data

4.40: enters Class box; selects Create Custom Class

4.47: within Create Custom Class, examines Skills

5.15: decides on Major Skills of: Block, Armorer, Medium Armor, Restoration, and Destruction. Minor Skills of: Longblade, Marksman, Spear, Athletics, and Sneak.

5.22: selects "ok" and returns to gameworld

5.44: speaks to Socucius Ergalla; examines training and persuasion options

6.21: attempts unsuccessfully to bully S. Ergalla.

6.25: successfully taunts S. Ergalla.

6.31: learns S. Ergalla will no longer train avatar (due to low disposition level).

6.35: returns to gameworld

6.43: picks up official release papers from desk

7.01: returns to gameworld

7.08: picks up inkwell from desk; the crime is reported. S. Ergalla scolds avatar but lets her off the hook.

7.21: enters avatar inventory for the first time. Skills and attributes are displayed in one window, the avatar's appearance and possessions in another. Examines meager inventory items; studies descriptions of iconic meanings (health bar, magicka bar, etc.)

7.59: returns to gameworld

8.05: speaks to generic Imperial legion officer. Asks about Imperial Legion.

8.24: returns to gameworld

8.27: enters inventory; attempts to drag release papers onto legion officer; returns to gameworld [this action has deposited the release papers on the ground.]

8.37: speaks to legion officer

8.41: returns to gameworld; opens door and goes into hallway

8.53: game prompts user to pick up dagger on table to learn combat.

9.05: picks up dagger

9.10: enters inventory; equips dagger; reads instructions for using it

9.30: returns to gameworld; examines items on "newbie" table and takes them.

10.17: has finished taking everything off the table; wanders around room.

10.41 dataset ends. [27 minutes 34 seconds overall]

The next dataset is 4.23 long, but contains no data, as the user left the computer and did not pause the game.

4.23 dataset ends. [31 minutes 57 seconds overall]

The next dataset is .08 long; no gameplay occurs.

.08 dataset ends. [32 minutes 05 seconds overall]

.01: enters game settings

.10: returns to gameworld; enters inventory

.12: returns to gameworld

.24: speaks to Sellus Gravius; asks about Imperial Legion; asks about Balmora; asks about silt strider; asks about joining the Imperial Legion

1.36: returns to gameworld

1.39: enters inventory; searches for release papers

2.48: returns to gameworld

2.52: attempts to steal candlestick from table; Sellus Gravius reports the crime, but overlooks it, reminding the avatar that being caught stealing will lead to arrest once the Census and Excise Office is exited. Continues to explore the room

3.15: speaks to Sellus Gravius

3.19: returns to gameworld

3.22: enters inventory; searches in vain for release papers

3.55: returns to gameworld

4.03: exits to Seyda Neen.

4.07: enters Census and Excise Office

4.25: steals plate in front of S. Ergalla, who scolds and releases the avatar.

4.36: finds release papers on the floor

4.49: explores C & E Office.

5.14: gives Sellus Gravius release papers; asks S. Gravius about his background; about the Imperial Legion; about Morrowind; and finally about his duties, which triggers instructions to deliver a package to Caius Cosades in Balmora. This is the first quest in the main Morrowind narrative. Asks about Gravius' trade.

6.35: returns to gameworld

6.47: exits to Seyda Neen: gaming programming instructs the user on how to access their journal, suggests they "check out Arrille's Tradehouse up on the left," and warns them that they are on their own now: no more tutorial help, and no more get out of jail free cards for crimes. The game can now be saved here for the first time.

6.52: enters journal (the opening entry reads, "My orders are to go to the town of Balmora in Vvardenfell District and report to a man named Caius Cosades. To find out where he lives, I should ask in Balmora at the cornerclub called South Wall. When I find Caius Cosades, I must give him a package of documents, and wait for further orders.")

7.05: returns to gameworld

7.06: talks to Vodunius Nuccius; ask for a little advice

7.21: returns to gameworld

7.32: enters T. G.'s house

7.39: speaks to T. G.; asks about specific place; latest rumors; little secret; my trade; services; someone in particular; specific place; background

8.53: returns to gameworld

9.10: exits to Seyda Neen

9.18: passes by Fargoth, who speaks to avatar; asks about ring; **gives ring to Fargoth** [happens at 41.63 gameplay] (choices were "Uhh, no, sorry. No ring." or "Yes I found it! Here it is."); asks about background; asks about latest rumors; little advice; little secret; my trade; ring; services; someone in particular; specific place;

10.09: returns to gameworld

10.22: speaks to Eldafire; little advice; someone in particular; Altmer; Altmer; latest rumors; my trade

11.12: returns to gameworld; wanders near Arrille's tradehouse

11.42: speaks to Indrale Rathryon; services; latest rumors

11.55: returns to gameworld

12.20: enters C & E Office

12.27: exits to Seyda Neen

12.45: takes out dagger for first time.

12.47: puts dagger away.

12.57: talks to Vodunius Nuccius; background; little advice

13.07: returns to gameworld

13.22: enters Draren Thiralis' house

13.29: speaks to Draren Thiralis; background; latest rumors;

13.57 dataset ends [46.02 overall]

.01: (still speaking to D. Thiralis); someone in particular;

.07: returns to gameworld; examines Thiralis' home and belongings

.42: exits to Seyda Neen

.45: speaks to a guard; Imperial Legion

.48: returns to gameworld

1.02: examines signpost (Gnaar Mok, Hla Oad, Seyda Neen, Vivec, Pelagiad, Ebonheart, Balmora)

1.29: speaks to guard

1.30: returns to gameworld

1.42: jumps over logjam of NPCs on bridge; first usage of "jump" feature

1.52: enters Foryn Gilnith's shack

1.56: speaks to Foryn Gilnith; fails to persuade him through admire

2.07: returns to gameworld; explores the shack

2.29: picks up book "A Dance in Fire" and gains one Mercantile skill point for doing so. **Quickly scrolls through the pages, not reading the text that is there.** [48.31 overall]

2.53: takes the book, rather than leaving it where it was.

2.59: draws dagger, accesses inventory

3.02: returns to gameworld

3.09: exits to Seyda Neen

3.20: talks to Teleri Helvi; specific place

3.24: returns to gameworld

3.43: speaks to guard

3.44: returns to gameworld

4.00: enters lighthouse with dagger drawn

4.10: **takes saltrice from sack on floor, not seeing owner nearby. She attacks. Desperate fight ensues:** avatar swings dagger, rarely connecting, but not getting punched

either. Soon, the avatar's Fatigue level is diminished, and attack is impossible. [first battle in Morrowind occurs after 50.12 of gameplay]

4.32: exits to Seyda Neen; **user seems to pause and reflect outside lighthouse door.**

4.57: enters lighthouse again; fighting resumes (with little damage). Once Fatigue is again used up.

5.30: exits to Seyda Neen; leaves lighthouse to explore nearby swamp

6.09: **picks Luminous Russula mushroom; first plant examined and taken in nature.** [after 52.11 of gameplay]

6.35: plunders surrounding area of all Luminous Russula's (value: 1) to be found.

6.53: discovers Daggle-tails nearby; picks them

7.25: attacked by mudcrab while picking mushrooms; flees a short distance lighthouse steps to draw sword; pauses here again until fatigue is replenished; wanders back into town

8.57: enters Arrille's Tradehouse

9.15: speaks to Tolvise Othralen

9.24: returns to gameworld

9.28: speaks to Arrille; little advice; practice your skills; popular potions; a long pause within this communication window, as if the user doesn't see the 'barter' button

11.25: returns to the gameworld

11.26: speaks to Arrille; selects barter; examines inventory items and shop sell items; sells mushrooms and folded cloth for $10; barters again; examines shop armor and weapons for long time

15.04: selects iron saber for purchase

15.37: selects chiton cuirass for purchase

15.47 dataset ends. (still examining armor) [1.01.49 overall]

.01: examining Arrille's scrolls for barter

.30: examining Arrille's misc. items for barter

.59: examining Arrille's spells for sale

1.32: returns to gameworld

1.38: enters inventory; equips iron saber, chiton cuirass, chiton boots

2.12: **examines the map window for the first time,** switching to the "world" map from the default "local" one [1 hour 04 minutes 01 second overall]

2.35: returns to gameworld

2.41: talks to Hrisskar Flat Foot; recover some gold; Fargoth's hiding place; **the user decides not take Hrisskar up on his offer to reward the avatar for finding where Fargoth hides his gold.** 1.04.30 overall]

3.29: returns to gameworld

3.34: talks to Raflod the Braggart; Seyda Neen; services; Training options considered

4.06: return to gameworld

4.12: talk to Tandram Andalen; latest rumors

4.23: return to gameworld

4.25: talk to Albesius Colullius

4.26: return to gameworld

4.29: talk to Elone; Pelagiad; Caldera; Ebonheart; Vvardenfell District; Vivec

5.01: return to gameworld

5.29: exit to Seyda Neen

6.00: **the user "quicksaves" the game: the first time this happened.** The user then returns to the swamp near the lighthouse, searching for the mudcrab that attacked earlier. [1.07.49 overall]

6.56: the mudcrab is found, and the avatar attacks with the iron saber

7.11: **the avatar kills the mudcrab. This is the first death of any kind so far in the game.** [1.09.00 overall]

7.23: the avatar disposes of the mudcrab's corpse.

7.28: enters the inventory; examines newly taken crab meat; eats crab meat

7.38: returns to gameworld

8.06: **enters water for the first time;** goes under

8.13: returns to land, wanders around village

8.55: **speaks to Fargoth; Fargoth's hiding place — Fargoth reacts negatively, ending conversation.** (is the avatar trying to warn Fargoth?) [1.10.44 overall]

9.16: speaks to Fargoth; ring; persuasion success (bribe 10 gold)

9.34: return to gameworld; wanders in village

10.15: reexamines signs to towns; locates path to Balmora and starts off, sword in hand.

10.43: talks to Seyda Neen silt strider conductor; silt strider

11.01: return to gameworld

11.30: picks more L.R. mushrooms and Daggle-tail along path to Balmora from Seyda Neen

12.56: enters Addamasartus

13.12: engages in combat with smuggler inside cave.

13.29: **kills smuggler; loots corpse;** continues to explore cave

14.25: enters inventory, examines newly obtained items

14.57: returns to gameworld

15.44: **avatar is killed by fire-magic-wielding smuggler in cave** [1.18.23 overall]

15.51: user loads most recent saved game; load process begins

16.12 dataset ends. [1.18.01 overall]

.01: saved game is still loading

.24: **the quicksave point highlighted in the last dataset (6.00) loads — it is the user's only saved game at this point. The avatar is still in Seyda Neen.**

.39: enters game settings; examines key controls

1.06: returns to gameworld

1.09: **the user switches to third person POV for the first time.** [1.19.10 overall]

1.15: enters game settings; examines key controls

1.26: returns to gameworld; returns to swamp near lighthouse

2.22: **finds and (re)attacks mudcrab from earlier.**

2.36: kills mudcrab, this time in third-person POV. Continues to wander in village.

3.45: continues to pick mushrooms alongside the path.

4.00: **bypasses silt strider platform without speaking to conductor** this time around.

5.06: continues to pick all possible plants along the path.

5.52: waits outside entrance to Addama-sartus while Fatigue is replenished.

6.18: enters Addamasartus.

6.34: engages in battle with first smuggler again.

6.52: kills smuggler; loots body

7.25: **disposes of corpse** (why this time, but not the first?)

7.34: leaves Addamasartus

7.35: long pause — user is away from game or reading manual.

8.49: user resumes playing; enters inventory; **experiments by eating food there;** (The avatar's health is drastically reduced — the user is likely seeking a way to bring it up.); examines weapons; equips chiton dagger

10.41: returns to gameworld; continues on path toward Balmora

11.17: enters inventory; examines world and local maps

11.49: opens journal

11.54: returns to gameworld; reverses direction on path

12.05: enters inventory; studies world map

12.13: returns to gameworld; continues along revised course

12.28: enters inventory; studies maps

12.30: returns to gameworld

12.48: reenters Seyda Neen; studies signposts for other towns again

12.50: enters inventory

12.52: returns to gameworld

13.09: accesses game controls; **turns voice audio down**

13.21: returns to gameworld

13.30: accesses game controls; turns voice audio back up

13.37: returns to gameworld

13.51: enters Arrille's Tradehouse

14.01: speaks to Arrille; popular potions; barter; sells excess weapons, items, & clothes; user appears to be searching for potions that will restore health to no avail.

17.20: returns to gameworld

17.29: exits to Seyda Neen

17.58: enters Census and Excise Office

18.10: exits to Seyda Neen

18.17: **attempts to rest in courtyard of C & E Office.** Game Programming advises the avatar that "Resting here is illegal. You'll need to find a bed."

18.32: returns to Seyda Neen proper.

18.36: speaks to Fargoth; services (why Fargoth? A friend?)

18.50: returns to gameworld

19.24: reexamines signposts for town directions

19.30: enters inventory; examines world map, studying Balmora location

19.35: returns to gameworld; heads toward Balmora

19.35 dataset ends. [1.37.36 overall]

.01: still on the path to Balmora; gathering flora

1.08: attacks a mudcrab & kills it

1.35: encounters the remains of Tarhiel; studies and loots corpse

2.06: consults inventory; studies map

2.14: returns to gameworld; leaves path to try direct route to Balmora across mountainous terrain

2.34: enters inventory; studies map

2.57: returns to gameworld

3.12: fights and kills kwama forager

3.26: enters inventory; studies map

3.31: returns to gameworld

3.49: enters inventory; examines health description and other attributes

4.30: returns to gameworld

4.40: attacks and kills scrib

5.11: enters inventory; studies map

5.15: returns to gameworld

5.30: **saves game progress**

5.42: attacks and kills scrib

6.44: enters inventory (after failed progress over mountains); studies map

6.46: returns to gameworld

7.47: enters inventory; studies map

7.49: returns to gameworld

8.00: enters inventory; studies map

8.02: returns to gameworld (working through the mountains toward Balmora)

8.16: spots kwama worker on path below; pauses to study it and regain fatigue

8.38: enters inventory; examines magical items

8.53: returns to gameworld; long pause ensues, even after fatigue is fully restored. User is away from the computer.

9.38: enters inventory; drinks flin

9.46: returns to gameworld

9.55: attacks and kills kwama worker

10.11: enters Shurdan-Raplay Egg Mine

10.22: **saves game progress**

10.25: enters inventory; examines magical properties currently affecting avatar (flin)

10.34: returns to gameworld

10.42: attacks kwama worker

10.51: **avatar killed by kwama worker** [1.48.27 overall]

10.57: user reloads most recent saved game (just inside S-R Egg Mine)

11.16: exits to Ascadian Island Region wilderness (between Hla Oad and Balmora)

11.43: enters inventory; examines maps

11.48: returns to gameworld (heading north toward Balmora)

12.43: picks flora near bridge near bridge near Shulk Egg Mine

12.52: enters inventory; examines map

12.54: returns to gameworld; crosses bridge (going west)

13.21: enters Shulk Egg Mine

13.43: is attacked by kwama forager; kills it

14.00: loots kwama eggs from a nest

14.28: exits mine to wilderness

14.28 dataset ends. [1.52.04 overall]

.01: continues toward Balmora

.38: enters gates of Balmora; explores city streets

1.03: speaks to Stargel

1.08: returns to gameworld

1.41: enters shop of Nalcarya of White Haven: Alchemist; goes upstairs

2.04: exits to Balmora streets (above Nalcarya's)

2.20: **saves game progress**

2.46: enters Balmora temple

3.04: examines shrine of St. Riln's; makes no donation

3.15: loots crates in temple

3.43: speaks to Telis Salvani; Morrowind lore; barter; purchases health and fatigue potions

4.45: returns to gameworld in temple

4.51: speaks to Feldrelo Sadri; is refused training

5.00: returns to gameworld; explores inside of temple

5.53: speaks to Llarara Omayn in temple lower level; barter; buys health and fatigue potions; examines spells for sale

7.26: returns to gameworld

7.36: speaks to Llathyne Hlaalu; barter; examines books

7.53: returns to gameworld

8.17: exits to Balmora

8.40: enters inventory; takes health potion; observes effects

9.05: enters inventory; takes health potion; observes effects (health now half full)

9.32: continues exploring Balmora

9.34: enters inventory

9.36: returns to gameworld

10.09: **opens journal**

10.15: returns to gameworld

10.38: speaks to Llandrus Belaal

10.42: returns to gameworld

10.52: speaks to Shargam gro-Shagdulg; specific place, South Wall

11.35: returns to gameworld

11.36: enters inventory; studies city map

11.48: returns to gameworld

12.47: enters South Wall Cornerclub

12.56: **saves game progress**

13.15: examines crate, but does not take contents; seems to pause to allow fatigue to replenish

13.39: opens journal

13.47: returns to gameworld

14.11: speaks to Phane Rielle; Caius Cosades (he suggests speaking to owner Bacola Closcius—journal updated); Bacola Closcius;

14.28: returns to gameworld; opens journal

14.35: returns to gameworld

15.05: speaks to Bacola Closcius; someone in particular; Caius Cosades; barter; beds; rents bed for day

16.33 dataset ends. [2 hours 08 minutes 37 seconds overall]

Chapter Notes

Chapter 1

1. "Console" systems do not have their own monitors and instead plug directly into a television. The Atari 2600, Sega Genesis, Sony Playstation 2, and Microsoft's Xbox 360 are all console systems.

2. Activision, Coleco, Commodore, Imagic, Magnavox, Mattel, and Texas Instruments all produced console systems in 1983, helping to saturate and crash the video game market.

3. Many more important games and moments in the history and evolution of video games exist. For more comprehensive historical coverage, see Wolf & Perron (2003), Wolf (2001), Dombrower (1998), and Gamespot's "The History of Video Games."

4. The term "avatar" was first used in a virtual context in 1985 in the popular *Ultima* series of video role-playing games. *Ultima IV* (1985) named the player character "Avatar" and later games in the series followed suit. Other early video games to specifically use the term in-game were *Habitat* (1987) and *Shadowrun* (1989). The term was first used to refer to an online virtual body in Neal Stephenson's 1992 cyberpunk classic *Snow Crash*. These important texts helped to familiarize video game users and theorists with the term and it has been used with increasing frequency (albeit inconsistently) since the mid 1990's in MUDs, video games, and to refer to Instant Messenger icons. Another landmark cyberpunk text ought to be mentioned here as well. William Gibson's *Neuromancer*. Released in 1985, the novel engrained the term "cyberspace" into popular consciousness. Gibson's notions of the benefits and risks of cyberspace interaction resonate within much of the scholarship quoted in this study.

5. In RPG worlds, players create avatars to control and role-play. But many other characters are needed to flesh out the gaming experience and make the RPG world dynamic. For example, the player's avatar might discover a small inn located near the path they are traveling on. Staying at the inn is not free: the innkeeper must be talked to, and the price of lodging ascertained. The innkeeper is not being role-played by the user, but rather by the dungeon master, since the innkeeper is a "static" character whose attributes never change and who will likely never be seen in the RPG again once the avatar leaves the inn and ventures on. Many such non-player characters (NPCs) incorporate an RPG world, usually located in strategic spots to aid the avatar in some manner (such as providing food, shelter, and new equipment) or provide information to help further the current quest or narrative arc.

6. Among the more popular table-top RPGs that capitalized on *Dungeons & Dragons*' success were *Tunnels and Trolls* (1975), *Traveller* (1977), and *Runequest* (1978).

7. PLATO (Programmed Logic for Automatic Teaching Operations) was one of the first computer-assisted instruction systems and was created at the University of Illinois.

8. As you've likely already guessed, I am an avid videogame player. I estimate that I logged over 200 hours playing *Morrowind* and over 100 hours so far in *Oblivion*. I remain fascinated by the large scope of both gameworlds and the open-ended nature of the choices available to the avatars. If one wants to study video games, one must also play video games (just as a film critic must watch a film to be able to critique it). All of my gameplay time in *Morrowind* was spent

with one avatar, a dark Elf female named Zaara. All of my *Oblivion* experiences have been with a Wood Elf named Zach (who looks suspiciously like me).

9. Bethesda's *Elder Scrolls* series pioneered open-ended worlds and freeform gameplay, where players could go and do whatever they wanted. The series began in 1994 with the release of *Arena*, continued with *Daggerfall* in 1996, *Morrowind* in 2002 and *Oblivion* in 2006. Each game is popularly known without the Elder Scrolls designation; henceforth in this study I will refer to the games simply as *Morrowind* and *Oblivion*.

10. Bethesda Softworks website (www.bethsoft.com/news/) lists several of the gaming magazines and websites that selected *Morrowind* as 2002's best videogame and *Oblivion* as 2006's best videogame. Among them are Gamespot, Gamespy, Game Chronicles, and USA Today.

11. For example, on August 22, 2007, there were 296 different topic threads in the Elderscrolls *Morrowind* forum. Among these were questions related to the game ("What does the Pool of Forgetfulness do?" "Can you become a vampire while carrying vampire dust?"), surveys related to the game ("What is the best weapon in the game?" "What is the worst town or city in the game?"), and threads solely devoted to the statistics and attributes of the users' avatars. Many other types of threads exist as well.

12. In *Morrowind* and *Oblivion*, skooma is an extremely addictive illegal narcotic, similar to crack cocaine or heroin. Many NPCs in the game will not even speak to the user's avatar if the avatar has skooma in their possession.

13. As previously noted, part of the appeal of v-RPGs is the ability to customize the avatar, both at the beginning of the game and as the gameplay progresses. The avatar continually gains experience in *Morrowind* by repeatedly using their skills (whether the skills be swinging a sword, casting spells, repairing armor; bartering with NPCs, etc.). When a certain number of skills have been increased, the avatar may then "level up": the user is allowed to choose which primary attributes to strengthen. A level five character indicates very little progression in terms of strengthening the avatar's skills and over-

all abilities. The maximum level for all attributes and skills is 100.

14. In the Elder Scrolls universe, the khajiit are a feline-like species: the user's avatar may be khajiit if they wish. Khajiit NPCs encountered in the game will often say, "Khajiit has no words for you" to someone (usually the avatar) they are disgusted by. It is the greatest verbal insult the species can utter.

15. Corprus is a contagious, incurable disease which distorts the features of the victim and effectively turns them into a mindless zombie. Catching corprus is one of the greatest fears of *Morrowind*'s denizens.

16. This quest in *Morrowind* can only be completed if the avatar avoids detection by any NPCs on the way to the shrine. This requires stealthy movement and no speaking to any other diegetic characters.

Chapter 2

1. I discuss theories of narrativity and their relationship to identity in greater detail later in this chapter.

2. Stuart Moulthrop's Storyspace, a hypertext writing environment, was one of the first programs to allow authors to produce the types of narratives Murray describes. Michael Joyce's *afternoon, a story* (1986) and Moulthrop's own *Victory Garden* (1992) were among the earliest examples of hypertext fiction.

3. Most v-RPGs have narrative plots that revolve around the user's avatar. In *Fallout 2*, for example, the avatar is known as The Chosen One (the intriguee), and the game's opening cinematic reveals that the avatar has been selected to save his/her village from extinction. Thus, the game's central plot line (the intrigue) cannot be achieved without the avatar. In this way, users are made to feel essential to the gameplay experience: the "non-trivial impact" mentioned by McMahon earlier as necessary to create immersion.

4. Wolf lists and describes the following eleven types of videogame space: no visual space (all text-based); one screen, contained; one screen, contained, with wraparound; scrolling on one axis; scrolling on two axes; adjacent spaces displayed one at a

time; layers of independently moving planes (multiple scrolling backgrounds); spaces allowing z-axis movement into and out of the frame; multiple, nonadjacent spaces displayed on-screen simultaneously; interactive three-dimensional environment; and represented or mapped spaces. Most videogames may represent several of these types of diegetic space at the same time.

5. Interactive 3D space can take many forms in video games and is applicable in both first and third-person point of view games. Some examples of interactive 3D spaces can be found in *World of Warcraft*, *Halo*, *Oblivion*, *Star Wars: Knights of the Old Republic*, *Crysis*, and *Gears of War*.

6. Many video games allow users to access a map of some kind to help them orient themselves in the gameworld. These maps appear in a separate window and may be viewed while the game is paused. Typically in games where exploration is important, unexplored sections of the gameworld map remain unviewable (referred to as "the fog of war") until the user's avatar or agent explores them. Examples of video games that feature map components are *Doom*, *Baldur's Gate*, *SimCity*, *Grand Theft Auto III*, and *Bioshock*.

Chapter 3

1. Indeed, a qualitative study seemed appropriate for this study's research questions, especially when considering how Denzin and Lincoln characterize qualitative research in their *Handbook of Qualitative Research*: "Qualitative researchers attempt to make sense of or interpret phenomena in terms of the meanings people bring to them. Qualitative research involves the studied use and collection of a variety of empirical materials that describe routine and problematic moments and meaning in individuals' lives" (2). My study investigated the construction of avatars (virtual identities) by users (nonvirtual identities) to ascertain how the relationship between the two develops and how they inform each other via passage through a liminal space, the projective identity. This study fits Denzin's and Lincoln's criterion of interpreting a phenomenon that has meaning in the participants' lives. Creswell's dis-

tinction between qualitative and quantitative studies also serves to clarify an appropriate methodological approach for my study as he points out that "quantitative researchers work with a few variables and many cases, whereas qualitative researchers rely on a few cases and many variables" (15–16). There are many variables that may impact user identification with their avatar in a v-RPG: the game's narrative, the gaming interface, the avatar, and the spatial environment of the gameworld all may play a role. These constitute the "many variables" mentioned by Creswell here, who goes on to suggest that qualitative studies are appropriate if "the research question often starts with a how or a what so that initial forays into the topic describe what is going on" and "the topic needs to be explored, [the] variables cannot be easily identified" (17) Again, my research questions and topic fit these guidelines for qualitative research.

Of course, there are many disciplinary and/or methodological approaches to qualitative research. I also had to decide which tradition of inquiry was most appropriate for this study. Creswell's *Qualitative Inquiry and Research Design* clearly identifies five different types of qualitative traditions of inquiry: biographies, case studies, ethnographies, phenomenologies, and grounded theories. The focus of each tradition is quite different. Biographies explore the life of an individual in great detail. Phenomenological studies attempt to understand the essence of experiences around a phenomenon. Grounded theory research develops a theory grounded in data from the field. Ethnographies describe and interpret social groups, and case studies develop in-depth analysis of a single case or multiple cases (Creswell 65). My study met Creswell's criteria for a phenomenological study since it "focuses not on the individual but rather on a concept or phenomenon and seeks to understand the meaning of experiences of individuals about this phenomenon" (38). As mentioned above, the phenomenon of my study is liminal projective identity. Of course, my project also presents brief case studies to study this phenomenon: there is a "bounded system" (the diegetic gameworld and limitations of the v-RPG itself) and in-depth data collection from multiple sources of information (61), both characteristics of case studies. However, I have focused on the phenomenon produced by the users' gameplay sessions rather than the users themselves and thus I privilege phenomenological methodologies in this study.

2. Drawing on Dukes (1984) and Riemen (1986) Creswell recommends a phenomenological study of three to ten subjects, suggesting that "with an in-depth interview lasting as long as 2 hours" three to ten subjects represents a reasonable size of participants (122). Ten subjects interviewed for two hours each would produce twenty hours of data that would need to be transcribed and analyzed. For my study, I collected data not only through interviews with my participants (initial interviews lasting an hour each and follow-up interviews lasting approximately two hours each), but also by recording and transcribing each participant's first ten hours of gameplay in the v-RPGs Morrowind and Oblivion. Given this additional videogame data collected and the time needed to transcribe it for analysis and follow-up interviews (approximately 40 hours needed to transcribe each participant's ten hours of gameplay), I selected two participants for this portion of the study so that the scope of the project remained manageable while still allowing me to collect relevant data.

3. Both Morrowind participants' names have been changed at their request to protect their identities. To honor the Sanskrit and Hindu origins of the word "avatar" I selected Vishnu and Shiva as pseudonyms for the participants. Both are the names of the avatars of Hindu deities. It was also important to select a pseudonym for the female participant that showed the close relationship between the name she selected for her Morrowind avatar and her birth name. Selecting Shiva as a pseudonym for her accomplished this.

4. The Star Wars trilogy takes place on many different planets and Hoth is one such planet. In The Empire Strikes Back, Hoth is the location of the Rebel Base until discovered by the Imperials. One of the film's epic battles takes place as the Imperial All Terrain Attack Transports (AT-ATs) attack the Rebel base, defended by the Rebel snowspeeders. It is this battle that Vishu refers

to, as many Star Wars video games over the years have recreated this famous battle.

5. Certainly, Tom's experiences in Oblivion discussed in chapter four seem to illustrate this fact.

6. It was also crucial that both participants have the technological capacity to play Morrowind on their home computing systems. The participants would be playing Morrowind's Game of the Year Edition which included Morrowind's two expansion packs, Tribunal and Bloodmoon. The following list contains the minimum system specifications needed to play this edition of Morrowind:

- An operating system of Windows 98, Windows 2000, or Windows XP with 128 megabytes (MB) of Random Access Memory (RAM).
- A processor of at least 500 megahertz (MHz)
- An 8x CD/DVD Read-Only Memory (ROM) drive
- One gigabyte (GB) of free hard disk space
- DirectX 8.1
- 32 MB Direct 3D compatible video card with 32-bit color support
- A DirectX 8.1 compatible driver and sound card
- A keyboard, monitor, and mouse

Morrowind's Game of the Year edition was released in 2003. Both Vishnu and Shiva had purchased new home computing systems in 2005. Vishnu's PC ran on Windows XP and contained 512 MB of RAM. His computer's processor was a Pentium 4 with 3.2 gigahertz (GHz), and his video card was a 128 MB nVidia GeForce FX 5300. The computer Shiva gamed on ran on Windows XP and contained one GB of RAM. The computer's processor was a Pentium 4 with 2.4 GHz with a 128 MB Image Quest L70S Radeon 9200 video card. These system specifications more than met the requirements to play Morrowind.

To record my participants' Morrowind gameplay, I excluded the possibility of using a video camera mounted on a tripod for a few important reasons. First, this method is somewhat obtrusive, and the presence of the camera lurking behind the participant could serve as a reminder that the user's virtual actions were being scrutinized thus preventing immersion or influencing the diegetic choices. Second, as anyone who has ever attempted to video record a television monitor or computer screen in this manner can attest to, the recorder is able to pick up the constant flicker of the screen that is typically imperceptible to our eyes. This pulsating flicker is distracting at best, and headache-inducing at worst; attempting to analyze over 20 hours of such tape would be extremely difficult as *Morrowind* has many icons that appear regularly on the screen and text boxes with small print. Being able to follow the user's diegetic choices is crucial and video recording in this manner would have presented an opportunity for data to be misinterpreted or lost. Instead, I used a computer software program named Fraps (www.fraps.com) that enabled me to record the participants' gameplay directly onto an external hard drive.

7. Users are free to pick any five of the available 27 skills to tag as Major Skills. These five Major Skills start with a higher proficiency rating than the other skills; the avatar also improves these skills more quickly. Only improvement in these five skills contribute to the avatar "leveling up."

8. Among the many scholar works devoted to MMORPGs are R.V. Kelly's *Massively Multiplayer Online Role-Playing Games* and all of the articles in edition 1.4 of *Games and Culture* (2006).

9. *The Morrowind Prophecies* lists 391 side quests that can be undertaken outside of the main quest storyline. Of these, 292 are factional quests, taken on if the avatar chooses to join one of the guilds (Fighters Guild, Thieves Guild, or Imperial Cult, for example) or Great Houses (House Redoran, House Hlaalu, House Telvanni). 65 miscellaneous quests also exist, random encounters with NPCs waiting to be kairotically discovered in the gameworld. Finally, 34 themed miscellaneous quests are listed, such as collecting a copy of each book in *Morrowind* or freeing all of the slaves in the game, "unofficial" quests that are never specifically referenced within the diegetic gameworld.

10. Chronos in *Morrowind* pauses when the user enters the inventory screen, giving the user time to study their inventory, the avatar's attributes and skills, the game maps, their spells, and the journal. As soon as the user exits the inventory and returns to the "normal" gameworld view, chronos begins to run again.

11. Sandbox or God games place the user outside of the gameworld in an omnipotent position from which the user sees the entire gameworld and manipulates it at will, making all decisions that affect that world. *Sid Meier's Civilization, RollerCoaster Tycoon,* and *Populous* are among the popular strategy games in this genre.

12. *Morrowind's* decision to force the user to play in first-person point of view (POV) until completing the avatar's initial construction is well considered. Until the user has selected from the gender, racial, facial, and hair options, no picture of the avatar can exist. Once all of these decisions have been made and Socucius Ergalla instructs the avatar to take their release papers off his desk, the user is free to access their inventory and change the POV.

13. Shiva's comment here refers to her desire to select a race strategically based on how she wanted to play. Shiva wanted to play a balanced character, one that could engage in both physical combat and magical combat effectively. Knowing this ahead of time, she studied each racial option looking for one that had strong ratings in Intelligence (important for casting spells) and Strength (important for melee combat).

14. The pre-existing classes already have names assigned to them. Combat classes have names like Warrior, Knight and Archer; magic classes have names like Mage, Nightblade, and Sorcerer; stealth classes have names like Thief, Bard, and Acrobat. Users creating their own custom classes can name the class anything they want (thus increasing the identification potential).

15. For example, six combat answers, three stealth answers, and one magic answer firmly situate the avatar as a combat-class Barbarian. Six combat answers, three magic answers, and one stealth answer is still a combat-based class but is a Crusader. Each of the 21 classes corresponds to a ratio of the types of answers (combat, magic, and stealth) given to the ten questions.

16. None of the ten questions are directly

tied to the *Morrowind* gameworld. The user must answer these questions before any involvement in the game's story or world or any awareness of what the answers mean in terms of assigning the avatar's class. Therefore, the user must by default draw on the proclivities of their real-world identities when answering these questions.

17. "Turn Undead" is a popular fantasy RPG spell. It is usually available to members of the clergy and refers to the spell's ability to "increase an undead creature's flee rating (its inclination to flee from an attacker)" (Hines and Cheng 30).

18. As is typical of first-person perspectives, only the arms and hands of the avatar are visible from the elbows on down. The appearance of the arms does change however depending on the types of gloves or gauntlets the avatar is wearing and the type of weapon they are holding.

19. In this instance chronos refers to the passage of day and night in the *Morrowind* gameworld of Vvardenfell. Certain quests make use of the game's chronos. For example, if the avatar joins House Hlaalu and rises in rank, eventually House members will construct a house for the avatar. Construction of the house takes place in phases, each lasting several weeks. By paying attention to the gameworld's chronos the avatar can monitor when tasks will be completed or how long they have to achieve quest goals.

20. Each NPC the *Morrowind* avatar speaks to has a pre-established Disposition toward the avatar from zero to one hundred. The higher the number, the more the NPC likes the avatar, and the more likely the NPC is to talk to you or offer you particular services. Users can attempt to alter their Disposition with a particular NPC through selecting one of four different types of Persuasion: Admire, Taunt, Intimidate, and Bribe. If these attempts are successful (determined by the avatar's Speechcraft and Mercantile skills), the NPC's Disposition towards the avatar goes up. If the attempt fails, the NPC's Disposition drops even lower.

21. One room in the Census and Excise Office is free of guards, which allows the avatar to successfully steal all the items in the room if they wish. In this way the avatar can obtain their first weapon (a dagger), some food, and other miscellaneous items

to sell for a few gold. New avatars/users in video games are commonly referred to as "newbies" and this room in the Census and Excise Office is clearly designed to give newbie players a few items for their inventory.

22. Addamasartus is a large cave just outside of Seyda Neen. It contains several slavers (who attack the avatar on sight) and a room full of slaves who the avatar can free if they so wish. Crates and barrels scattered throughout the cave contain miscellaneous items that can be looted. Addamasartus is located near Seyda Neen's siltstrider port (which offers fast travel to nearby towns). Perhaps predictably, both Vishnu and Shiva discovered Addamasartus within their first two hours of *Morrowind* gameplay.

23. If the avatar can find a safe place to rest, doing so will replenish their health, magicka, and fatigue points. Resting can take place anywhere in the wilderness as long as creatures are not nearby. In towns, the avatar must find a bed to rest in legally (in a tavern or a guild if the avatar is a member).

24. Vishnu is correct: *Morrowind* does make an ethical distinction between killing and murdering. If an NPC attacks the avatar (initiates the physical combat), the avatar has the right to defend herself. If this combat leads to the death of the offending NPC, the avatar has committed no crime. This is killing and carries no legal penalty. If the avatar initiates combat with an NPC in a town and kills that NPC, this is murder. Town guards will attempt to arrest the avatar for this crime. However, this rule only applies to attacks and kills made in civilized areas (towns and forts). The avatar is free to attack and kill any NPC discovered in the wilderness (caves, strongholds, ruins, and encampments are all considered part of the wilderness) without the action being recognized as legally criminal.

25. The many dozen books that can be discovered and read in *Morrowind* bring the gameworld to life. Many of the books provide historical lore about Morrowind. Others describe native flora and fauna. Still others tell exciting tales of adventure and mystery (clearly intended to be fictive works written by the fictional denizens of the land). *Morrowind* users who spend time

reading the books enrich their knowledge of the virtual land they are exploring.

26. *Morrowind* avatars can only carry a limited amount of items in their inventory. This is referred to as the avatar's Encumbrance. The total weight the avatar can carry is determined by their Strength attribute: the higher the Strength rating the more weight (and the greater number of items) the avatar can carry. If the avatar exceeds the Encumbrance weight, the avatar is unable to move until they drop enough items to reduce their Encumbrance below its maximum value. By carrying books in his inventory yet never reading them or selling them, Vishnu is in essence carrying dead weight that takes up space without reward.

27. Both Shiva and Vishnu admitted they read the *Morrowind* game manual before beginning the game. On the second page of the game manual in a five paragraph "Introduction to Morrowind" the designers stress the vast freeform gameworld: "Huge, detailed, and open-ended are words that frequently come up when talking about *Morrowind*...One minute you may be gazing up at the moon and stars over the plains or out for a swim in the Sea of Ghosts, and running for your life from a cliff racer or slaughterfish the next. Vvardenfell is a culturally and geographically diverse place. Morrowind is filled with things for you to do ... hundreds and hundreds of things. No matter what your preference, there's no right or wrong way to play Morrowind" (Hines and Cheng 2). With this awareness both participants were alerted to the fact that they were free to wander in the large gameworld in non-linear fashion and each was eager to do so.

Chapter 4

1. Four of the Skills available in *Morrowind* were removed in *Oblivion*: Spear, Unarmored, Enchant, and Medium Armor. The Long Blade and Short Blade Skills were combined into a single Blade skill, and the Axe skill was combined with the Blunt Weapon skill.

2. Tom's admission that he had played *Baldur's Gate* (another PC-RPG) surprised me, as he had been adamant that *Alternate Reality* had been his only v-RPG experience before this project. When I questioned him on this, it became clear that Tom was referring to the Playstation 2 version of *Baldur's Gate*, which was very light on the RPG elements and heavy on combat action: very much a "hack-n-slash" gaming experience rather than a roleplaying experience.

3. For example, there are icons that convey an item's value in gold, an item's weight, how much damage a weapon causes, how much armor protection an item provides, the quality of the item, and an item's health (an item's condition degrades with usage; the lower its health, the less effective or powerful it is). There are also icons that indicate if items are magical, poisoned, stolen, or broken. Each spell also has its own icon as well. As a result, there are a few dozen different icons for the gamer to memorize.

Chapter 5

1. Future dystopia has long been a popular genre in science fiction novels. Along with Stirling's works, George Stewart's *Earth Abides* was one early critically acclaimed novel in this genre. Of course, Orwell's *1984* is also clearly future dystopian. Long a staple among the fanatical science fiction community, future dystopian works continue to gain mainstream popularity, as demonstrated by the Will Smith vehicle *I Am Legend*, the TV show *Jericho*, and the British film *Doomsday* (an homage to John Carpenter's *Escape from New York*).

2. These Skills are Small Guns, Big Guns, Energy Weapons, Unarmed, Melee Weapons, Throwing, First Aid, Doctor, Sneak, Lockpick, Steal, Traps, Science, Repair, Speech, Barter, Gambling, and Outdoorsman. You can clearly see how similar these are to the skills of Morrowind and Oblivion. Most deep v-RPGs provide improvable skills in this vein. After all, the more choices the gamer has to make and the more different ways the avatar can improve, the greater the potential for immersive identification.

3. The sixteen Traits available in *Fallout* and *Fallout 2* are: Fast Metabolism, Bruiser, Small Frame, One Hander, Finesse, Kamikaze, Heavy Handed, Fast Shot, Bloody Mess, Jinxed, Good Natured, Chem Reliant,

Chem Resistant, Sex Appeal, Skilled, and Gifted.

4. *Fallout*'s "Best of All Time" rankings include number twenty-one on gamesradar.com and number thirty-three on IGN.com's 2007 ranking.

5. The new thirteen Skills in *Fallout 3* are Barter, Big Guns, Energy Weapons, Explosives, Lockpick, Medicine, Melee Weapons, Repair, Science, Small Guns, Sneak, Speech, and Unarmed.

6. Nintendo's Wii gaming system allows users to create simplistic avatars that can be used in the Wii *Sports* games. Each avatar is called a "mii." Rather than the highly customizable Oblivion avatars, mii avatars are caricature-like and much more cartoon-like and cutsey.

7. Question One on the GOAT asks, "You are approached by a frenzied vault scientist who yells, 'I'm going to put my quantum harmonizer in your photonic resonation chamber!' What do you do?" As Bianca didn't understand the question, she was at a loss as to how to answer.

Bibliography

Aarseth, Espen. "Computer Game Studies, Year One." *Game Studies* 1.1 (July 2001). <http://www.gamestudies.org>.

_____. *Cybertext: Perspectives on Ergodic Literature.* Baltimore: The Johns Hopkins University Press, 1997.

_____. "Playing Research: Methodological approaches to game analysis." *Fine Art Forum* 17.8 (Aug. 2003). 19 Mar. 2004. <http://www.fineartforum.org/Backissues/Vol_17/index.html>.

Activision. *MechWarrior 2: 31st Century Combat.* Activision, 1995.

_____. *Pitfall.* Activision, 1982.

Advanced Microcomputer Systems. *Dragon's Lair.* Cinematronics, 1983.

American Laser Games. *Mad Dog McCree.* American Laser Games, 1990.

Anais. "Real vs. virtual identity." Online posting. 14 Dec. 2005. Morrowind general discussion. 16 Dec. 2005. <www.elderscrolls.com/forums>.

Apogee Software. *Duke Nukem.* Apogee Software, 1991.

Atari. *Battlezone.* Atari, 1980.

_____. *Gauntlet.* Atari, 1985.

_____. *PONG.* Atari, 1972.

Baudrillard, Jean. *Simulacra and Simulation.* Sheila Faria Glaser, trans. Ann Arbor: The University of Michigan Press, 1994.

Bazerman, Charles. "Genre and Identity: Citizenship in the Age of the Internet and the Age of Global Capitalism." Richard Coe, Lorelei Lingard, and Tatiana Teslenko, eds. *The Rhetoric and Ideology of Genre: Strategies for Stability and Change.* Cresskill, NJ: Hampton Press, 2002. 13–37.

Berger, Arthur Asa. *Video Games: A Popular Culture Phenomenon.* New Brunswick, NJ: Transaction Publishers, 2002.

Bethesda Game Studios. *Fallout 3.* ZeniMax Media, 2008.

Bethesda Softworks. *The Elder Scrolls: Arena.* Bethesda Softworks, 1994.

_____. *The Elder Scrolls II: Daggerfall.* Bethesda Softworks, 1996.

_____. *The Elder Scrolls III: Morrowind, Game of the Year Edition.* ZeniMax Media, 2003.

_____. *The Elder Scrolls IV: Oblivion.* 2K Games, 2006.

Bioware. *Baldur's Gate.* Black Isle Studios, 1998.

_____. *Star Wars: Knights of the Old Republic.* LucasArts, 2003.

Black Isle Studios. *Fallout 2.* Interplay, 1998.

Blizzard Entertainment. *World of Warcraft.* Vivendi Universal, 2004.

Bloom. "Real vs. virtual identity." Online posting. 14 Dec. 2005. *Morrowind* general discussion. 16 Dec. 2005. <www.elderscrolls.com/forums>.

Bobg. "Real vs. virtual identity." Online posting. 2 Sept. 2008. *Oblivion* general discussion. 4 Sept. 2008. <www.elderscrolls.com/forums>.

Bolter, Jay David, and Richard Grusin. *Remediation: Understanding New Media.* Cambridge: MIT Press, 2000.

Bordieu, Pierre. *The Logic of Practice.* R. Nice, trans. Stanford: Stanford University Press, 1990.

Brayf. "You know you've played too much Morrowind when..." Online posting. 2

Dec. 2005. *Morrowind* general discussion. 16 Dec. 2005. <www.elderscrolls.com/forums>.

Bullfrog. *Populous*. Electronic Arts, 1989.

Bungie Studios. *Halo: Combat Evolved*. Microsoft Game Studios, 2001.

Burke, Kenneth. *A Rhetoric of Motives*. Berkeley: University of California Press, 1969.

Butler, Judith. *Gender Trouble: Feminism and the Subversion of Identity*. New York: Routledge, 1990.

Charrette, Bob, Paul Hume, and Tom Dowd. *Shadowrun*. FASA Corporations/Fantasy Productions, 1989.

Chow, Rey. *Writing Diaspora: Tactics of Intervention in Contemporary Cultural Studies*. Bloomington: Indiana University Press, 1993.

Clarke-Willson, Stephen. "Applying Game Design to Virtual Environments." *Digital Illusion: Entertaining the Future with High Technology*. Clark Dodsworth Jr., ed. New York: Addison-Wesley, 1997. 229–239.

Cobb. "Real vs. virtual identity." Online posting. 2 Sept. 2008. *Oblivion* general discussion. 4 Sept. 2008. <www.elderscrolls.com/forums>.

Coe, Richard, Lorelei Lingard, and Tatiana Teslenko, eds. *The Rhetoric and Ideology of Genre: Strategies for Stability and Change*. Cresskill, NJ: Hampton Press, 2002.

Core Design. *Tomb Raider*. Eidos Interactive, 1996.

Creswell, John W. *Qualitative Inquiry and Research Design: Choosing Among Five Traditions*. London: Sage Publications, 1997.

Crytek. *Crysis*. Electronic Arts, 2007.

Csikszentmihalyi, Mihaly. *Beyond Boredom and Anxiety*. San Francisco: Jossey-Bass Press, 1975.

Cyan, Inc. *Myst*. Broderbund, 1995.

Danile. "Real vs. virtual identity." Online posting. 14 Dec. 2005. *Morrowind* general discussion. 16 Dec. 2005. <www.elderscrolls.com/forums>.

Dante Nerevar. "Real vs. virtual identity." Online posting. 14 Dec. 2005. *Morrowind* general discussion. 16 Dec. 2005. <www.elderscrolls.com/forums>.

Data East. *Burgertime*. Bally Midway, 1982.

DeLeuze, Gilles. *Spinoza: Practical Philosophy*. R. Turley, trans. San Francisco: City Light Books, 1988.

_____, and Pierre-Felix Guattari. *A Thousand Plateaus: Vol. 2 of Capitalism and Schizophrenia*. London: Athlone, 1987.

Dennis, Robert. "Technology paragraphs." Email to Zach Waggoner. 13 Aug. 2006.

Denzin, Norman K., and Yvonna S. Lincoln, eds. *The SAGE Handbook of Qualitative Research*. London: Sage Publications, 2005.

DMA Design. *Grand Theft Auto III*. Rockstar Games, 2001.

Doctor44. "Real vs. virtual identity." Online posting. 2 Sept. 2008. *Oblivion* general discussion. 4 Sept. 2008. <www.elderscrolls.com/forums>.

Dombrower, Eddie. *Dombrower's Art of Interactive Entertainment Design*. New York: McGraw-Hill, 1998.

Ducheneaut, Nicolas, Nick Yee, Eric Nickell, and Robert J. Moore. "Building an MMO With Mass Appeal." *Games and Culture* 1.4 (2006): 281–317.

DynaMix. *MechWarrior*. Activision, 1989.

EA Sports. *Tiger Woods PGA Tour 09*. Electronic Arts, 2008.

EA Tiburon. *Madden NFL 06*. EA Sports, 2005.

_____. *Madden NFL 07*. EA Sports, 2006.

Eco, Umberto. *Semiotics and the Philosophy of Language*. London: MacMillan, 1984.

Entertainment Software Association. "Top Ten Industry Facts, 2005." 17 May 2006. <http://www.theesa.com>.

Epic Games. *Gears of War*. Microsoft Game Studios, 2006.

EXistenZ. Dir. David Cronenberg. Alliance Atlantis, 1999.

Faigley, Lester. *Fragments of Rationality: Postmodernity and the Subject of Compo-*

sition. Pittsburgh: University of Pittsburgh Press, 1992.

Farterman. "Real vs. virtual identity." Online posting. 2 Sept. 2008. *Oblivion* general discussion. 4 Sept. 2008. <www.elderscrolls.com/forums>.

Filiciak, Miroslaw. "Hyperidentities: Postmodern Identity Patterns in Massively Multiplayer Online Role-Playing Games." *The Video Game Theory Reader.* Mark J. P. Wolf and Bernard Perron, eds. New York: Routledge, 2003. 87–102.

Firaxis Games. *Sid Meier's Gettysburg!* Electronic Arts, 1997.

Flinn, Kelton. *Air Warrior.* Kesmai, 1987.

Flynn, Bernadette. "Language of Navigation Within Computer Games." *Fine Art Forum* 17.8 (Aug. 2003). 19 Mar. 2004. <http://www.fineartforum.org/Backissues/Vol_17/index.html>.

Freedman, Aviva, and Peter Medway, eds. *Genre and the New Rhetoric.* Bristol, PA: Taylor and Harris, 1994.

Friedman, Jonathan. "Global Crises, the Struggle for Cultural Identity and Intellectual Porkbarrelling: Cosmopolitans Versus Locals, Ethnics and Nationals in an Era of De-Hegemonisation." *Debating Cultural Hybridity: Multi-Cultural Identities and the Politics of Anti-Racism.* Pnina Werbner and Tariq Modood, eds. London: Zed Books, 1997: 70–89.

Fuss, Diana. *Essentially Speaking: Feminism, Nature & Difference.* New York: Routledge, 1989.

_____. *Identification Papers.* New York: Routledge, 1995.

Gamespot. "The History of Video Games." 23 January 2002. <http://gamespot.com/gamespot/features/video/hov/>.

Garriott, Richard. *Akalabeth.* California Pacific Computer Co., 1980.

Gee, James Paul. *What Video Games Have to Teach Us About Learning and Literacy.* New York: Palgrave Macmillan, 2004.

_____. Personal Interview. 21 Feb. 2006.

Gibson, William. *Neuromancer.* New York: Ace Books, 1984.

Giddens, Anthony. *Modernity and Self-Identity.* Stanford: Stanford University Press, 1991.

Goldberg, Athomas. "Avatars and Agents, or Life Among the Indigenous Peoples of Cyberspace." *Digital Illusion: Entertaining the Future with High Technology.* Clark Dodsworth Jr., ed. New York: Addison-Wesley, 1997. 161–180.

Graham, Beryl. "Playing with Yourself: Pleasure and Interactive Art." *Fractal Dreams: New Media in Social Context.* Jon Dovey, ed. London: Lawrence & Wishart, 1996. 154–181.

Green, Nicola. "Beyond Being Digital: Representation and Virtual Corporeality." *Virtual Politics: Identity & Community in Cyberspace.* David Holmes, ed. Thousand Oaks, CA: Sage Publications, 1997. 59–78.

Grodal, Torben. "Stories for Eye, Ear, and Muscles: Video Games, Media, and Embodied Experiences." *The Video Game Theory Reader.* Mark J. P. Wolf and Bernard Perron, eds. New York: Routledge, 2003. 129–155.

Grosse Pointe Blank. Dir. George Armitage. Walt Disney Studios, 1997.

Gygax, Gary, and Dave Arneson. *Dungeons and Dragons.* Lake Geneva, WI: Tactical Studies Rules, 1974.

Haraway, Donna J. *Simians, Cyborgs, and Women: The Reinvention of Nature.* New York: Routledge, 1991.

Hayles, N. Katherine. *How We Became Posthuman: Virtual Bodies in Cybernetics, Literature, and Informatics.* Chicago: University of Chicago Press, 1999.

Hines, Pete, and Ashley Cheng. *The Elder Scrolls III: Morrowind Game of the Year Edition Game Manual.* Rockville, MD: Bethesda Softworks LLC, 2003.

Hjelmslev, Louis. *Prolegomena to a Theory of Language.* F.J. Whitfield, trans. Madison: University of Wisconsin Press, 1961.

Holmes, David. *Virtual Politics: Identity & Community in Cyberspace*. Thousand Oaks, CA: Sage Publications, 1997.

Humphreys, Sal. "Productive Players: Online Computer Games' Challenge to Conventional Media Forms." *Communication and Critical/Cultural Studies* 2.1 (Mar. 2005): 37–51.

Ice Troll. "Real vs. virtual identity." Online posting. 14 Dec. 2005. *Morrowind* general discussion. 16 Dec. 2005. <www.elderscrolls.com/forums>.

id Software. *Doom*. id Software, GT Interactive, Activision, 1993.

_____. *Quake*. Activision, 1996.

_____. *Wolfenstein 3D*. Apogee Software, 1992.

InXile Entertainment. *The Bard's Tale*. Vivendi Universal Games, 2004.

Joyce, Michael. *Afternoon, a story*. Watertown, MA: Eastgate Systems, 1990.

Kelly, R.V. "Chapter 4: Attraction and Addiction." *Massively Multiplayer Online Role-Playing Games*. Jefferson, NC: McFarland, 2004.

Kennedy, Helen. "Lara Croft: Feminist Icon or Cyberbimbo? On the Limits of Textual Analysis." *Game Studies* 2.2 (Dec. 2002). Mar. 15 2004. <http://www.gamestudies.org>.

Klein, Jan. *Immunology: The Science of Non-Self Discrimination*. New York: Wiley-Interscience, 1982.

Knapp, Peter. "The Disembodied Voices: The Problem of Context and Form in Theories of Genre." Richard Coe, Lorelei Lingard, and Tatiana Teslenko, eds. *The Rhetoric and Ideology of Genre: Strategies for Stability and Change*. Cresskill, NJ: Hampton Press, 2002. 275–296.

Konami. *Contra*. Konami, 1987.

_____. *Frogger*. Sega/Gremlin, 1981.

Linden Lab. *Second Life*. Linden Lab, 2003.

Lionhead Studios. *Fable*. Microsoft Game Studios, 2004.

Lonesniper. "You know you've played too much Morrowind when..." Online posting. 2 Dec. 2005. *Morrowind* general discussion. 16 Dec. 2005. <www.elderscrolls.com/forums>.

Loughry, Tom. *Advanced Dungeons & Dragons: Treasure of Tarmin*. Mattel, 1981.

Lucasfilm Games. *Habitat*. Quantum Link, 1987.

Mackay, Daniel. *The Fantasy Role-Playing Game*. Jefferson, NC: McFarland, 2001.

Maxis. *Sim City*. Broderbund, Maxis, and Electronic Arts, 1989.

_____. *Spore*. EA Games, 2007.

McMahan, Alison. "Immersion, Engagement, and Presence: A Method for Analyzing 3D Video Games." *The Video Game Theory Reader*. Mark J. P. Wolf and Bernard Perron, eds. New York: Routledge, 2003. 67–86.

MC2-Microids. *Still Life*. MC2-Microids and The Adventure Company, 2005.

Melucci, Alberto. "Identity and Difference in a Globalized World." *Debating Cultural Hybridity: Multi-Cultural Identities and the Politics of Anti-Racism*. Pnina Werbner and Tariq Modood, eds. London: Zed Books, 1997. 58–69.

Microids. *Syberia*. The Adventure Company, 2002.

MicroProse. *Sid Meier's Civilization*. MicroProse, 1991.

Miller, Marc. *Traveller*. Game Designers' Workshop, 1977.

Moulthrop, Stuart. *Victory Garden*. Watertown, MA: Eastgame Systems, 1992.

Mulvey, Laura. *Fetishism & Curiosity*. London: BFI, 1996.

Murray, Janet H. *Hamlet on the Holodeck: The Future of Narrative in Cyberspace*. New York: Simon and Schuster, 1997.

Namco. *Ms. Pac-Man*. Midway, 1981.

_____. *Pac-Man*. Midway, 1980.

_____. *RBI Baseball*. Tengen, 1988.

Newman, James. "The Myth of the Ergodic Videogame: Some Thoughts on Player-Character Relationships in Videogames." *Game Studies* 2.1 (July 2002). 15 Mar. 2004. <http://www.gamestudies.org>.

Nicholls, Brett, and Simon Ryan. "Game, Space and the Politics of Cyberplay." *Fine Art Forum* 17.8 (Aug. 2003). 19 Mar. 2004. <http://www.fineartforum. org/Backissues/Vol_17/index.html>.

Nintendo. *Donkey Kong*. Nintendo, 1981.

_____. *Popeye*. Nintendo, 1982.

_____. *Super Mario Bros*. Nintendo, 1985.

_____. *Super Mario Bros. 2*. Nintendo, 1988.

_____. *Wii Sports*. Nintendo, 2006.

Nutting Associates. *Computer Space*. Nutting Associates, 1971.

Olafson, Peter. *The Morrowind Prophecies Game of the Year Edition: Official Guide*. Rockville, MD: Bethesda Softworks, 2003.

Origin Systems. *Ultima IV: Quest of the Avatar*. Origin Systems, 1985.

_____. *Ultima Online*. Electronic Arts, 1997.

Padalin. "You know you've played too much Morrowind when..." Online posting. 2 Dec. 2005. *Morrowind* general discussion. 16 Dec. 2005. <www.elderscrolls.com/forums>.

Papastergiadis, Nikos. "Tracing Hybridity in Theory." *Debating Cultural Hybridity: Multi-Cultural Identities and the Politics of Anti-Racism*. Pnina Werbner and Tariq Modood, eds. London: Zed Books, 1997. 257–281.

Paradise Programming. *Alternate Reality*. Datasoft, 1985.

Pearce, Celia. "Game Noir: A Conversation with Tim Schafer." *Game Studies* 3.3 (May 2003), 15 Mar. 2004 <http://www.gamestudies.org>.

Perrin, Steve, et al. *RuneQuest*. Chaosium and Avalon Hill, 1978.

Polygon Magic. *Galerians*. Ash. Sammy Studios, 2003.

Rare. *Perfect Dark*. Rare, 2000.

Rehak, Bob. "Playing at Being: Psychoanalysis and the Avatar." *The Video Game Theory Reader*. Mark J. P. Wolf and Bernard Perron, eds. New York: Routledge, 2003. 103–127.

Robinett, Warren. "Foreword." *The Video Game Theory Reader*. Mark J. P. Wolf and Bernard Perron, eds. New York: Routledge, 2003. vii-xix.

Rockstar North. *Grand Theft Auto: Vice City*. Rockstar Games, 2002.

Ruggill, Judd Ethan, Ken S. McAllister, and David Menchaca. "The Gamework." *Communication and Critical/Cultural Studies* 1.4 (Dec. 2004): 297–312.

Russell, Steve, et al. *Spacewar!* The Massachusetts Institute of Technology, 1962.

Ryan, Marie-Laure. "Beyond Myth and Metaphor: The Case of Narrative in Digital Media." *Game Studies* 1.1 (July 2001). 16 Sept. 2004. <http://www. gamestudies.org>.

St. Andre, Ken. *Tunnels and Trolls*. Flying Buffalo, 1975.

Sawyer, Chris. *Rollercoaster Tycoon*. Hasbro Interactive, 1999.

Sega. *Zaxxon*. Sega, 1982.

Snowblind Studios. *Baldur's Gate: Dark Alliance*. Vivendi Universal Games, 2001.

Sonic Team. *Sonic the Hedgehog*. Sega, 1991.

Sony Online Entertainment. *EverQuest*. Sony Online Entertainment, 1999.

Square Co., LTD. *Final Fantasy VII*. SCE America, 1997.

_____. *Final Fantasy X*. Square EA, 2001.

Squire, Kurt. "Cultural Framing of Computer/Video Games." *Game Studies* 2.1 (July 2002). <http://www.gamestudies.org>.

Stephenson, Neal. *Snow Crash*. New York: Bantam Books, 1992.

Stone, Allucquere Roseanne. *The War of Desire and Technology at the Close of the Mechanical Age*. Cambridge: The MIT Press, 1995.

Syronj. "Real vs. virtual identity." Online posting. 14 Dec. 2005. *Morrowind* general discussion. 16 Dec. 2005. <www.elderscrolls.com/forums>.

Taito Corporation. *Space Invaders*. Midway, 1978.

Taylor, Laurie. "When Seams Fall Apart: Video Game Space and the Player." *Game Studies* 3.2 (December 2003).

Mar. 15 2004. <http://www.gamestud
ies.org>.

The vrrc. "Real vs. virtual identity." Online posting. 14 Dec. 2005. *Morrowind*
general discussion. 16 Dec. 2005.
<www.elderscrolls.com/forums>.

Thorhauge, Anne Mette. "Player, reader
and social actor." *Fine Art Forum* 17.8
(Aug. 2003). 19 Mar. 2004. <http://
www.fineartforum.org/Backissues/Vol_
17/index.html>.

Toastman. "Real vs. virtual identity." Online posting. 14 Dec. 2005. *Morrowind*
general discussion. 16 Dec. 2005.
<www.elderscrolls.com/forums>.

Tri-Ace. *Star Ocean 2: The Second Story*.
Sony Computer Entertainment America, 1999.

Troika Games. *Arcanum: Of Steamworks
and Magick Obscura*. Sierra Entertainment, 2001.

Turkle, Sherry. *Life on the Screen: Identity
in the Age of the Internet*. New York:
Touchstone, 1995.

2K Boston. *Bioshock*. 2K Games, 2007.

Van Gennep, Arnold. *The Rites of Passage*.
Chicago: University of Chicago Press,
1908.

"Verisimilitude." Def. 1a. *The Oxford English Dictionary*. 2d. ed. 1989.

Walker, Jill. "Performing Fictions: Interaction and Depiction." *Fine Art Forum*
17.8 (Aug. 2003). 19 Mar. 2004. <http://
www.fineartforum.org/Backissues/Vol_
17/index.html>.

Walther, Bo Kampmann. "Playing and
Gaming: Reflections and Classifica-
tions." *Game Studies* 3.1 (May 2003). 15
Mar. 2004. <http://www.gamestudies.
org>.

Williams Electronics. *Joust*. Williams Electronics, 1982.

Wilson, Laetitia. "Interactivity or Interpas-
sivity: A Question of Agency in Digital
Play." *Fine Art Forum* 17.8 (Aug. 2003).
19 Mar. 2004. <http://www.fineartfo
rum.org/Backissues/Vol_17/index.ht
ml>.

Wolf, Mark J. P. "Abstraction in the Video
Game." *The Video Game Theory
Reader*. Mark J. P. Wolf and Bernard
Perron, eds. New York: Routledge,
47–65.

_____. "The Video Game as a Medium."
The Medium of the Video Game. Ed.
Mark J. P. Wolf. Austin: University of
Texas Press, 2001. 13–33.

_____, and Bernard Perron. "Introduc-
tion." *The Video Game Theory Reader*.
Mark J. P. Wolf and Bernard Perron,
eds. New York: Routledge, 2003. 1–24.

Yates, JoAnne, and Wanda Orlikowski.
"Genre Systems: Chronos and Kairos
in Communicative Interaction." Richard
Coe, Lorelei Lingard, and Tatiana
Teslenko, eds. *The Rhetoric and Ideology
of Genre: Strategies for Stability and
Change*. Cresskill, NJ: Hampton Press,
2002. 103–121.

Index